# ESCAPING VIET NAM

## H'YOANH'S STORY

March 2013

For R.T. & Scottie,
    With gratitude for your
enthusiasm and your support –
        Harriet

# ESCAPING VIET NAM
## H'YOANH'S STORY

A Memoir of Determination,
Defiance, and Deliverance

Harriet Hill and H'Yoanh Buonya

TATE PUBLISHING
AND ENTERPRISES, LLC

Published by Tate Publishing & Enterprises, LLC
127 E. Trade Center Terrace | Mustang, Oklahoma 73064 USA
1.888.361.9473 | www.tatepublishing.com

Tate Publishing is committed to excellence in the publishing industry. The company reflects the philosophy established by the founders, based on Psalm 68:11,
*"The Lord gave the word and great was the company of those who published it."*

Published in the United States of America

ISBN: 978-1-62295-829-0
1. Biography & Autobiography / Personal Memoirs
2. Biography & Autobiography / Historical
12.12.03

# AUTHOR'S NOTE

It has been one of my greatest privileges and joys to write this story about a remarkable woman who has been my friend for twenty-three years. I was involved in the building of her family's Habitat House, and although I had a questionable title of "nurturer," she was the one who allowed me to hear her personal story. When I tutored her in English, I often remarked that someday she should write a book, and she always said, "My English not good." To which I responded, "It will be."

I have watched H'Yoanh and Y-Jim's family participate in the American dream—as productive, responsible, contributing, caring citizens of the United States.

After a beautiful, inspirational twenty-fifth anniversary celebration of their marriage at St. Joseph's Catholic Church in Raleigh on December 20, 2008, followed by a feature story in Raleigh's *News and Observer* about their journey, I called her and said, "It's time." She agreed.

On January 25, 2009, we began, often meeting together in her home on Sunday afternoons—hearing her story, listening intently to her words, reading her written texts, asking myriad questions to each other. Then the transposing of her memories became a major part of my life for the next three years.

The writing comfortably stepped into first person, and I often found myself in her skin when I cried, laughed, gave thanks, and lamented the horrors and deprivations that challenged her spirit

H'Yoanh and I have experienced unconditional love and affection throughout our friendship. This book is an offering to that spirit and a tribute to her reverence for life. May you who read these memoirs allow a thread of hope and a beam of light always to shine on your path.

—Harriet Hill

# ACKNOWLEDGMENTS

My heart is filled with gratitude—a small word that cannot possibly express the enormous appreciation I have for my family and friends. I have acknowledged only a few who welcomed us to the United States and into their lives with their love and support. My family also is a source of joy and strength.

Kathy Miller Ktul was one of our first guardian angels, teaching us—with humor, care, and grace—how to cook unfamiliar foods, how to drive a car, and how to approach learning English.

Clair and Dan Hinspeter have been with us almost from the beginning. They offered guidance for parenting skills and for educational opportunities, for ministry through our church, and are godparents for our children.

At St. Joseph's Catholic Church, we have been blessed to know and to serve with Father Saxon, Father Thanh, Father Vang, and finally, Monsignor John William. Msgr. John William has been a sustaining power in our faith. He officiated at a beautiful service to bless the twenty-five-year marriage of Y-Jim and me. We will forever be grateful for his presence in our lives.

Harriet and Jim Hill have been guiding influences since the building of our Habitat House—encouraging education, teaching English, insisting on U.S. citizenship (1995), promoting cultural events, supporting our children. Harriet and I have a spiritual connection, which became even more significant during the writing of this book.

Sometimes I cannot believe the accomplishments of my family—my husband who has supported me for over twenty-eight years and our five children whom God entrusted to me for care and direction. I thank each of them for their love and support.

And, finally, I am grateful to all who protected me and who allowed me to survive the struggles and adversities of my young life, especially to Sister Helen. I hope that the supporting names in this book will be remembered for the love, joy, sacrifice, and healing that occurred in Viet Nam. These devoted family and friends fought and died so that all of us had a chance to be free.

—H'Yoanh Ksor Buonya

With gratitude and deep appreciation, we especially wish to thank Bonny Harrison for her outstanding editing skills; Surry Roberts for his exceptional research and excellent composition of the Prologue, his advice and his enthusiasm; Mike Benge for sharing his articulate script and expertise for the Prologue; Jack Zapple for his writing proficiency of the Prologue; Allen Hill for his literary advice and support; Viet Nam veterans, Bill Thaxton, Mike Benge, Mark Sprague and Surry Roberts for contributing pictures.

—Harriet Hill

# CONTENTS

# PROLOGUE

## *Montagnards in Vietnam and Cambodia, 1941–1992*

—Surry P. Roberts, M.D.
CAPT. MC, Fifth Special Forces
Grp. (Abu) RVN (1968–69)
CIDG HOSP, Pleiku, Central Highlands
Jack Zapple, NC State University, 2008–2012

In every compelling story, there is a revival of the human spirit after incredible hardship in the face of crushing odds. This story surely ranks near the top of the list. For the reader to fully understand the circumstances that H'Yoanh Ksor Buonya faced during her flight from Vietnam to the United States, it is necessary to gain insight into the background and history of Vietnam and Cambodia during this period.

During Japanese occupation of Vietnam in WWII, the Viet Minh, an independence movement, emerged in 1941 under the revolutionary leader Ho Chi Minh, a Vietnamese agent of International Communism. Ho founded the Indochinese Communist Party, with the objective to colonize Indochina (Vietnam, Laos, and Cambodia) after the war. In August 1945 the Japanese empire fell, and the Viet Minh occupied Hanoi, seeking independence from French rule. The French military returned in force in 1945 to quell the Viet Minh. Soon after, the Viet Minh guerrilla campaign against French forces began in earnest and allowed Ho to eliminate potential patriot political leaders, one by one. The first Indochina War (December 1946–August 1954) ended after the fall of Dien Bien Phu on May 7,

1954, which allowed the French to negotiate a cease-fire with Ho Chi Minh, which created a favorable political position for him at the Geneva Conference of 1954.

The 1954 Geneva Accords separated the country at the seventeenth parallel, providing for rule in the north by the Communist forces of Ho Chi Minh and allowing the resumption of rule in the south by Emperor Bao Dai, who had been titular head under the French since 1920. The region remained tumultuous. The prime minister in the south, Ngo Dinh Diem, staged a coup in 1955 replacing Bao Dai with himself as leader of the Republic of Vietnam.

In the late 1950s, the Hanoi-controlled Viet Cong mounted a guerrilla campaign to overthrow Diem's government in the South. In this period both North and South turned into police states, conducting raids and killing anyone who seemed subversive to the regime in power.

To combat the Viet Cong, the United States CIA, in 1961, helped to organize and arm the Montagnards (ethnic minorities) in the Central Highlands as the Civilian Irregular Defense Group (CIDG) program. There were twenty-four U.S. Special Forces detachments scattered throughout Vietnam, the majority made up of Montagnards. At the height of American Special Forces operations in the Central Highlands, there were approximately thirty thousand Montagnards serving as CIDG and Mobile Strike Force Command (MIKE) forces. By 1963, the American relationship with the Catholic Diem regime broke down due to the latter's suppression of the Buddhist majority. A CIA-backed mission by the Army of the Republic of Vietnam (ARVN) resulted in Diem's arrest and assassination on November 2, 1963. Without American support the regime fell and was replaced by a line of military dictators, none of whom lasted. During this time of chaos in South Vietnam, the Communists in the North were relatively stable and expanded their presence in the South. The Gulf of Tonkin incident on August 2, 1964, gave the

United States an excuse for a full-scale intervention against the Communist forces in the North. In February 1968, the North Vietnamese Tet Offensive against the South, with its political impact, turned American public opinion against the war. At the height of the war in 1968, there were approximately 560,000 American troops on site.

The 1973 Paris Peace Accords formally recognized the sovereignty of North Vietnam and also South Vietnam. U.S. combat troops were removed by March 1973. Limited fighting continued, but without American support, South Vietnam could not hold out and suffered greatly at the hands of the Communist forces. The North Vietnamese Army (NVA) captured Phuoc Long province, on the Cambodian border in December 1974, which had served as a buffer area to protect Saigon and the populous delta. Shortly afterward, the North Vietnamese Army met with leaders of the Montagnard resistance organization, FULRO (*Front Unifie de Lutte des Races Opprimees*), and made promises of Montagnard autonomy in the Central Highlands and direct aid to the Montagnards. The purpose of this was to blunt the defense of Ban Me Thuot by FULRO. A portion of the FULRO movement agreed to stand down. The Montagnards were betrayed, and their resistance was no longer effective. The North Vietnamese Army took control of the Central Highlands from Kontum to Dalat in March 1975, and the killing of Montagnards increased significantly. President Thieu of South Vietnam removed support for the Central Highlands. Select Montagnards were promised evacuation by a navy warship off Nha Trang and from Saigon by helicopters, but these evacuation routes never materialized. Prior to the evacuation of Saigon, representatives of the American Embassy met with Montagnards and advised them to make their way into the jungle and wage guerrilla warfare against the Vietnamese Communists. Aid was promised for this, but never happened. The NVA on the Cambodian border, along with troops coming down Highway 1 along the coast, took Saigon on April 30th, 1975. North and South Vietnam were merged to form the Socialist Republic of Vietnam in July 1976. For their support of United States troops during the Vietnam War the Montagnards were the target of Communist Vietnamese vengeance and stiff reprisals in subsequent years. Thousands were hunted down and killed or spent extended time in "reeducation" (concentration) camps.

Following extensive training by Mao Tse-Tung, in China, Pol Pot became head of the Khmer Rouge Communist Party in Cambodia in 1963. The Khmer ethnic group made up 90 percent of the Cambodian population at that time. During the Cambodian Civil War from 1970–75, Lon Nol, the leader of the Khmer Republic, invited about fifty Montagnards, including Y-Bham Enoul and the rest of the FULRO leadership, to Phnom Penh for talks, which might benefit both groups. Y-Bham Enoul and his senior staff were held under house arrest in Phnom Penh for about a year. At the end of the Cambodian Civil War between the Khmer Republic and the Khmer Rouge, Pol Pot, with military assistance from the North Vietnamese, entered Phnom Penh as head of his Khmer Rouge government (Democratic Kampuchea) on April 17, 1975. He instituted the Killing Fields in which about two million city dwellers were exterminated, as were countless others living in the countryside. At the outset of the Killing Fields, Y-Bham Enoul and the other Montagnards were taken to the Phnom Penh soccer stadium and murdered. The remaining Montagnards were left without significant leadership. Pol Pot established a power across the country, distancing himself from the Vietnamese; his Khmer Rouge was organized like a confederation of independent bands led by local commanders. In a series of escalating military actions along the border between Cambodia and Communist Vietnam from 1975 through 1978, interaction between the two countries deteriorated. The Vietnamese-controlled "eastern" Khmer Rouge were ordered by Hanoi to stage an attack across the border in order to provide an excuse for Vietnam to send fifty thousand of their regular army sweeping into Cambodia in late 1978.

In January 1979, Pol Pot retreated to the Thai border. The Vietnamese established a proxy government in Phnom Penh led by Heng Samrin. During the 1980s, the Khmer Rouge fought the Vietnamese in a war of attrition, and the Vietnamese army suffered great losses. Nevertheless, the Vietnamese pushed to the Thai border, driving the remaining Khmer Rouge into the mountains and destroying the effectiveness of the Khmer Rouge government in 1985. Pol Pot died soon after. In the late 1980s with the demise of Russia and its international support, and with heavy casualties, Vietnam withdrew its troops from Cambodia and reduced their colonial aspirations. Soon after, Vietnam discharged six hundred thousand troops, many of whom shed their uniforms and took up residency in Cambodia. Refugee camps that were set up on the Thai-Cambodian border in 1979 by the United Nations/Red Cross received thousands of Cambodians and some members of the displaced Khmer Rouge and into the early 1980s small numbers of Montagnards.

After 1975, countless numbers of Montagnards fled deep into the jungles of Cambodia to continue their fight against the Vietnamese. They were joined by those escaping from the concentration camps and a continuous stream of villagers in small bands fleeing the severe repression in Vietnam. Montagnards by the thousands died of starvation, disease, or were killed by the Vietnamese. Some of the Montagnards chose to cross Cambodia to the Thai border for survival, essentially one of the three known depleted battalions of FULRO, with a few women and children. This meant walking through unfamiliar jungles and crossing the Mekong River on homemade rafts. The Montagnards had to negotiate permission to pass through the territory of each independent band of the Khmer Rouge. They were under constant threat of being pressed into service by the Khmer Rouge, and many were. The men were used as porters or point men, and others were used to clear mine fields and booby traps. In 1986, 212 survivors at a refugee camp on the Thai border were evacuated to the Philippines, where they were provided several months of preparation for their arrival in Greensboro, North Carolina, in November of that year. A second group of 400 Montagnards, deemed by the press as the "Lost Battalion," were found by the United Nations in 1992 in Cambodia along the Vietnamese border and were soon flown to the United States to join the first group. A third battalion of Montagnards and their dependents attempted to cross Laos for the safety of Thailand but were met by a large Vietnamese army unit and annihilated.

"The Vietnam War extracted its toll, and one of the most tragic and little-known consequences was the decimation and destruction it brought to the Highland People. By War's end in 1975, around 85 percent of their villages were either in ruins or abandoned. Of the estimated one million highlanders, between 200,000 and 220,000 had died or were killed, including around one-half of their adult male population. But a great many were not killed by bullets or bombs. They perished because their world was shattered" (Dr. Gerald Hickey, *Shattered World* [University of Pennsylvania Press, 1993]).

# INTRODUCTION

I come from a heritage of people who settled in the Central Highlands of Vietnam and Cambodia about two thousand years ago. Of Malaysian decent, these mountain people, called Montagnards, prospered in their world of shared resources, community responsibility, respect for individuals, harmony with nature, and moral justice. For generations, they farmed in the fertile soil of the Highlands and practiced rotation of crops, which fed the thousands of villagers who lived peacefully in the jungles and fields in the central mountainous area of Vietnam.

They had their own beliefs and practices, which included several deities, and were exposed to Catholicism through French missionaries around 1850 and to American Protestantism early in the 1930s. Music, dance, and art were important in communication between families, dialects, and tribal understanding.

In 1958, the Central Highlands of Vietnam was a beautiful area of well-kept farms, Montagnard villages, and supportive communities. But the Vietnamese government, led by President Ngo Dinh Diem, in the name of "modernizing the Montagnard nomads," began to take land from the Montagnards and to resettle massive groups of South Vietnamese in the confiscated areas. They gave Montagnard farming communities substandard lands, which flooded and lacked good soil for the crops that they planted. The government resettlement led to the formation of a Montagnard defense group called Bajaraka (named after four of their major tribes—Bahnar, Jarai, Rhade, and Koho). In addition, Vietnam was rapidly advancing toward war.

It was into this world that I was born, sometime in August 1958. My official day is August 8, but since many Montagnards were illiterate, few birth certificates were officially recorded, and reliable birth and death dates were committed to memories.

# THE EARLY YEARS

My mother passed away when I was four or five months old. My dad (Nay Dong) was in the Vietnam military service away from home.

I was maybe seven or eight when I heard the first story about my mother as a young girl.

She was with a group of friends who gathered to see a psychic read palms and make predictions for the future. He read my mother's palm and told her that she would have one baby, and then she would die. The prediction seemed absurd until she married and was pregnant with me (her first child). During her pregnancy, she became seriously ill. The palm reader's words haunted her, and fear took over her life—fear of dying and fear of losing her baby.

My family said that shortly after I was born, my mother held me close and named me H'Yoanh Ksor. I nudged at her breast for nursing and clung to her, but she was unable to feed me regularly. The fear lived within her, and sickness overpowered her.

My grandmother (I don't remember her name) helped care for me. I was told that she chewed bananas into a paste and mashed rice for me to eat, and she wrung out sugarcane stalks for whatever sugar milk she could get just to keep me alive. She carried me everywhere she went and showed me great love and kindness.

My mother soon died, and my grandma, my uncle Ksor Mtuat (my grandma's son), and I moved to a room in another aunt and uncle's house. That aunt (my mother's sister, Ksor H'Jok) and her husband (Siu Ing) had a daughter (H'Kong) three months younger than I. My aunt nursed both of us for a short while, but she had a difficult time taking care of two baby girls.

Uncle Ksor Mtuat said that after we moved in, my grandmother became ill and coughed day and night for many months but still watched over me. Before her last breath, she said, "Take good care of my granddaughter; don't hurt her!" My Aunt H'Jok and Uncle Ing Siu became Ami and Ama, my mom and my dad.

Some of those younger years are confusing to me, but I know that Ami and Ama could not look after me very well. When my ama went into the military service, my mom needed help. She took me to the Catholic Center, an orphanage and a school in Cheo Reo, a small town about a two-hour dusty walk away from our village, and left me. There I stayed most of the time from about two or three years of age.

The nuns at the center, Sister Helen and Sister Goretti, were very kind and showed me great love. They first called me H'Ton, which means "mother died—no milk." Later, Sister Amanda gave me the name of H'Tien (meaning *holy one* or *spirit*). That name remained with me throughout my years in Vietnam.

## *Inside the Barrels*

About the time that I was four, I was moved from the orphanage to the school to begin my lessons. We were separated by ages, but one evening after dinner, my friend H'Nhun and I were left in the dormitory with some older girls. It was novena Wednesday, and the nuns had gone to church. The girls gave both of us plastic bags and said, "Go get some dry milk from the storage room and bring it back to us! We are hungry. It stays open until after nine when the nuns come back from church."

We did not know where the storage room was, so they took us down the stairs, opened the door to a large room where the food was kept, and turned on the light. Inside were barrels and boxes and cans, and it smelled of meat and spices that made our eyes open wide and my mouth feel watery. My whole body trembled as my hands clapped together at the sight of all that food and at the dream that we could take something sweet back to our dormitory. We also thought that the girls would help us open boxes and tins. Instead, they took the lids off two barrels that were about two feet apart, put each of us in a barrel, walked out, turned out the light, and closed the door.

It was dark—very dark. We screamed. No one came.

H'Nhun and I could not see each other, but I called to her, and she said that she was standing up, but she could not climb out of the barrel. I could also stand up, but something soft and powdery came up to my knees, and my eyes barely reached the rim. I put my hands on the inside of my container. It felt cold and slippery and hard like metal.

We screamed again—long screams—but no one came.

"What do you have in your barrel?" she called across to me.

I tasted a handful with my tongue. "It's dry, sweet milk, and it has a good taste. What do you have?"

"It doesn't have any flavor, and it's dry in my mouth. I think it might be flour," she said while making a spitting sound.

I reached for another handful and began to lap it up like a dog. I ate and ate until I felt a little sick. "Yum, this is so good."

"I wish that I had it over here," she said. "Why don't you throw some to me?"

"How?" I felt around in the powder; then packed the dry milk into a ball. "Okay! Here it comes." And I threw it in her direction.

"I didn't get anything," she complained. "Do it again!" Our voices echoed from the barrels, and we both giggled and laughed and forgot that we were scared.

"Okay! Here's some more." I threw with all my strength, but my arms kept hitting the side of the barrel. I threw again, and she got some of it and licked it off her hands. Then she tossed a ball of flour back at me, but it didn't pack together very well. It did hit the barrel, and I could feel it in my hair and on my face.

"Send me some more," she said.

"You throw some to me too," I laughed.

And that is how we passed the time until we heard footsteps in the hall. We became very quiet, didn't move, didn't breathe. The nuns, returning from church, talked as they passed the storage room. The door opened, closed, and the key turned the lock. Our fear quickly rose into screams. Someone unlocked the door, walked in, and turned on the light. "Who is here? What is this?"

My eyes became accustomed to the bright bulb hanging on a cord from the ceiling, as I slowly stood on my tiptoes and peered over the rim of the barrel. Three nuns stared through the doorway and stood in silence, their wide-eyed gaze stunned by the white carpet.

I could see the top of H'Nhun's head in the other barrel. It was white. I was white, the barrels were white, the floor was white, and the sisters looked like storm clouds of white drifting toward us. They reached into the barrels and lifted out two unidentifiable little white ghosts—a mist of dry milk and flour floating from our bodies.

The sisters could not control themselves and be mad at us. They started smiling and then laughing. All they could recognize were big black eyes surrounded by angelic white robes—without wings. They took us to the dining room where they could see us better and then to the bath to clean us up.

Sister Helen arrived and brought with her a very mad face. "Why are you here? It is past time for you to be in bed."

We just stared at her because we were nervous about telling on the big girls who got us into trouble. She said that we would see her early the next day, and we were put to bed immediately. Falling asleep was not a problem.

The following morning, we stood very straight and still in front of Sister Helen, not even imagining what might happen to us. "Who did this to you? Who told you to go into the storage room? Why were you in the barrels? Tell me the truth!" Her mad face was still showing.

We had whispered to each other about being scared of what the older girls would do to us if we told and about how mad we were at them for putting us in the dark room in the barrels. But we finally had to tell Sister Helen their names, and she told us to never listen to the older girls anymore. We both nodded our heads yes and shook our heads no and were so happy that she did not punish us. But we heard that the pranksters had to do extra work at the school, and the rules became more strict. We never were left alone again, and we walked out of our way to keep from passing close to the mischief makers.

Sister Helen named H'Nhun "Little Cat" and gave me the name "Little Rat." And the nuns teased us about our adventure for a long time.

## *My Papa*

At the Catholic Center/Thanh Gia School, there were many of us who were considered orphans. We were like a family without families, except that I did know that I had relatives in a village somewhere else and that they cared for me, and I visited them from time to time. But I was loved by the nuns and by friends, and I didn't remember much about my other life.

One day, about 1964, while we were playing in the field before our 5:00 p.m. dinner and our study time, Sister Helen called for me to come and line up with a dozen other boys and girls in front of two large boxes on the ground—gifts for the children at the school. I stood in the middle of that line. Then a white man in an American uniform, who had three uniformed men standing in the courtyard near him, walked up and down in front of us, from right to left to right and looked at each of us very kindly. Sister Helen pointed to me and said something that I did not understand.

I was the smallest of the girls and watched him with only my eyes moving. He stopped in front of me, reached out to take my hand, and encouraged me to come out of the line. He stooped down, reached into one of the boxes, and handed me the most beautiful baby doll I had ever seen. When her feet touched the ground, her head was under my chin. I did not know what to say and just looked at her, and then at him, and then at her, and when I put my arms around her, she felt happy, and I felt less nervous and scared. The man gave both of us a hug and a gentle smile, and Sister Helen signaled for the rest of the children to look in the boxes for more toys. She led the man over to a bench where they sat down, while all of us laughed and giggled, and I continued to stare at my doll.

Sister Helen called another girl's name, H'Phian Nay. We all rushed back into line, and H'Phian Nay came over and stood beside me, as Sister Helen directed. I did not say a word. I just smiled at her and showed her the doll. The man and Sister Helen talked a long time and then signed a paper and gave it to another nun. The man smiled at me and at Phian, went back to his friends and to their two jeeps, and left. I was so excited about my gift that I did not eat much dinner that night and barely finished my little bit of study. But when I climbed into bed, I tucked the doll baby under my covers, hugged her tight, and went into a happiness sleep.

The next morning, everything seemed normal, except that I had to leave my doll in my bed. After my lunch, I went back to her, and we all took naps. I was awakened by the *beep-beep* of a car blowing its horn. I was lying there looking at my new baby when Sister Helen came in and said, "Let's get your things together. Your new dad has come to get you."

Sister Helen said that my friend Phian, who was a little older than I was, would go with me, that the man who had brought me the doll wanted to be my daddy, and that Phian would stay with me until he could take me to America and adopt me. I did not know what that meant or what to say, so I wrapped one arm around my doll baby and held Phian's hand, and we left the dormitory. The friendly man was waiting by his jeep with another man in a uniform. They lifted us into the seats, started the engine, and we drove off waving to Sister Helen—feeling a strong arm around both of us, the wind blowing in our faces, and the road bumping us up and down.

My new daddy was a captain in the U.S. Army. He was very kind and seemed to want to make us happy. He wanted me to call him Papa, and he named me Anna and gave the name Mary to Phian. We all lived in his bunker house with sandbags around the outside. Papa tried to teach me some English words. I learned a little, but he arranged for us to be driven to our school each day to study in our own language. John, his friend in uniform, looked after us when Papa was away. And whenever Papa returned, he let me ride on his shoulders and walk around the village that was close by and dance in the shower. He bought new clothes for us, and we all laughed a lot. Our interpreter told me that Papa had a daughter in the United States who was my age and whom he missed very much and a wife who was going to have a baby. They wanted to bring me to their home as another daughter. There was a love between us that I had never experienced. He had many friends who called him Judge, and now he had a new little girl who adored calling him "my papa."

I don't remember the time—it could have been five weeks or nine months, but my mom and dad back in the village also wanted my papa to adopt one of their daughters and take her to America. He said he would not, and they insisted that he return me to them. Papa became very upset, and when my dad Ing Siu and his daughter, H'Kong, showed up at the camp, Papa took all of us back to the Thanh Gia School in his vehicle and talked to Sister Helen and my ama. When he came out, he was so angry that he threw Ama's bike into the bushes in front of the school. I knew that something terrible had happened, but I could not understand all of the words between the translator and Sister Helen and my papa. Sister Helen tried to give him another girl to take, but he refused. I cried and hugged him and begged him not to be angry and not to leave me. He hugged me long and kissed me with a wet face, but then drove off, and someone told me that my papa did not eat or sleep for three days. I never saw Papa again.

## *Dreams Broken, Life Lived*

Courtesy of Bill Thaxton

I turned six, and my ami and ama told Sister Helen that I was needed at home to help. It was the custom in our culture that the oldest had a big responsibility to help with the chores. I heard Sister Helen's voice arguing that I was too young, but it was decided that I would go to them whenever a group was walking in that direction, and I should come back to the center as soon as the chores were done. She was very strong about not letting me walk the two hours to and from the village by myself. But Ami did not always return me promptly to the center. I could hear her say that no one was going that day, and no other words were necessary.

By that time, there was a baby boy, Buk, who arrived about a year and a half after H-Kong, and then four girls: H'Plip, H'Nhim, and later H'Lip and H'Ty—all very close together. I dreamed of life with my papa; I lived life with the family of my birth. I sang to my baby as much as to my sisters, and I learned to let my memories bring happiness to my days.

The people in my village were not happy to see me come out to work with them, because they would have to stop and explain how to do the jobs expected of me by my family. I would stand there until someone was willing to give me directions. "Why has this little girl been sent out to work around the village? She is too young," they would complain. They seemed to love me, but while helping me, they could not stop talking about my mom. "Don't come next time," they told me, "you poor baby." But I wouldn't say anything and came again when I was told.

I learned how to pull weeds in the rice paddies and to pick and pound rice. I thought that it was a lot of fun, a chance to be in the water and to make talk with the neighbors. Even though the villagers disapproved, they allowed me to work by their sides, and they shared their food and chatter with the "one so small."

The villagers were also unhappy when they found out that my mom had sent me out to tend the family's water buffalo, one female and four smaller ones. On the first day, I did not know what to do, but I watched how the other families of children and adults moved their herds. So with the small lunch that my mom had fixed for me tucked safely in a little woven basket that I strapped on my back, I stood on my tiptoes, opened the gate, waved my arms to tell the buffalo to come out, and tried to make my voice sound older. They shifted from side to side and moved slowly through the gap and toward the meadow behind our neighbors and their own buffalo. It was scary at first. I was only a little taller than their knees and was sure that the buffalo would run when they got the chance to be free from their pens. But they just strolled out into the field, nudging and nibbling clumps of fresh grasses as they went, and I, dressed in a short dark skirt and print blouse, went after them, the flip-flops on my feet flapping on the ground as I ran.

Those smart buffalo seemed to know when it was time for lunch. I was glad for that, as I was always tired and hungry. I ate whatever my mom had packed for me and then took a nap near the animals.

One day, all of the buffalo crossed the river on the other side of the field. We followed, but the water was deep, and my cousin, Ksor Puin, had to carry me on his shoulders. Just after the herd settled down to eat the fresh grasses in their new surroundings, and we were drying our clothes, we heard a lot of loud screeching noises from the nearby trees. We looked up to see groups of monkeys swinging from limbs and yelling at us as if to say, "Get out of here, this is our place!" They dropped to the ground from their hiding places, and we ran. They charged at us and then ran back to their trees, then charged again. The adults screamed and ran and waded back across the river, but my young cousin stayed and helped carry the children to the other side. Before he came back for me, I stood on the bank shaking and crying and wondering if the frightful monkeys would eat me. They kept charging, teeth showing, mean lips on their faces. I was the last terrified child on the bank when Puin finally swam across and carried me to safety on his back.

In the late afternoon, some of the men waded the river to get the buffalo. The monkeys stayed in the trees as though they were afraid of the men and only found fun in chasing women and children—maybe because we made similar screeching noises as we ran away.

After the buffalo were collected and herded across to our side, they ambled toward the village as though they knew that the day was at an end. The five in my care followed the others and hardly stopped to nibble more grass. At least I didn't have to chase them. When I got to the gate I had left opened, they walked through and back to their pens, seemingly glad to be home. I climbed on the gate, wrapped the rope over the end of the fence, and closed them in for the night.

The villagers protested loudly to my mom and grumbled about her to one another. I had charge of the buffalo only a few more times.

## Our House in the Village

(Type of Jarai Tribal Village House)

(Type of fire box used for cooking)

Our house, about five feet off the ground, was built on stilts made of tree trunks. The thatched roof, over bamboo walls and floor, helped to protect us from the heat, rain, and all of the weather. A ramp, crossed with bamboo footholds, led up to the entrance in the front of the house where there was a door and a large window, both made of panels that slid from side to side. The same was in the back half of the house and allowed for ventilation, for the heat and for the stoves. Guests were admitted only at the front entrance, but relatives and close friends could come through the back door anytime.

There were three open rooms for sleeping along one side, divided by bamboo walls, and one long room on the other side for activities and for eating. One of the three rooms was for Ami and Ama, and all of the children slept on mats in the middle room. The third small room was in the front corner and saved for guests. When the children lay down on the bamboo floor for the night, we were head to toe to head, or we cuddled up together and shared a blanket for warmth. Sometimes I would curl up into a ball, wrapping myself in whatever clothes I had, to keep away the bugs and the cold. Ami did not seem to notice when we grew larger.

In the middle of our living space, we had two wooden boxes, which were filled with dirt and were safe for burning wood and charcoal. Near the front of the house was one that gave off light and heat, and at the back of the room was a stove for cooking. The cooking stove also partially heated the house, which was good in the winter, but in the summer months, the heat disturbed our sleep, and the smoke in the evenings was often suffocating. When it rained, the smoke could not escape to the damp outside.

Our cooking area was built inside a heavy three-foot-by-three-foot-square wooden frame, about eight inches tall, filled with dirt, and large enough to hold several pots and bowls on flat stones set in the dirt. The wood fire was built in the center between three foot-long stone posts (each one two and a half inches in diameter). The ends of the posts were embedded in the dirt and positioned to lean toward the middle to form a triangle that supported a cooking pot, while other prepared dishes sat in the charcoal keeping warm on the flat stones. The hot dirt would also give enough heat to help steam other food. We ate from dishes and bowls that we bought in the market, and sometimes used chopsticks to pick up our food, but most of the time we ate with our hands. Ladles were made from bamboo cut into sixteen-inch lengths with the bottoms whittled into scoops to lift food from the big pots onto our plates.

We used gourds to collect water for cooking and for drinking. The villagers packed fresh gourds in mud until the seeds inside dried and shriveled up. Then the seeds were shaken out of the necks, and the gourds were washed out many times until the insides were totally clean. Different villages had their own distinct gourd colors and designs. Our village had white gourds. Dark and shiny outer colors covered the gourds in the wealthier village near the city.

Inside our house, next to the cooking area, sat a large metal pot like a caldron, about two feet in diameter, filled with water that we changed most days. We took turns bringing buckets of water from a stream on the other side of our fields. I could take just a few steps at a time that allowed me to rest my heavy load and to keep the water from splashing out. When it was fresh, we drank it, but mostly we used it to wash our pots and dishes.

I should have learned to cook, but at that time, the importance of good food did not come first to my mind. My mom's food was only a little different each day. We ate rice at every meal—our bread. Sometimes she varied the dinner with eggplant, pumpkin leaves, hot peppers, bamboo shoots, or fruit. Occasionally she made a broth with bits of buffalo meat, fish, pork, or chicken, all of which she hung from our bamboo rafters to dry. Our living was simple—no milk or cheese, no refrigerator, no electricity.

The animals that we raised—chickens, pigs, cows, or buffalo—were slaughtered only for special guests or for important occasions and feast days. If a family had several guests, a chicken or two might be cooked. Guests always ate first with the man of the house, and the rest of the family ate what was left after they finished.

But animals were usually offered as sacrifice (most villagers worshipped nature), and after the ceremony, everyone would eat the meat and any other dishes prepared by individual families. If the whole village was involved, a buffalo or oxen would be slaughtered by a villager, especially for the yearly harvest feast.

When my ama went in the army, they paid him a small amount, which helped us buy what we needed. Our possessions were limited, but my ami had a few pieces of jewelry made of brass chains with decorations, which she wore on festival days and for special occasions. I was often curious about the small enclosed basket where she kept them in her room, but I never asked her where they came from.

At night an oil lamp lit the house with flickering colors of orange and familiar shadows. Most of the time, we were comfortable enough, and sometimes, ahead of the sun, I would fall asleep before the evening meal was finished. But someone would always wake me and take me to my room to roll out my mat on the bamboo floor. During the warmer months, I sometimes had a blanket under me that helped to soften the floor, and some nights I don't think I slept at all. We had bedbugs that crawled up through the bamboo and bit me and sucked my blood. My mom would say, "Take a heavy stick and hit it hard on the floor around your mat, and they will fall to the ground—good food for the chickens!" It did help a little, but some nights I scratched a lot—like the hens below me.

# Friends, Education, and Family

## *Transition*

I was in my sixth year when a man began to visit our house to talk to my mom about me and something concerning education, which I did not fully understand at the time. I learned that his name was Cheo Siu and that his wife was some relative of my grandpa's. One of his daughters was already taking classes at a nearby school.

After he and his wife came several times to our village, I called the man Awa (uncle) Cheo. During one of those visits with my mom, he discussed with her something about me and God and going to Catholic meetings at a friend's home, and Ami said that I could go. There were no school classes at that time. Awa Cheo came for me on Sundays and took me to his home for religious services, where a German priest, who traveled on his bicycle from the city, conducted the lessons and mass for numerous friends and family members.

One day I heard Ami and Uncle Cheo talking in voices that seemed urgent. My mom said to him, "My child does not know anything. I won't let her go."

But after their voices got louder and their words shorter, the man looked at me and said, "Come with me!" I did not know what to do. I looked at Ami and then at Awa.

My mom seemed angry and said, "Yes, just go with him!"

Awa and his wife had been good and kind to me, but I was afraid. He said to me, "I want to help you. You are old enough to go back to Thanh Gia School and to learn, but you must stay there to sleep and eat, like you did at the center before, because it is too far away to come home every night. I have been trying for a long time to get your *ami* to agree. You are a smart little girl, and I know that you can do well there."

Ami said, "Go! Go with him! I don't know what to do. Take some clothes and go with him." And she turned her back.

I just stood there, looking through watery eyes, but I did as she told me and put my few clothes in a small cloth bag that hung on my shoulders. Ami could hardly look at me. She gave me a quick hug. Uncle Cheo took my hand, and we walked out of the door. He settled me on the back of his bicycle, and he paddled off to Thanh Gia, which means "Holy Family School." The almost two-hour ride to Cheo Reo was bumpy over the dirt roads, but there was relief after we reached the pavement closer to the city.

When we arrived, there were many children, and the building looked bigger than I remembered. I was nervous and scared and did not see anyone I knew. Not many young girls from homes in the villages went to school at that time. Education was not important, but working in the fields was necessary for a family's survival.

I stood in the door of the school, holding Awa's hand, my eyes wide, and my heart coming out of my blouse. Then, like a robed angel flowing down the hall came Sister Helen, and I ran to hug her and to lose my face in the folds of her habit. I peeked out and saw Awa's smile. It would be all right; I would make new friends— and best of all, Sister Helen was standing right beside me.

I did stay at Thanh Gia, where I began my love for learning and my devotion to education. In fact, my mom and dad, seeing how well I did at the Catholic school, sent their first daughter, H'Kong, to stay also.

My beloved Sister Helen

## *Thanh Gia School*

Thanh Gia was a blessing in my life. I was at an age to absorb everything, and the lessons fascinated me, as well as gave me direction. I loved learning. The buildings grew smaller the longer I stayed, and the friends increased in number.

At night, with the mosquito netting drawn around each of our beds, our large dormitory room looked like a cemetery with one hundred or more tombstones lined up in rows, bodies of small and large children resting on the surface of leggy cots. The nights after we filled our bag mattresses with new straw, I could feel the dust from the straw creep through the cloth cover, and my nose would feel twice as large as I breathed the air in the room. It was like sleeping in a barn. But the covers were softer than a bamboo floor, and I was happy to have a warm place at night and a bed of my own.

Every morning a nun woke us up early by clapping her hands. There was no bell, or soft voice, and there was no time to snuggle down into the covers to stay dreaming for another few minutes. We had to get up immediately, straighten our mattresses over the wooden slats of our beds, fold our blankets, tie back the mosquito netting from around our beds, see that our few belongings were straight, and get dressed for school and for our chores.

We had little time for the bathroom, as there were few places to relieve ourselves, and there were so many of us. Our toilets were concrete slabs with places to sit over a trough that ran to a cistern outside. Cleaning the toilets was one of our shared responsibilities. After we washed down the floor and around the toilets, we poured water from two buckets down the toilet holes and into the trough. If sticks, used for wiping, were left in the hole, we had to retrieve and discard them before we carried the two water containers to the nearby well to refill them for the children who would clean the next day. That was not my favorite job, but we were expected not to complain. At least the boys took care of their room next door.

Outside we had our own basins, each with our names, for washing our faces and brushing our teeth. We spit on the ground and poured the water from our bowls out onto a garden area nearby. Rainwater was always collected for drinking and for washing, but we relied a lot on the water from the well.

Chores, in groups of ten, were done before breakfast and rotated each week by the nuns. The assignment that I liked best was cleaning up trash and raking sand and dirt in the main courtyard in front of the school. I often found small xu coins that someone had dropped. It was not much money, but I liked having something that I could call my own.

The breakfast food was different most mornings with a variety of potatoes, sweet potatoes, yucca roots, bread once a week, and oftentimes, rice with fish sauce. We were fully awake by the time that we ate, and our chattering tongues often made us reach the classroom just in time for the beginning bell.

The first classes that are in my memory were on the second floor, up a long flight of stairs that challenged my little legs. I learned how to read and to write and to relive the fun I had during summer days in my village at my friend H'Don's school. Classes were long for us who were so young, but in those early years, the excitement of learning took me into areas that put joy into climbing stairs.

Every morning, we first prayed our faith and then recited from the plaque on the wall: *"Tifn Hoc Lf Hau Hoc Vain"* ("First Respect, Education After"). Respect for teachers was absolute.

Wednesdays were bathing days, and the Ayun River, about an hour's walk from our school, was swift enough to allow the dirt and soap from our bodies to float quickly away. There were no school classes on those afternoons, and each of us was with an adult, for the river was deep in places and rapid in others. Our teachers shared their soap and shampoo with those of us who had little. I always looked forward to the cool water and to lying down in the shallow part in my clothes, even though I could not swim. Tiny waves rippled over my arms and legs, and my long hair drifted around my face. After cleaning our bodies and a brief time of splashing, we all emerged from the river and let the sun dry our clothes while we walked back to the dormitory. My dress, even though draped almost to my ankles, was one piece of cloth, dropping from a strapless wrap to a sheath that hung close to my body. By the time I reached the school, it was no longer wet. I slid my feet into my flat thong sandals, and I was clean for another week.

## My Mother's Name

My last name, Ksor, is the name of the family ancestors of my mother, Ksor H'Tlok. In the Montagnard custom, anyone with our same last name of Ksor is considered to be a cousin for a lifetime. We are all a family and are responsible for helping one another wherever we are. The women and the female children have an *H* at the beginning of their names, which designates the female gender and the village where they were born.

My friend H'Don Ksor was a sister to me. She was three years older than I was and went to school before I was old enough to go. She liked to pretend that she was my teacher. H'Don would make me sit on a step outside, or at a table inside her house, to learn the ABCs and numbers, and when I missed something, she would rap me on the head with her wooden ruler. I think that she liked the rapping as much as the teaching.

I could not talk well or tell stories like the other children because I stuttered, and my tongue seemed to twist in my mouth. But I loved to sing, and when H'Don gathered other children at her house, she taught all of us songs and dances (like the cha-cha) and how to play hide-and-seek, kick ball, and lots of other games. I was the happiest when I was with her, and her summer classes helped me after I entered Thanh Gia in the first of the grades.

H'Don lived with her aunt, H'Prep, because her aunt did not have a daughter. H'Prep's sister, H'Don's mother, lived with her father in the village but visited often. The house of H'Prep was beside ours. When I was living with Ama and Ami, H'Don would call to me to come and play with her, and I would skip over with happiness when I could. Our friendship was bound by love and loneliness.

Occasionally, after our chores were done, we would get to play in the fields and the village until our evening meal. It was a time to run and laugh and feel free. I miss my "sister" very much and wish that we could share our close relationship again.

About the time I was seven, H'Don, my cousin, and I were playing in the field behind my house when my cousin and I got into a fight about something that I could no longer remember. What I do remember clearly is that he said to me, "Why didn't you die with your mother?"

And I said back to him, "Why did you not die with yours?"

While we were shouting at each other, I just considered those to be hurtful words from mad children. But H'Don's face froze, and her hand went to her mouth, while her eyes seemed glued to mine.

"What is the matter?" I asked as my cousin ran off.

"He should not have said that." And she turned away.

"Tell me why you are so upset. He was just being mean. I don't like him."

"You said you are staying at your Uncle Mtuat's house tonight. Ask him about your cousin's words."

H'Don ran across the field toward her house, leaving me to stare after her. I wanted to follow, but her voice told me that it was important for me to go directly to Awa's house.

My mother's brother, Awa Mtuat, carefully explained to me about my mother's illness and about her fears and about how much my grandmother loved me, and how we three lived with Ami and Ama from the time after my mother died, when I was still a tiny baby. I had heard the story before but had not thought past those early details. I listened quietly, unsure of what he was exactly saying, and then asked if I could go to H'Don's to stay the night.


We sat down on the lowest step to H'Don's house, and she could not seem to get her breath. "H'Tien, I have tried to tell you several times but always thought that someone else—some of your family— should tell you, but they never did. I know that you have heard the villagers talk about your ama and ami, and you have heard them say how sweet your mother was, but you never seemed to think that your mother and Ami were two different people. We sat silent for a few minutes. "My mother told me that your grandmother looked after you before she died, and then your ami nursed you and H'Kong together and kept you as her own until she had more children and ran out of strength. She took you to the Catholic Center because she knew that you would have food and care."

I could feel her looking at me, but I stared at the ground. "My uncle told me all of that, but I'm not sure that I believe him. I know that somehow I am different from the rest of the family, but I have not thought much about it and accepted that maybe I am not good enough."

"No, your ami loves you, but since you are the oldest, she has expected more from you."

I was so young to hear her words, and she was not old enough to say them with such kindness, but there we were, two little girls—two sisters at heart—sharing the realities of life.

That night, I ate dinner at H'Don's house and stayed until morning. I must have slept some, but I remember lying beside her on her mat and letting various conversations, that I had previously ignored, struggle for interpretation in my mind.

I loved my family, including Ami and Ama, but I didn't feel connected to them. There were six other children (five girls and one boy), and I made their seventh—a lot of mouths to feed.

*Maybe I can stay more evenings with H'Don's family and with friends and eat more meals away from home. Now I understand why the village is my family too. They have been very kind to me.*

Uncle Mtuat had told me also that Ami and Ama had asked H'Bro R'com, a close family friend, to marry my birth father and to look after me. She refused the former but treated me as a daughter. Her goodness and her love I treasured in my heart.

## *My Father*

I don't remember much about my father, Nay Dong, except that he was in the South Vietnamese Army. My family said that he came to my ami's house, maybe twice, and picked me up and cried, but I did not understand and was always afraid of him. After the last baby, H'Lip Ksor, was born, he came to the house a few times and picked her up and cried, maybe thinking of the baby girl that he once had. On those occasions, he never spoke to me. But the few times that he visited the village while I was young, when other people were around, he would hold me on his lap and brag about me.

He was handsome, with dark complexion, and I remember wanting him to like me, but he seemed only to talk about himself while he caressed the small gun that he carried at his side. It frightened me. His parents, my grandparents who lived in the village, would brag about him and about me, but after he went away, they would not speak to me or act as though I was their granddaughter. I heard later that Nay Dong told the army that he had a daughter, and they gave him extra money for my care, but I never saw any of it.

I am not sure how old I was when my father returned from the army for my mother's death anniversary—maybe three or four. But I do remember that he came in Montagnard ceremonial clothes, and he had dark hair around his mouth, making him look scary. He led the way to the graveyard for friends and family. They chanted mourning words in loud voices, and at the ceremony, they cried and read poems of farewell. My father sipped rice wine and seemed to mourn the most.

Friends and family had rebuilt the wooden house that sheltered the family's graves (often as many as ten) and had painted it with a dark paint, adding pictures of birds and flowers for decorations. The house, with its walls halfway up the sides, was large enough for people to sit around on benches inside and sometimes to sleep there (during the mourning time once a year) to be close to their loved ones.

During the ceremony, my distressed father pulled out his gun and shot it into the air, frightening all who were there. I was terrified by the noise. I don't know where I was standing at the time, but I remember villagers telling me to run—run and hide. The jumping in my stomach made my feet not touch the ground as I darted behind shops and houses. Later, friends told me that my father had wanted to shoot himself and to shoot me so that the two of us could be with my mother. He never heard my heavy breathing; he never found me. I never went back to the place where my mother was buried.

As I grew older, I saw him in the village a few times when he would return from the army, and he came to my school once or twice, telling the school that he was my father, but he did not recognize me, and I thought he was a stranger. I was confused when he introduced himself as my father.

In 1972, in my seventh year in school, the government reported that Nay Dong was missing in the war in Cambodia. His body was never returned. After they told me, I had no emotion for the loss. I did pray for the peace of his soul, and occasionally a sadness came into my heart for all of the times that we could have known each other. But by that age, I was not alone. I had developed a strength that walked with me and gained many friends, who showed me great love.

## *Thang Tien Middle School*

From 1969 to 1973, I attended Thang Tien Middle School (sixth to ninth grades—called high school) in Cheo Reo/Phu Bon. It was a small private Catholic school that belonged to a priest, and most of the teachers were nuns and brothers, but a few were from the army and some from the Catholic Church in the city. Our principal was the Rev. Nguyen Hou Vien.

Sister Helen or the nuns or Awa Cheo must have arranged for me to be enrolled, for my family had no money to send me, and they did not understand that private school education was not free—or why I wanted to go when they needed me at home.

Getting to Thang Tien every day did not seem to be a problem for me because I had a bicycle, and even though Cheo Reo was a two-hour walk, I could make it there in much less time.

On the first day of school, I felt very smart in my below-the-knee dark skirt, white blouse, and a backpack containing my lunch strapped over my shoulders, riding my old bicycle all the way to my new learning adventure. Unfortunately, the bicycle did not last much longer than that day, so after it completely became a pile of twisted metal, I began the back-and-forth trips from my home on foot. My mornings then began at 5:00 a.m. so that I could make the two-hour walk before the eight o'clock class. Someone must have told the principal what I was doing, because I soon learned that I could stay at the school during the week and walk home only once on Fridays—and walk back to school on Mondays.


Every morning, before we could go in to class, all of the students assembled in straight lines in front of the school to do controlled exercises, prayers of our faith, and a pledge to our country.

The small sixth-grade classroom was overcrowded with forty students, so the principal divided us into two groups: 6-A and 6-B. There was enough excitement and nervousness to fill three rooms. After I was assigned to 6-B, I realized that some of my classmates from Thanh Gia would be with me. We whispered and held hands and giggled until order was demanded, but when I looked around the room, I saw that the Montagnard girls wore black skirts and white blouses while the Vietnamese girls wore long white dresses. I saw in their eyes that they noticed me, but I did not have money to buy new clothes. I could pretend that I didn't care, but I tried extra hard to be sure that my clothes were always clean.

When we began our first day of schoolwork in our new room, I sat at a desk with my classmate Dung who had notebooks and pencils in her backpack. I did not know where she got her things, but I borrowed a pencil and paper from her to write down what we were supposed to do and what I needed for my backpack.

As the class began, one by one we stood up and gave our names to one another. And during the day, different teachers entered our room to introduce themselves and to tell us about the subjects that we would study: math, social studies, language, science, history, and English as a second language. Each teacher said, "Hello and welcome to the sixth grade!" Then they introduced the textbooks that we would use for classes. It did not seem too different from the fifth grade. Oh, but was I very wrong.

I noticed that the other students had school supplies also, and I assumed that the school had given them the notebooks and pencils. But because I was shy, and I did not want my stuttering to be noticed, I didn't ask who to see about the requirements. So that Friday night, when I went home for the weekend, I told my mom that I needed money for supplies. She gave me twenty dong (Vietnamese money), which I took to school on Monday to buy pencils for myself. The teacher said, "This will buy only a notebook and one pencil. You will need much more." I bought those from my teacher and then began to understand about the money that was necessary for textbooks and more notebooks. The classes had already begun, and I took all the notes I could on the paper that Dung had given to me and in my notebook during the next week.

So the following weekend, I asked my mom for more money. She said, "I gave you twenty dong last week. Why did you spend it so fast? Your sister is in school too, and she still has her money."

My sister, H'Kong, had been retained in the fifth grade and was in a different school, along with Buk (third grade) and H'Plip (second grade). I could not answer my mom why H'Kong got her supplies for free, and I did not. I just paced up and down, telling Ami that I needed more—a lot more—for books, but she held tight to her money. So the four of us walked back to our schools the next week, I with a heavy heart and empty pockets.

A friend, Siu Piu, worked in the afternoons in the supply store at the public school. I told him that I only had one notebook. He gave me pencils and notebooks from the store and wrote a letter to my father in the military in another city, explaining about my school situation. A long time passed, two more weeks, and then my ama came to our house in the village and left me five hundred dong to buy the books that I needed. The books and supplies cost three hundred and fifty dong, so I had a hundred and fifty left to buy some clothes. Montagnard students were in the minority, but we were still required to wear the white shirt and long black skirt school uniform.

It took me a month to catch up with my lessons, but my teachers that year were very patient with me. I worked hard to be a good student and passed each year to the next grade at Thang Tien.

# GIRL SCOUTS

Between seventh and eighth grades, I was chosen from my school to join the Girl Scouts. I did not have any close friends in the scouts, but I heard that it was fun and that you could learn a lot of helpful ways to do things. And I really liked their uniforms—better than our school dress. Twenty girls in my troop came from Thang Tien and about thirty from the Buddhist school. There did not seem to be a problem between any of us, and the dress code made us all look similar. In fact, we looked like small adults.

The basic uniform was a white shirt with buttons and a collar, dark blue skirt, and tan hat with pointed crown, a two and a half inches brim, and a leather strap under the chin to keep it on. The outfit was completed by black shoes and white socks that were knee high. The Boy Scouts wore short pants similar to our style and colors, and we all had new backpacks. Some of the leaders wore uniforms like ours, and some seemed to be attached to their whistle necklaces, which they wore with importance.

Among the leaders was Brother Nguyen Cao Nguyen, who was very strict and dressed in a long black robe. It seemed that the whistle was the reason he was in the scouts. He blew it a lot, especially when we were learning different dances and songs. Being perfect was his goal for each of us. Since I stuttered, I tried not to talk much, but I loved to dance and to sing, so I made him happy when I was the first one to memorize all of the songs. Everyone was required to be accomplished in music. But we could either win or lose at our games.

Three games that I liked best were blind mice's bluff, drop an object, and hopping over bamboo poles.

For the first, we put two girls inside a circle. One "mouse" was blindfolded, and she had to find the other one who could not leave the circle. The noise was like a sports match, as everyone squealed and clapped and tried to direct the blind mouse.

In another circle game, we each put our hands behind our backs, and one person went around the outside of the circle with an object and dropped it into someone's hand. That girl then chased the person around the circle back to her place. If she could not catch the runner, she had to stand in the middle of the circle and sing a song in front of everyone. Some of the girls would rather eat worms than sing.

And the most difficult one for me was the bamboo pole dance. Two girls held the ends of two long bamboo poles close to the ground and smacked them together while a third girl jumped in and out of the clapping poles and tried not to get her foot caught when the poles snapped shut. There were a lot of bruised ankles.

When schools took a break, the Girl and Boy Scouts could go to a camp, sponsored by the Catholic Church and the Buddhist temple, both private schools. It was normal for us to be with teachers who wore black robes and with monks who were dressed in long brown or gray cloaks, but other adults outside of the schools also helped and wore the official scout uniforms. All were professional and believed in strict discipline.

Scouting taught us how to be responsible citizens and that we should always try to help others. After one of our meetings, we joined the Boy Scouts in our area, all dressed in our uniforms, even with gloves to wear, for a march to the main street. Most of the scouts thought that we were to be in a parade. It was a parade—to pick up trash and to set an example for all of the residents to pick up their living spaces and to be neat. The signs that our leaders carried for us read "Keep the street clean and save the environment!" When we heard Brother Nguyen Cao Nguyen's whistle blow in Morse code, we all said, "All done!" The cheers from the scouts were louder than the adults thought were appropriate, but it was done, and we only received punishment from our leaders' tongues.

In our first year of scout meetings, one of our projects was to learn the Morse code. We thought that it was an exercise in dots and dashes that was more like a game than a real message system. Then during our school break, twenty Girl Scouts from Thang Tien were to join other scouts for a three-day retreat at Camp Solidarity. We heard that on the first day, we had to pass a test on the Morse code before we could do anything else. The thought of missing anything at camp made me practice often, but with twenty-four letters in the alphabet, my dots sometimes got confused with my dashes, and then my confusion became confused.

The night before camp, Sister Helen came to my room to help me get my things ready and into my backpack. We had a list on paper that told to bring towels and soap and toothbrushes and cool clothes, but it did not have a suggestion on what to do with out-of-control twirling stomachs and stuttering words.

Sister Helen took both of my hands in hers as she bowed her head. "Our dear Mother of Jesus, watch over your child, H'Tien, and bring calm and happiness to her life, that she may sleep well this night and wake tomorrow reassured of your love and confidence and full of joy for the days to come!" She smiled and hugged me, and my fears seemed to remain in the folds of her habit.

The next morning, we checked to be sure that our notebooks and pens were in the top of our packs, and we gathered with other scout groups for a walk to the hamlet of Bon Ama Djong. After a signal from a whistle necklace, we marched down the main road looking very smart and important. People lined the road to see us—fifty girls and fifty boys smiling, waving, and trying to be impressive.

On the other side of the hamlet, our leaders pointed to a piece of land covered in grass, which would be our testing site. It was a pleasant place to sit and have a "classroom."

We arranged our notebooks on our laps and waited for the whistle that would dot and dash the Morse code into the air for us to remember and to read from our minds. Then we had to follow what it said. I could hardly breathe, and there was much talking.

A long, high noise on Mr. Thong's whistle made us all close our mouths quickly. Then, over a megaphone, Mr. Thong announced, "Attention please! Each of you campers have your notebooks ready. Listen carefully for the Morse code blown on my whistle. I will go slowly and will repeat the letter twice. Write the letters down as I give them, and when I have finished, you must decide what words the letters form and must follow the directions that the words say. You do not talk or share. Thank you and good luck!"

My heart beat fast, and my hands felt prickly. I made the sign of the cross and murmured, "Oh God, help me!" What would I do if I did not know the words?

The whistle blew in short and long tweets, and I wrote down each letter carefully as I thought it to be. After Mr. Thong finished, boys and girls started getting up and walking down the road with some of our leaders. That made me more nervous because I could not put together all of the letters into words. There seemed to be three words missing—or written down wrong.

When I looked up at Mr. Thong, I saw a little smile on his face, and he must have seen how hard the rest of us were struggling. He said, "Okay, listen, and I will repeat the code one more time." I almost dropped some tears, but when his whistle stopped, I had the other three words: *"Honi nay chung ta cani trai tai song Tong Dring."* (Our camp is settled at Tong Dring River.)

The *U* and two *R*s had escaped from me, but when I remembered, I finished writing and jumped up, moving in Mr. Thong's direction and mumbling "Tong Dring" loud enough for a few around me to hear. They got it too. I felt sorry for everyone else who could not break the code.

I could only have silence with Mr. Thong, but he motioned toward an arrow that pointed down the road path where people rode motorcycles and bicycles. I wished for someone to be with me, to talk together, but no one came. So I walked for about thirty minutes and saw my teacher, Nguyen, standing beside another arrow. He told me that this was the first of four "gates" that I would need to pass on the trail to Dring River, and I was to speak only if spoken to.

Nguyen said, "Do you know any songs or a dance?"

"Yes." I laughed. "'Yum Balabi Nebo Yaya.'"

I began, and after the fourth time, he said, "That's quite enough," gave me a paper that said I had passed, and pointed down another trail.

I laughed and skipped in the new direction. And then my shoes, real lace-up shoes, began to scream, and I knew that I had blisters on my feet. I had no Band-Aids in my pack, so I took off my shoes and socks, and I heard my feet say, "Thank you!"

Two arrows, one with a skeleton head, were at the next marker point. A moment after I studied their directions, I chose the arrow aiming away from the skull. Gate 3 was not far and had a friendly lady handing out bread when I met her. She had the best smile, and although I was not supposed to speak, I said, "Thank you!" and gave her a hug out of my happiness. She told me to keep the pass that Nuguyen had given me and follow the arrow to the last gate.

There I was given cold water and a snack and asked my supervisor's name. I told her, and she laughed at my bare feet and asked about my shoes. I pointed to my backpack, and she pointed to my right, where I saw some of the girls from my troop. I ran and waved and jumped into their arms, and we laughed at our success. There were four missing from our group, but a lot more were still at the testing site. However, we heard later that all of the scouts finally passed, and no one was sent home.

Each troop had to wait on supplies from the other members of the troop to put up their tents. Some bragged about how fast they were because their group was already there. But we hurried when the rest of our girls came and were not the last to finish.

Once our troop of twenty had completed our tents, we had to cook our evening meal so we dug a hole where we could build a fire and gathered wood. The five of us in our tent stretched our blankets out and made room for our clothes and packs. We arranged and rearranged, changed into our camping clothes, and rearranged again.

After we realized that there would never be enough space like we imagined, we left the tent and sat down on the ground outside. The sound of the river in front of us took over our conversation, and our voices became calm murmurs. The days at that camp were a time of great joy and peace in my life.

I could not have known at the time how helpful the lessons that I learned there would be in my future. I learned how to test water for drinking and to cook food over an outside fire. We were taught about plants and bugs and ants that were safe to eat and how to cook them. (I only nibbled the bugs.) We made different crafts and useful tools from the natural areas around us. We could not go near the water alone and were taught extra safety in the water, but many times in the future I would regret that I never learned to swim.

When we heard one long whistle, we had to find the person who was our assigned friend, to be sure that she was safe. We shared stories, songs, and dances at night around a big campfire.

On the last day of camp, each group wrote or told about their experiences, and what they liked most, and what they would like not to do again. The stories were funny, especially about eating bugs (mostly boy tales), and some of the girls cried because they would leave good friends the next morning.

And after the sun made early dawn sparkles on the river, we stuffed our clothes into our packs, folded our tents, and filled our fire holes with soil, and left the camp nearly the same as we had found it. In our uniforms, we walked back to our different schools, to Thang Tien, or our villages—a shorter way, it seemed. Our minds had been challenged, our bodies begged for sleep, but our hearts were smiling.

# GROWING INTO AWARENESS

## *Eighth Grade*

In the eighth grade, my partially sheltered life began to encounter tattered edges, and the outer layers of my innocence became exposed. My math teacher was Brother Nguyen Cao Nguyen, who had been one of my Girl Scout leaders. He was strict then, but now he was stricter and mean. He also was a choir and dance leader, and I was in those classes too. He did not favor me in any way because of the scouting.

Often during our math lessons, we got spankings in front of the whole class. The girls cried, but not the boys. Brother Nguyen was exceptional in math, and he demanded that all of us pay close attention to what he wrote on the blackboard, and we did. But we were too scared to ask him to explain problems that we didn't understand, and when our answers were wrong, that's when we received our spankings. I got a lot of them. Every time I saw him coming toward me in his long black robe, I turned away. His red nose on his red face made him look even more evil. I think that he liked knowing that I was afraid of him. Some students were so fearful that they quit the class and took math at another time. I had no extra time for classes, so I stayed. This was my only chance to learn.

The principal knew of the stressful situation between the teacher and the students. In the middle of the year, he told our teacher to take a week's vacation, and he told us that the Brother would be away for a few days. Nguyen Cao Nguyen planned to leave the following Monday from Phu-Bon for a five-hour bus ride to his home in Qui Nhon City.

Beginning on Monday, our mathematics class was taught by a substitute teacher. Late in the morning of that day, during our lessons, we heard piercing noises from emergency sirens. Our teacher was as startled as we were, but he kept on teaching, and we were expected to sit in our places until our recess.

Our classroom was across the road that led to the dispensary, which had only a floor and a roof held up by posts but no walls. During our early-afternoon break, we went outside to play but nervously talked about the earlier disturbance. Then we saw a military truck pass by with sounds of wailing and moaning coming from the inside. The truck stopped at the first aid shelter, and as we watched from the edge of the schoolyard, we saw what looked like bodies being unloaded. My friends and I were curious and moved cautiously toward the truck to see what was happening. To our horror, we saw that those were not corpses but body parts—legs, arms, heads—being laid out next to one another on the floor of the medical pavilion. Women and men cried loudly and held on to one another in their grief.

A classmate ran back across the road and vomited. I followed her but glanced back twice in disbelief at the carnage. How could that be possible? I did know that bad things were happening around our village and that the roads and towns seemed to multiply uniforms. But these people who were shattered beside the road were people like me.

None of us had ever seen anything that frightening. We returned to our room for the next class, hearts pounding, silent, and stunned by the horrific visions of destruction. We passed other students leaving their classrooms to see what was happening at the dispensary, but we dared not speak of the devastation that we had seen.

As we walked back to our dormitories, the villagers told us that a bus had been blasted to pieces by a roadside bomb, an act of the Viet Cong. I had only heard that name and barely understood what people meant about the "militant VC murderers."

The next day, we heard that the cook at our school had lost a daughter in the explosion. Our innocence was caught in the web of destruction. Numb and silent, we held hands and hid our fear behind blank stares. We had smelled death.

A week later, the principal of the school, Nguyen Hou Vien, who was a priest, came to our class to announce that Brother Nguyen Cao Nguyen had returned from his vacation. After the announcement, he walked out of the room. We murmured to one another about the suddenness of the principal's departure, but we returned to silence when our substitute teacher began the class again.

The following week, we saw Brother Nguyen in the schoolyard and did not speak to him but wondered when he was going to teach our math class again. A few days later, without warning, he opened the door to our classroom, walked right in, and stood in front of us with one hand inside a pocket of his black robe. The whole class stared through the stillness. He had changed. I still felt nervous in his presence, but his manner was gentle and mild; his face was not red and grumpy, but his eyesight shifted from us to the floor, out the window, and back to us.

After taking a deep breath, his unsteady voice broke the silence, "Good afternoon!"

We responded with, "Good afternoon to you!"

He continued, "How are you doing without me?" No one answered.

A moment passed. A student next to me softly said, "We are doing fine."

He shifted his stance, took another deep breath, and said, "I came to your class today to tell you of my experiences of two weeks ago. I thank God that I am so lucky and blessed to see all of you again. It is a mystery to me why I am still alive."

I could hardly believe what he was saying. He spoke deliberately.

"I should start from the beginning. All of you know that I was to take a vacation and planned to go to my home in Qui Nhon. I knew that it would be a boring, bumpy long trip, about five hours, changing buses, going from Phu-Bon through Pleiku to Qui Nhon City, so I got on the bus with a newspaper to read and put my belongings under my seat. The bus was packed—about forty passengers with luggage. There were bags in every possible space, in compartments under the bus and also strapped on the roof. As the bus began to move, I opened my newspaper and settled into my seat.

"Somewhere between a half hour and forty-five minutes, riding toward Pleiku City, a roadside bomb, planted by the Viet Cong, went off as the bus passed over it, near a bridge. I did not feel anything, hear an explosion, or see any destruction. I just found myself sitting in my seat, on a rock platform beside a running stream next to a bridge. I still held my newspaper in my hands. It was as though nothing had happened.

"When I became conscious of my surroundings, I heard myself mumble something about where were all the people and tried to reach for my handbag under my seat, but my fingers only grasped sand, rocks, and bushes. I put my newspaper down, looked around, and slowly stood up, my robe touching the ground and sand spilling from my hands. I could not understand where I was. Maybe I was dreaming. I was not hurt; I could move all of my limbs; my robe was not torn, and I was not bleeding anywhere that I could see. Then, as in a trance of sounds and motion, I remembered the bus and the crowd of people and that I was going on a vacation, and I took a step, and I heard screaming and crying. It came from the road above me."

His eyes met the floor as he paused and took another deep breath, letting out the air slowly.

"I took several steps from under the bridge, and a flood of nausea ran over me as I saw the shattered bus and the gigantic hole beside it. I stumbled into the remains and saw blood everywhere, limbs torn from bodies, flesh splattered, and burned corpses still in their seats. A few were still alive and screaming for help. I ripped my robe into pieces and tried to help stop the bleeding of some, but there was so much destruction and little hope, as the few people who pleaded for life died before my eyes. I prayed; I felt overwhelmed, and I could not control my emotions. I stumbled around the wreckage looking for my belongings, under bodies and metal parts. I found my suitcase and handbag, only partially disturbed, under the body of the woman who was sitting beside me. I moved her enough to pull them out and sat down beside my possessions, next to a wheel of the bus, alone in the middle of the screaming."

Tears ran down his face as he tried to finish his story, and tears flowed from my eyes and from my heart. Not one of us stirred.

He composed himself a little and continued, "I did trust in God, but I was still afraid that someone would come and attack me. Why was I alive? Could I have helped more? I prayed for an ambulance to come, but it seemed hours—maybe one or two—before anyone arrived. When a truck finally came, it was the Red Cross, and they brought others to help. I explained to them what happened, at least how I remembered it, and they told me to get into the Red Cross truck with my bags and stay until they could take me home. What was left of my robe hung on my body and smelled of blood, but I did not want to leave it behind. Maybe I thought that it was part of the mystery and part of the miracle."

He paused again, wiping the tears with the back of his hand. "I have shared this with you so that you will understand my absence and that you will know that I am grateful that God has spared my life."

He stood before us and bowed, humbled in the heavy air of a powerful testimony. First one, and then two, and then all of us eased to the front of the room, shook his hand, and said, "Welcome back!" We gathered around, lost for words to comfort him, as our substitute teacher came forward to lead us in a prayer of thanksgiving for Brother Nguyen's safe return.

## The Snake

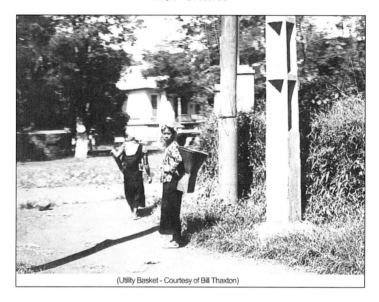

(Utility Basket - Courtesy of Bill Thaxton)

At age thirteen, school was more expensive than the money I had. Selling bamboo shoots was a fairly simple way to get extra dong, but I had to harvest the shoots first.

Bamboo came in all kinds and sizes, from tall trees to shorter clumps, and I knew that the most tender shoots were behind small clusters of trees. Often, the land that they grew on belonged to people around our village. H'Don and I would take baskets and wooden-handled knives down a path away from the village and stop when we saw a grove that looked promising.

On one particular day, we came to a fork in the road and thought that if we separated, we would be more successful— she went left, and I went right. I had walked only about one hundred yards when my excitement made me laugh out loud. In front of me was a very large stand of a bamboo tree cluster that looked untouched.

Only thinking about the wood and shoots that I could get, I began to carefully cut the surrounding stalks away to get into the inside area where the tender shoots were. My knife had a sharp blade that was six inches long and had a rounded handle about the same length. I worked the knife back and forth across each bamboo culm (stem joint) until it fell and then made a pile of the wood by the cluster. The anticipation of finding six- to eight-inch shoots, which brought good money, made me cut down hard and move fast. My goal was to work my way into the area of greatest possibility. Carrying the pile of bamboo wood back in my arms would not be a problem.

I could see a clearing up ahead and began to crawl on my belly, pulling myself along with my elbows, like army men do. I reached the edge of the clearing toward a mound of dirt beside a hole (probably made by rats) and slid in closer to get a better angle for cutting. There were enough shoots to fill my basket and H'Don's if I could get her to come back with me. In that moment of gladness, I looked up just in time to see a bright red eye not three feet away that was reflecting the sun from somewhere above. The eye was on the head of a giant black snake, over a foot above his coiled body, with its long feathery tongue shooting straight down at me. We both froze, but I was stiff for less than a second.

As I rapidly slithered backward along the path I had made, I scraped my legs and tore my dress, and the newly cut stalks grabbed at my hair. At the edge of the bamboo cluster, my heart pounded so hard I could barely breathe. I jumped up and down, shaking my hands and hugging myself, as my feet forced the rest of my body in the direction where I last saw H'Don. The knife and the woven basket were gifts for the snake—gifts that Ami did not miss for a long time.

I stopped by a tree to catch my breath and remembered what the villagers had been talking about just the day before in my front yard. I had not listened much then, but it became very vivid to me as my breathing began to slow. That red eye, the size, the shape, the color—it was one of the most poisonous snakes in Vietnam. I saw H'Don down the road and waved. My story would last us all of the way home.

The men had warned that two of the same snakes had been spotted in those bamboo groves and that they were probably nesting, so "don't go near those areas." Whenever snakes were seen, men would throw grenades into the suspected nests to kill them. Even though I was frightened beyond my beating heart, we did not tell anyone else about the snakes so that the villagers would not blow them up. The snakes did not harm me, and I did not harm them.

## *Ending Ninth Grade*

During those middle school years, I tried very hard to keep up. The Sisters offered us help for thirty minutes or an hour whenever they could, but most of the time we had to learn our subjects by ourselves. I found it difficult to ask anyone for extra time. I was used to making my own way, but all of the classes were taught in Vietnamese (not in the Montagnard dialect of my village), so I had to listen carefully as well as learn the subjects.

There were no computers, no phones, and no watches to tell time. In the afternoon, I worked on my lessons; in the evening, I practiced my dance and music, and often I studied until midnight. Even though our final exams were most difficult, my teachers assured me that I passed my grade, but there was no time to rest.

Two hours after my last exam, Brother Nguyen Cao Nguyen and Sister Rosa, my group dance and choir leaders, told me that they had selected me and seven others to perform in a competition and that we needed to rehearse right away. They had chosen a particular dance and song for the Thang Tien High School program and one dance for the Thanh Gia Elementary School. I remember thinking that my legs would not hold me up to go over the songs and to memorize the steps.

While I practiced for that performance, another Sister came to the rehearsal to tell me that I had been chosen to enter into another competition between four schools that was sponsored by the Ministry for the Development of Ethnic Minorities. (That was the name given to a government-run program that was forcing the Montagnards into learning submission to the new Vietnam government.) The program was to be held at the military auditorium a week later. In fact, I found out that the competitions were all at the auditorium with the same sponsor, the Vietnamese military. Being selected was an honor, but exams had sucked out a substantial amount of energy.

At the auditorium on the evening of the competition, dancers from our school changed clothes in a room behind the stage where children from other high schools dressed for their acts. It was very busy and crowded and sounded like free-play time at Thanh Gia. I had several costumes with me, as I was in two group dances and one group song with my high school and a group dance with the elementary school.

As I changed between each number, my friends had to help me fix my hair into various styles. For the Thanh Gia act, we rushed very fast, but the judges waited ten minutes while my blouse, stockings, shoes, hair, and costume were completed.

I was the first on the line in front of eight girls (four dressed as boys), and when the curtain opened, the music began, and we were very collected and poised. No one in the audience realized how frantic we had been.

The judges announced at the end of all of the performances that our school had excellent marks, but the best was "O_Me_li" performed by Thanh Gia Elementary, which won the entire competition. We clapped and hugged one another and cried happy tears.

After we were thanked for our participation and the performers gathered their belongings, I searched in corners and under chairs for my clothes and costumes but could not find many items from our dances. Finally, I stopped and glanced around a room that had become much too quiet, with only a few girls moving toward the exit door. My elementary and high school groups were gone, along with the dance outfits. I went outside and saw that our small buses were gone; the lights in the building's windows were disappearing, and I was left alone.

I did not know anyone who was leaving the auditorium and was afraid to get in a car with a stranger. All I knew was that I had to start walking along the street. My feet were without shoes or sandals—only red stockings. I had no blouse to cover my undershirt, and my short skirt was part of my last costume. The direction to the school was simple, but I was not sure about the details in the dark. I walked straight forward as fast I could, trying not to look to the side or to the back, but with my eyes wide open.

*How could my friends and teachers have left me? Maybe each group thinks that I am with the other one. Which school has my clothes, my costumes? What will I do if a car comes by and stops?*

I walked and walked, almost running at times. I don't remember how long, but when I finally saw the school in front of me, my body felt totally drained. It was near midnight by then, and I knocked hard and long on the school door until it opened, and Sister Helen stood there in a nightgown with a shawl over her head. Electric shock seemed to flow through both of us.

"What...? Come in right now!" She closed the door. "Come with me!" The color in her face had faded by the time that she woke Sister Rosa to ask how this could have happened.

There were no immediate answers; words would continue in the morning. Sister Rosa gave me a banana to eat from a basket in her room, and they walked me to my dormitory, speaking very fast in low voices, their gowns quietly waving from side to side.

I sighed deeply and shuffled to my bed. The next morning, I awoke still in my clothes, with the banana in my hand.

# Ahead with Determination

By the end of my ninth year, I had had more formal education than most of the girls in my village, and I wished for much more but wondered how I could continue. Learning had become my life. One of the nuns at my school said, "You need to stay here and to help teach at the preschool." But at fourteen, I did not consider that to be an option for me. When I told her that I wanted to be a sophomore in the public high school, she said, "No, you must stay." My sadness and disappointment covered me like dark clouds as I left her office. I took a long, slow walk down the road, shuffling my feet and kicking up dust, and ended my journey at my old Thanh Gia dormitory. I knew that without an education, my expectations for a better life would come to a dead end.

I had to talk to someone else. Sister Helen, my trusted friend and "other mother," had gone to another city, but no one seemed to know where—or would not tell. I missed her so much and did not understand why she left us.

I saw Sister Amanda walking toward her office, and I waved and asked if I could talk to her. She had also been a caring friend since my years at the Catholic Center. We sat on a bench beside the school, and for most of an hour, I poured out my uncertainties and frustrations and the exact words of direction from the other nun. When I finally stopped, I looked at her, wondering if she understood my rambling words.

The breeze gently ruffled her habit around her kind face as she said to me, "You have a gift for learning. You embrace life as it comes to you. Remember that the name you have, H'Tien, means 'holy one' or 'spirit.' You are too young to have a class of preschool children. You can help sometimes, but you need more instruction and more education. And you may not want to teach preschool the rest of your life."

She paused and reached for my hand in my lap. I sat up straight and found it difficult to speak. She had touched my heart. Sister Amanda had listened—she had heard me, and I whispered, "Thank you!"

She continued, "Right now, don't say any more words to anyone, and let me see what I can do."

I assured her that I would wait and pray and try hard to be patient. A smile was back on my face and was spreading inside.

About two weeks later, Sister Amanda asked me to come into her office. "I have contacted a priest, a friend, Father Son, who is from Qui Nhon City. Father Son knows Mother Gabrielle (Nguyen Thi Phi Huong), the head of Trinh Vuong Qui Ntton, a big school in that city. He wrote to Mother Gabrielle about you, and she agreed that you could come to the school if your grades are good enough."

I could not contain my excitement. I almost knocked over a chair when I danced around the room. Sister Amanda said, "Wait! We must send your grades." But we both knew that I was near the top of my class. I would start in the fall.

I still had to be quiet about the school until I was sure, but I began to think about how lonely I would be so far away from all the people I knew. H'Don, my closest friend, was at her house when I arrived there. She agreed not to tell my secret, so I confided to her and babbled my words so fast that she could hardly understand me. I said, "You must come with me. I don't want to go alone. We can have so much fun if both of us are there."

She looked at me in astonishment. "What are you thinking? I don't want to go so far away from my home and my family."

"Oh, please, H'Don, we have been close friends for so many years."

"I'll need to think about it." She stared at her shoes for a long time and looked at me and then out of the window. "I'll think about it. I don't want to miss you either."

The next day, H'Don came to my house, and we took a walk. "I have thought a lot about you and our friendship. I would miss you too much, so I will go with you if my parents approve."

We hugged each other, giggled a lot, hugged each other again, and jumped up and down, but I could feel the apprehension in our celebration. Qui Nhon City was very far away. There was much to think about.

I returned to Thanh Gia and told Sister Amanda that I had a friend who wanted to come with me. She was a little surprised but said that she would try to arrange it through Father Son. Of course, H'Don's grades would have to be sent, and I knew that they were not quite as good as mine, but I prayed that they would be good enough.

Also, I went home and told Ama of my plans and said that I would need money. He just looked unbelieving and said, "I don't have any money for *your* school." He told me that his daughter H'Kong, my cousin, was going to school in Saigon, and he wondered why I did not go there too.

In the village, I had heard that I could apply to Renes Pagis in Saigon, where they had a program for students who had good grades. H'Don and I rode bicycles to the Ty Phat Tnen Sac Toc Office. A paper outside on a bulletin board said that the classes were full. I saw my cousin's name as having been accepted. She was younger than I was, so I knew that it was not a place for a high school education. It was for learning skills such as cooking, sewing, and farming. H'Don and I were a little disappointed as it was so much closer to home and not as expensive, but we knew that the possibilities for us were far greater than studying for a trade.

## *Summer in Cheo Reo*

It was *hot*. Summers in Cheo Reo were *very* hot. I returned to my village to wait for an answer from Mother Gabrielle. There was much work to be done, especially in the rice fields—weeding the paddies, pounding the rice, and redirecting the water from the stream and river so that it could be more available to us.

Every morning I followed Ami and Ama to the garden or to the fields that they farmed. It was difficult to tell the difference between the rice and the weeds, especially in the paddies. When I looked out across the land, the rice fields were like flowing green meadows, but after wading through the paddies and bending over for hours, I experienced another view. My body ached all over, and the sun was unforgiving.

I knew that it would get better as I became used to the heat, but I was amazed at Ami and Ama who had been doing that kind of work for years. I was sorry to see them work so hard under the scorching sun, but Ami never looked at a watch. She knew when twelve noon came, and we could all go to a hut beside the fields to have a thirty-minute lunch and rest. I usually found a shady tree and had no trouble closing my eyes for a nap, which frequently lasted longer than the break. However, no one woke me when they returned to the fields, and often the sun was down a bit when my eyes opened again.

I dreamed about the fun that I could be having with young people more my age. My friends H'Blin and H'Don and I talked to several of the youth nearby who spoke to their friends about getting together to work in the fields as a team and about helping in the village. Many went to different schools, and some had never been to school, but all liked the idea of sharing the work. We formed a group of twenty who discussed our idea with people around our village. We found twenty families who needed our help—some wanting us right away.

So we gathered at the first rice field early the next Monday morning. A lot brought pointed hoes, which we sharpened before we started. The hoes allowed us to go down under the weeds and grab the roots. I used my hoe very slowly, and some made fun of me, but I still have all of my toes. We spread across the field, one person at each end of a row, working toward one another. When the acres were small, we could finish by one or two o'clock and have the rest of the afternoon free.

Often the boys would act silly and throw dirt and dig dirt worms to make the girls scream. They only scared me once. The second time was no surprise. We all worked hard, but there was a lot of laughter and joking. Sometimes, the ones who finished first would smoke. They rolled tobacco inside banana leaves and made the air smell terrible. H'Don, H'Blin, and I did not smoke and didn't understand how the others could work so hard under the hot sun and not have the smoking lay them out on the ground.

# *Work for Pay*

It was okay to help families and to have fun doing it, but I kept thinking about the school and what my expenses would be. After we worked together several days, I confided in the group that I needed money to go to school and that my family had none to give me. Everyone seemed enthusiastic and wanted to help.

So I found three families who could pay and who knew of my plan to attend a more advanced school. They gave each member of our group two hundred dong for the job, and I received four thousand dong for working several days late into the evenings. I was thrilled. I took off a week to rest and to help my ama and ami before I gathered our group for the second paying family. For my extra hard work, I received another four thousand dong.

The third family only needed ten people for their fields, but the owner was H'Don's wealthy uncle. All of H'Don's family was in a high class with money. I worked the rice field with my hoe and weeded one of the two gardens that they owned. Even though it was very hard, I was so happy that I was earning money, and H'Don did help me with some of the gardening.

Across a row of vegetables, I winked at her. "Thank you, my friend! Now I am sure that high school is a true possibility."

Three months of summer gave me more understanding of who I was and what I could do. The village reached out to me with loving care, and I loved them back. Numerous young people from the area took long, restful summer vacations, but for me, a vacation was returning to school.

Toward the end of the summer, my calculations were that I had worked half of a month for my family, half of a month for school supplies, a month for my room and food, half of a month for clothes, with a little left for unexpected expenses. It was time for a break. I put aside the heat, the sweat, the calluses on my hands, the sun-baked skin, the insect bites, and the aches and pains. I was singing happy.

But a problem developed for me at home. A woman in the village shook her finger at Ami and raved to her, "Why do you let your daughter accept money for working in the fields and gardens?"

Ami was surprised and asked me about it. "What is this I hear about you and your friends being paid for helping in the rice paddies this summer? I did not know that was happening. How much did they pay you?"

At first, I looked away, and then I faced her directly. "I need money to go to school. Ama said that he had none to give me. Sister Amanda has applied for me to go to high school in Qui Nhon City."

Ami gasped. "That is so far away. I don't understand. Why do you need more school? You need to stay closer to us. We need you here."

"I am going! I want to go! I need to go!"

She did not know that I had found out that Ama had given H'Kong ten thousand dong to go to her school. I knew then that I was on my own, and I never discussed with her the amount of money that I had made. I had worked very hard, and my friends had been especially generous.

## *One More Step—Without Sister Helen*

The next week, I went back to my old dorm at Thanh Gia to see Sister Amanda. When I walked through the doorway, she took a step back. "What has happened to your skin?"

I laughed. "I'm not sure, but it may have something to do with working in the fields this summer. But I have money for school." I beamed.

"And I have good news for you and H'Don. You may go to the high school in Qui Nhon, but you may not be in the same classes. Even so, both of you will have to work very hard. They will need birth certificates to prove your ages. Here are two forms each that need to be filled in and signed by your ama and H'Don's. Bring them with you when you return.

"I have taken Sister Helen's place at the dorm for now. She is going to her hometown, so if you want to stay here, I will help you get ready. You are to leave in a week. I will worry about you and H'Don the whole time and will pray for you. Father Son is bringing a letter of introduction that you are to give to Mother Gabrielle when you get to the school."

I just stood there. I did not realize that it would all happen so quickly. A smile crossed my face, but my hands tingled, and my legs felt wobbly. Sister Amanda walked past her desk and wrapped her habit-covered arms around me like a cocoon. My body quivered as my eyes grew moist, and when we separated, I knew that her strength would always be with me.

Then I stopped in the middle of my happiness. "What did you say about taking Sister Helen's place? Where is she going? Why would she leave us?"

"Oh, H'Tien, I am not free to discuss that with you. You will have to ask her."

"But she has taken care of me since I was very little. I need her. I want her to stay."

My eyes and my heart were unbelieving. "How can I find her?"

"She may be somewhere around the school, but she stays in prayer a good deal of the time. I know that she loves you and the other students very much."

"I must go and try to see her." I turned and hurried toward the door but stopped before I closed it. "Thank you, Sister Amanda! Thank you for caring about me too!"

After I left her office, I kept thinking that maybe I did not understand all that she said. She only spoke Vietnamese, not the Montagnard Dega language. I did speak both, but sometimes I did not hear all of the Vietnamese words.

I looked all over the school and asked everyone I saw if they had seen Sister Helen, but she hid from us. Had any of us done something to make her leave? I knew that when she got angry with us, she would speak in French. We did not understand the words, but we knew what she was saying. It had been awhile since I had heard any French. I thought it must be that the school did not want her anymore, but how could that be, when she taught all of us, and she taught skills and typing to adults? That seemed too distant an idea. No matter what was in my mind, she was leaving, and I wanted to say good-bye. But she was nowhere.

When the news was heard by everyone, there was much sadness. I barely ate or slept for three days, and it seemed that tears accompanied every breath. It was unfair for her to just walk away.

But that is how it was, and Sister Amanda, although nothing like Sister Helen, was kind and began her new role as head of the school with courage and patience. Her medical education allowed her to teach nursing skills and to prepare many for other jobs in the cities.

# In Pursuit of a Dream

## *Going to Qui Nhon*

I stayed at the dorm that night, and in the evening, Father Son came to bring me the letter. He said to me, "Keep this letter close to you until you meet with Mother Gabrielle. I have drawn you a map of how to get to the school from Pleiku. You will need to take a bus that will stop overnight on the road. It will not cost you anything to get to the bus in Pleiku that will take you to Qui Nhon. There are two priests, friends of mine, who are going that way, and you will ride in a car with them."

I listened, but I could not take it all in.

That night, I struggled to write a letter to Ama and Ami, trying to explain why I had to go and where I would be. I knew that if I tried to reason with them when I saw them, it would be a conversation that would go nowhere. I tucked the letter in my backpack beside Father Son's letter.

The next morning, I returned to my village and to my home and asked Ama to put a date of birth for me and to sign two papers. He did not understand the need for the papers, but I just said that I had to have them for school. He put down the date that he remembered, signed his name, and returned them to me. I would give Sister Gabrielle one and keep the other.

Then I went to H'Don's house to talk about what we would take. We thought that one suitcase each and a carrying pack would be enough. That was easy for me, but her belongings filled her room. Even so, she kept unpacking things that she at first thought she couldn't leave behind.

We had friends to thank and good-byes to make—until the Christmas holidays. They all wished us well. But I had a difficult time during my last night with Ami and Ama. Ami thought that

I had come home to stay and to go to my same school. She just could not understand how important it was to me. I would see that they got my letter after I left. Ami offered me no money, not even ten dong, and only briefly came to the door when I took my things to H'Don's house.

H'Don's family had helped her decide on what to take and gave her enough money to last until the holiday. They were not real happy, but they knew how important education was. Most girls stayed in the same place forever without it. And they were somewhat reassured that we would be together.

We left in the early morning, in her father's small car, and met Sister Amanda at the dorm. She approved what we were taking, gave us her blessing, and we all walked to Father Son's house, where two priests waited with our transportation. The car could barely hold four people, but with the suitcases on top, and with our handbags in our laps, we were somewhat comfortable.

The priests drove back through our village, and I asked them to slow down while I reached out of the window to a friend who was walking along the road. I asked her to deliver my letter to Ama and Ami. The words were few but clear: "I want to go to school. I must go. There is no grade higher than ten at Thang Tien where I can have more education. I will be careful. I will miss you! I love you! I'll be back on Christmas Day."

H'Don and I did not talk much to the priests, as we did not know what to say to them. They had a conversation between themselves about the meeting they were to attend, and we mostly sat in silence and stared out of the window.

By midmorning, the priest who drove turned the engine off at the bus stop on the other side of Pleiku. Both priests helped us with our bags as we got out of the car, and the driver reminded me, "Look at the map that Father Son gave to you and follow it carefully. It will be very valuable to you. Be smart, stay alert, watch your money, and try not to talk to anyone unless you speak Vietnamese. If anyone thinks that you are Montagnards, they may be unkind to you." He made the sign of the cross, gave us his blessing, returned to their car, and disappeared into traffic.

I was not quite prepared for his words, but I understood their meaning. H'Don just stared at the people, at the vanishing car, and at me. She did not speak as much Vietnamese as I did, so I knew that she was startled, but we were committed, and we had to go on.

My mind and my stomach struggled to stay calm. I glanced at our bags sitting at the side of the street with only us to look after them and unfolded the map again to see if anything had changed since the last time I looked. We rested on the suitcases for about thirty minutes until the bus arrived and then made sure that our two large bags were securely stored before we got on. At the door of the bus, we paid a man for our tickets and quickly found two seats together. As the bus pulled away from the stop, I looked out of the window and felt the tension begin to relax. The first step had been taken, and we were finally on our way to an exciting adventure.

"H'Don, we have a long trip ahead, so I'm going to take a nap. Wake me if anything unusual happens—if you are still awake. The rest should be easy." Or so I thought.

## *The Gate at Qui Nhon*

It was barely light in the evening when the bus stopped at a gate outside what seemed to be the city of Qui Nhon. We were both awake and staring out the window at the lights in the houses and shops. The gates to Qui Nhon had barbed wire across them so that no vehicles could go across the bridge into the city. The bus driver said that everyone would have to get off.

As we stepped to the ground with our things, two people grabbed our luggage that was being taken off the bus. It happened so fast. H'Don ran after a man who took hers and pulled it away from him. A woman hurried with mine toward a hut-type building with a metal roof, where there were few lights and no sign to tell what it was. I chased her down, took my suitcase, and yelled out for H'Don, who was looking for me.

"Where are you, sister? H'Don, over here!" There was a lot of confusion.

Suddenly, a man stopped and looked at me. "What? What did you say?"

I realized that I had not spoken in Vietnamese.

*H'Tien, be smart, be careful, don't let them know that you are a Montagnard! They may not treat you well.* The priest's words came rushing back to me.

In a mumbling Vietnamese voice, I said, "I was just talking to myself."

I heard the woman who had grabbed my suitcase say, "Come, come, we all sleep here!" By then, H'Don was at my side, and we stopped and got out my map before we went in.

The map said, "Stop for the night at the Old Market at Qui Nhon." A sign down the road, on the other side of the locked gate, read "Old Market." But the only place opened for us to stay was the hut. And there were several other huts where the bus travelers were going. I folded up the map and wondered what to do.

The bus driver pointed out a toilet facility to the side, near a creek. Everyone was using it, so we waited for it to clear a little, but when we went in, it was so dirty that I nearly got sick, and H'Don went around to the back and gagged. We tried to act mature and in charge of ourselves, but I don't think that we fooled anyone. Since most of the travelers had found a place, we walked up a few steps where the woman had called to us, dragged our suitcases and handbags, and entered a musty, dark building.

The woman inside took our things and said, "You pay me, and I take you to your room."

There were no "rooms." The wooden floor creaked as we slowly followed her to a small area where she put down our bags and where she took our money. It was separated from other areas by bamboo walls and had material draped across the front side (a kind of doorway) to allow some privacy. There were thin pieces of wood laid across the planks on the floor and two blankets that we didn't dare touch. I guessed that it was where we were to sleep. H'Don's parents had been right about adding thin blankets to our handbags, but I knew right away that sleep would not be easy.

"This is where you stay." That was all. She turned and went back to the front door.

I could barely swallow, and H'Don had big watery eyes. I lowered my voice, "Stay here, H'Don, and don't speak to anyone!"

The building was round, and at one side I saw light that framed the edges of dark hanging cloth. I heard a noisy mixture of voices and smelled food. When I went to the opening and slowly moved the curtain back enough to see a dingy lighted room, I saw a number of men—two were soldiers—seated at a round table, eating, drinking, and gambling. The smoke was so thick that it dimmed the lightbulb hanging from the ceiling.

A man covered by a dirty apron cooked something in a pot over an open fire. I pulled back the curtain a little too far, and some of the men saw me. The cook smiled widely, showing several teeth were missing in his mouth. The gamblers made some bad remarks about me and laughed. I didn't know all of the words, but their looks and gestures confirmed what I thought. I closed the curtain quickly and knew that H'Don and I would not be safe by ourselves.

I walked past a "room" where a couple sat with a baby. I already had spoken to them on the bus. They smiled, and we greeted each other again. I started to walk away but stopped and went back.

I whispered to them, "Please let my friend and me sleep with you. There are some mean-looking men in the room behind that curtain where you can see the smoke coming out. They saw me looking in for food and laughed and said that they would be seeing me later. It makes me very afraid for us. Please, we will be very quiet!"

They looked at the tiny area where they had to sleep, but after talking between themselves, they agreed. I went back and told H'Don to come with me. We left our luggage in our room, the couple put their bags with ours, and the four of us, with the baby, crowded into their tiny space.

"We have some sweet, sticky rice. Would you like some?" the wife said.

"Oh no, thank you." H'Don gave me such a look.

The husband offered again, "We have enough."

I didn't hesitate. "Thank you! We have not eaten all day." My trembling hands began to relax.

Our conversation was low, and we finished talking to one another after the rice had been eaten, and the baby had been nursed. I slept close beside the little one, who didn't cry all night. Very late, after the men stopped drinking and gambling, we could hear them looking behind each curtain and talking about the girl they had seen. I pulled the thin cover over my head, drew my body up into a small ball, and did not move. After I heard them stumble out of the front door, my shallow breathing relaxed into a deep sleep.

## Qui Nhon City

Morning began early, but we had no trouble getting ready to leave, since we had slept in our clothes. As we went outside, we found that the gate had been opened, and the bus was waiting for us. Along with our new friends, we again loaded our bags and climbed up into our seats. I got out the map to figure out what to do next.

I found "Old Market" again and followed the drawing to "New Market," an area where the school was. It looked like a short way, but we passed so many streets and traffic lights and shops that I couldn't be sure. My eyes burned, my stomach ached, and H'Don looked as though she could just disappear into her wrinkled clothes. I must have appeared the same. But we knew that we were almost there—wherever "there" was.

I saw it first. "Look, H'Don, a big sign that says 'New Market.' We're here."

The driver drove the bus over to an area where other buses had gathered and called back to us, "This is New Market."

I began to feel alive again. The sun was bright now, and our bags were easy to find. Our friends with the baby and others from the previous day's trip got off the bus also, but they all hurried away, seeming to know where they were going. I looked around for a sign that said, "Trinh Vuong School," but there was none in sight.

"Let's sit down a minute and look at the map!" A bench was close by and, at this point, H'Don showed little energy to do much else. The map had a line drawn to Trinh Vuong, but I could not tell where we were or how near we were. At the next corner, I saw a group of *tuk-tuk*s whose drivers could probably give us some information.

A few of the *tuk-tuks* were motorcycles that pulled two-seater (or more) carriages. The vehicles could move quickly in traffic, but I had never ridden in one.

"We want to go to Trinh Vuong School here in New Market," I said to one of the drivers. "How much will that be?"

He looked at us and seemed to decide that we did not know what a good price was, so he told us a sum that we didn't think we could afford. As he opened his mouth again to bargain, I saw a rickshaw that was operated by a man on a bicycle. His seat had room for two, and he gave a good price. I said, "Okay."

He lifted up our luggage into a large wire basket behind where we were to sit, and we stepped up to a seat like one in a very small ox cart.

"Yes, I know the school, and I will have you there soon," he said and began to pedal the rickshaw down the street and out into traffic.

The night before had been a bad dream; hunger was no longer on our minds. Neither of us had been in a city this large, and the sounds and rush of cars were frightening. But we held hands, watched through eyes larger than normal, and even giggled in our excitement of being close to our destination. We were just getting settled in the rickshaw and enjoying the scenes that passed when the driver came to a stop in front of a large stone building surrounded by walls topped with embedded glass and with a closed iron gate. Words carved in the stone over the door read "Trinh Vuong High School."

"This is where you go?" he asked.

It took us a moment to reply. The building was much larger than anything in Cheo Reo, and the windows with their metal bars did not seem very welcoming. But we had arrived, and as we got out of the rickshaw, I felt both of us become nervous at once.

As soon as the driver put our luggage on the street, and we had paid him, he pedaled off before we could say thank you.

"This is Trinh Vuong High School?" I asked a man who was just inside the gate.

He stared at us through the bars a moment before he answered. "Yes, what do you want here?"

"I have a letter for Mother Gabrielle. She is expecting us." I showed him the envelope with her name on it.

He looked at me and then at H'Don and walked up the stairs to the door. After he knocked and we all waited, a nun opened the door and asked what he needed.

"There are two girls here to see Mother Gabrielle. They say that they have a letter for her."

We stared back at the nun. We had never seen a nun's habit like hers. She was so covered in black-and-white clothing that we could barely see her face.

"Open the gate," she said, "and bring their bags inside."

I can only imagine how we must have looked to both of them. We definitely were not the freshest in appearance or fragrance.

Our measured steps followed her through the doorway into an entrance hall.

She motioned for us to go into a room on our left. I could not compare it to anything I had seen before. The ceiling was very high, dark curtains hung on either side of the two windows, pictures of holy people were on the walls, and another nun, in the same style habit, stood up as we entered and came around her desk to speak.

"Why are you girls here?" she greeted us in a kind, low voice.

I walked toward her with my letter. "This is a letter for Mother Gabrielle from Father Son. I would like to give it to her, please."

"Please sit down. I will see if she is available."

She left us alone. My stomach began to make noises, and H'Don sat on her chair like a wilted flower. I must have looked the same. There was silence for a few minutes.

"This place is so big," H'Don whispered. "Is this really a school?"

"I am sure of it, but I wonder where all of the students are. They must be on a holiday."

Maybe ten minutes passed—maybe much longer. The door opened, and a very large nun seemed to float into the room toward us. For some silly reason, I immediately pictured her taking up both seats in a rickshaw by herself, habit flying in the wind with her almost-floor-length rosary clutched to her side. H'Don and I stood up.

"Good morning, girls! I am Mother Gabrielle. I understand that you have brought me something."

"Yes,' I said, barely moving my feet. "It is a letter from Father Son. I am H'Tien Ksor, and this is my friend H'Don."

"Please sit down, and I will read the letter." She read only a bit and looked up at us. Her hand gestured toward our heavy jackets. She must have noticed the moisture on our faces. "You come from Pleiku, a cooler place than Qui Nhon City."

We nodded. "Yes, it is quite warm." I opened my coat a little. "But we are glad to be here."

She finished the letter and smiled. "I think that you might be hungry and that you would like to wash your hands and face. I will have Hai take your things to a room where you will stay for now, and we will talk together after our meal."

"Thank you!" I said, a little above a whisper. The strain of the trip, the tiredness, the comfort of finally being in a safe place, and the thought of food almost overwhelmed us both. As we followed the gatekeeper up the stairs to the second floor, my body felt weighted down, and I swallowed hard so as not to show my grateful relief.

# STRUGGLE TO SUCCEED

## First Weeks at Qui Nhon

We were not sure who knew why we were there, except for Mother Gabrielle. At first, the nuns and the housekeepers told us that we were to clean the rooms at the school and to help in the kitchen. We had learned to say only what was necessary. The words of Father Son's friend kept coming back to me: *Be smart, be careful, do not let them know that you are Montagnards! They may not treat you well.*

For two weeks, before the students returned for the next year's studies, we cleaned in all of the buildings. We did not realize that we had come too soon, but we followed directions as we were instructed. The three buildings had many floors. A building behind the one at the entrance to the school was four stories high. On the top floor lived three hundred young girls who, I was told, were called postulants. They were taught classes in sewing, cooking, music, and things that girls need to know how to do—in addition to studying how to be nuns. When I saw their swimming pool and room for exercising, I immediately knew that this was not an ordinary school.

During the first week that we were there, Mother Gabrielle called H'Don and me into her office. I was sure that we had done something wrong, and maybe she was sending us back home.

She smiled when we entered the room, and that put us more at ease. "When the students return in a week, you can no longer wear your black sarongs and blouses to class. You must look like the other girls. This afternoon, I want both of you to go to the third floor where sewing is taught and be measured for the school uniform. It is a white tunic that comes down to your knees over long white pants. A white undershirt is to be worn so that none of your skin will show under the top when you are raising your arms in class or in the city. There is a fifty-dong penalty charge if the rules are not followed. You will need two of these outfits and will wear them five days a week. You must pay for the material, but the postulants will make them for you. The only cost to you will be five thousand dong each for the two dresses. You must blend in with the girls and be like them. No one will know who you are. You may need to practice your Vietnamese."

I just said, "Yes, Mother Gabrielle." But when we got outside of her office, I leaned against the wall and took a deep breath. I had only saved ten thousand dong from my work during the summer in the rice paddies, and I knew that there was no more when that was gone. "Oh my!" I looked at H'Don. "Do you have that much money?"

"Yes, but I can write to my parents to send me some more, and I will help you whenever you need it."

H'Don and I looked at each other, our eyes questioning. "I did not know that being Montagnard would make a difference with the girls or nuns at the school." And I also didn't know when we came that these were girls from very wealthy families. Later I heard two of the girls talking about their parents paying ten thousand dong a month and that they could only go home for holidays.

Mother Superior directed us to sleep in a room down the hall from her office on the first floor, next to the dormitory for the forty K-5 children. Our classes would be in different parts of the school. H'Don would have classes for the grade level that she had achieved in Cheo Reo, and I would be on the third floor of another building with the tenth-grade girls.

A week later, the students arrived with lots of luggage and with clothes and radios and books that I had never seen before. It made me glad that we were not staying on the same floor because even though H'Don had brought more clothes than I owned, we did not wear the same style as the other girls.

Mother Gabrielle assigned H'Don and me to work in the kitchen a little longer. I think that it was to give us another type of identity than just a student. Even so, after a few weeks, she told us to concentrate on our studies. I was especially glad because I didn't understand the way the teachers taught the subjects, and my grades were not very good. And H'Don was having a terrible time keeping up. She cried every day.

In my school in Cheo Reo, the teacher tried to explain what was in our books and wrote a few things on the blackboard so that we could understand. The teachers at Trinh Vuong walked into class and wrote dates and places and anything about the subject on the blackboard and then talked about the information that we should know. I could not remember all of the things that I was told in all of the nine different subjects, so I did not do well on the exams. French and English were required, and every day I was learning more Vietnamese.

In science, Teacher Duy was a pleasant man, but I was too shy to ask him how I could do better. One day, he said, "I want to talk to you. Please stay after the class is over."

My stomach moved badly, and I was very nervous. *What if they send me home?*

He asked me to sit down and began by saying, "H'Tien, where are you from?"

I just knew that all was lost, but I had to tell the truth. "I am from Cheo Reo City."

He replied, "I know that place. I taught young men in a school in Pleiku, and I am familiar with the Montagnards."

My heart sank.

"I want to help you. I think that you are smart but do not understand the method of teaching at Trinh Vuong. You need to come to your classes with a notebook and pen. When the teacher writes something on the blackboard, write it down in your notebook before she or he erases it. Listen carefully to what is said and try to write down all that you can. It is not easy to listen and write at the same time, but I think that you will do much better if you try this." Then he smiled and put his hand on my shoulder to reassure me.

"Thank you. I have wanted to talk to you but was afraid."

"Come again when you have a question, and I will try to give you support."

It was the end of classes for the day. I almost ran to find H'Don to tell her what we needed to do to make our grades better. When I found her in the room, she was crying again. She was so miserable. "Look, H'Don, I know how to study now. Teacher Duy just talked to me with advice about learning in this school."

She didn't want to hear any of it, and I don't think that she tried very hard after that, but she didn't cry as much, and her grades were just a little better. I did what he said and read my notes and memorized dates and names and improved my grades so that they would not send me back to Cheo Reo.

## *Surprise Visit*

About two months after we were at Trinh Vuong, Mother Gabrielle sent a message to me and to H'Don to come to her office. We came down the hallway holding hands and whispering in wonder of what we had done. I was so scared that I had not brought my grades up enough, or that one of the nuns had seen my skin showing between my blouse and my skirt. I did not have fifty dong to pay for a penalty.

When we walked into her office, I froze. There was Father Son standing by Mother Gabrielle's desk. I lost all of my politeness and ran to him with my arms opened. H'Don followed more slowly, as she did not know him, but there was much happiness in the room.

"I was worried about you two. I thank God that you found this place. You look very grown up and healthy."

"Oh, we are. We are so glad to see you." I stopped and turned to Mother Gabrielle. "Please excuse me. Good afternoon, Mother!" She smiled and nodded. Father Son seemed pleased that I had not totally forgotten my manners. "Can you stay a little?" I pleaded.

"I have asked Mother Gabrielle if both of you can come to my family's house for dinner tonight. We can talk a lot then, and you can tell me about your trip and about school."

The smile on Mother Gabrielle's face assured me that she had given her permission.

"You may go now," she said, "but first, go to your room and wash your faces."

Father Son's house was close enough to the school that we could walk. It was the first time that I had been outside the gate. I had forgotten how busy the streets were and how much noise came from the cars, but I was so happy that H'Don and I almost skipped beside Father Son.

At his house, we received a cheerful welcome from his family. It seemed that everyone talked at one time. My heart was full, and the food smelled delicious. We put chairs around the table and sat down to thank God for our meal and for all of us being together.

The ten guests passed dishes of rice and chicken and steamed vegetables to one another, and everyone began to eat and talk, except me. Beside my plate were chopsticks. I looked around to see how the others were using them, and they seemed to have no trouble. I kept picking up a little rice with the sticks, but bits fell into my lap, and I used my fingers to get it to my mouth. H'Don wasn't doing much better. She whispered to me, "Ask them for a spoon or fork."

I lowered my head and whispered back to her, "No, I can't do that."

I managed to pick at the food awhile before Father Son noticed that most of my rice bowl and the food on my plate were not disappearing very fast.

"Why are you not eating? The food is good. Do you need help?"

His sister asked, "How do you eat at school?"

I was embarrassed, but I answered her, "We have a spoon and a fork."

"Oh, we didn't think of that. Let us help you."

"It's okay," I said. "I don't want to bother you."

Spoons and forks were brought to both of us, and we finished our dinner, but I didn't eat more and felt that I was not a proper guest.

Afterward, Father Son tried to cheer me and asked what I might need at school. I only wanted to be nice to him and to his family, but I shyly said, "Money. Everything at the school is very expensive." He nodded.

We thanked the family over and over, and Father Son walked us back to the dorm before the nine o'clock curfew. Hai let us in through the gate, and H'Don thanked him and went inside. Father Son handed me a piece of paper with his address. "Please write to me if you need help. Study a lot! Mother Gabrielle says that you are trying very hard. This is not much, but here is two hundred dong. It will help you buy something that you need."

In the light, he could see my tears. My speech choked. "Thank you! I know that God will bless you." I turned and went inside.

## *Unexpected Life at Trinh Vuong*

After we knew some of the girls a little better, one of them became my friend. She was so funny and liked to apply makeup to my face and fix my hair up on my head like hers. She told me that my long white blouse was not very stylish and that she could fix it. She snipped the side seams up to my waist, but not enough to show any skin. Even so, I still wore an undershirt. One day I passed a full-length mirror, and I think that I stood up taller after I viewed my reflection.

My friend did not include me in all of the girl-school tricks, but that saved me from being expelled.

One evening the microphone system began yelling out from the hallways. There were two words: *Romeo* and *Juliet*. I heard it over and over. I began to understand that something unusual was about to happen at the school. There had been high excitement during the day between the girls, kind of like the electricity in the science lab. I passed our hall supervisor, BaBa, who immediately got up from her desk at the end of the hall in time to see girls running from room to room and rushing down the hallway and down the steps to the first floor. BaBa was not anyone's favorite person. She was old and always grouchy and never seemed to enjoy being at the school, so the girls often tried to take advantage of her and referred to her by several names that she would not like.

One girl almost knocked the books I was carrying out of my arms as she slid past me on the opposite side from BaBa and ducked into a room. I heard the door lock. BaBa knocked and said, "Let me in!" There was no answer. Just silence. She looked at me. I shrugged and kept walking down the hall. Around a corner, I heard a lot of running going toward the stairs.

Within thirty minutes, the noise and running came to a silent stop. It seemed that a number of girls had planned to go out for the night. Some got past the gate; five came back in before the nuns finished their dinner and found out that a prank had taken place. Ten girls were caught by the nuns and taken out into the courtyard around the flagpole behind the main building.

The other news that I heard the next morning was that their parents had to come to the school and sign a paper to allow them to come back and stay until the end of the semester. Several girls in my classes had puffy red eyes, and there was little laughter in the halls. I thought about myself and imagined that if I had known the girls better, I probably would have been running for the front door myself. From then on, my love for the school and for the girls with electric spirits grew as flowers in rain.

The school year ended too quickly for me. In May, before our semester exams, Mother Gabrielle met me in the hallway and asked if I could walk with her to the gardens outside. As we talked, she asked me about my exams and if I needed extra help. She didn't wait long before she stopped and asked, "You have learned well. If your exams are also good, do you think that you will come back next year and continue in the eleventh grade?"

I had not expected this conversation. "I don't know. I love the school. It is very hard for me, but I have learned a lot. I must talk to H'Don. You know that we are like sisters."

"Yes, I know, but she has been sad here and has not done as well."

The sun lingered above the wall around the school and made afternoon shadows. As I looked across the square of grass and trees, it made me sad to consider leaving this place. "I'll talk to H'Don, and we will let you know after exams if that is okay."

The subject was closed.

When H'Don and I were together that night, she looked away and said, "No, I cannot stay. It is too hard for me, but you stay and go to the next grade. I want to go home; I don't want to go to school anymore."

"But we are sisters. We need to stay together." Our words ended there.

I tried to study for my science exam, but it was very difficult to concentrate. When I got into bed, I tossed and turned as the thoughts swirled around my head for hours.

The next morning, I continued to remember that I had a decision to make—and an exam to take. H'Don was getting dressed. "I must go home with you," I said. "We are sisters. I will find a high school there where I can work on more subjects. We go together."

"But you can stay. It will be all right."

All I could think of to say was, "No, we must go together." She went to her class's test, and I followed her not long after.

I knew the answers to most of the questions on the test, and after I left the classroom, I went to Mother Gabrielle's office. She invited me to come in.

I approached her desk. "I will go home with H'Don. We came together, and we will stay that way."

"Please sit down, H'Tien. This school has helped you to grow, and we have enjoyed having you here. I am so proud of what you have done. I can see that you could accomplish much more next year. Are you sure?"

The lump in my throat from the first day seemed to return as I looked at the floor, then straight at Mother Gabrielle. "I am sure." I stood up and went to her desk. "I want to thank you for allowing me to come to school here and for letting me come for free. You have been very kind to me, and I will never forget you or the friends that I have made here. I will miss all of you."


Two days later, everyone's exams were finished, and most of the suitcases were packed. The postulants performed a program for us to enjoy in the auditorium in the evening. I could hardly believe how good they were. Some wore stage makeup and dressed like men. Others dressed as women. They sang and played guitars, drums, and other instruments in a band and acted in comedy skits. We laughed hard and clapped a lot. I sat next to my best friend at the school and felt my heart dancing and crying at the same time. Maybe, someday, in another place, in another time, we would meet again.

As I walked to my room after the play was over, I passed by a window in the front of the main building and saw that there were more men at the gate than usual—security. Mother Gabrielle was ready for any creative tricks. The halls remained quiet.

# RETURNING HOME

## *Journey to Cheo Reo*

The next morning, there was no time to be sad, although tears were everywhere. H'Don and I said all of our good-byes and thank-yous and took our packed bags to the gate. Many cars—parents and taxis—lined up in the street outside. We had our map and knew that we must return to New Market then to Old Market to reach the bus stop. We asked a taxi driver how much it would cost to go that far. It was a lot of money for us, but we decided that it was good. H'Don's parents had sent her enough to get home, with a little extra for me. They understood. The driver put our bags in the back, and we climbed in and shut the doors. I was nervous and started to shake. I hoped that we were going the right way. It helped take my mind away from leaving Trinh Vuong.

We were better prepared for this trip. Our backpacks carried snacks, and we had directions in our heads. One of the nuns had called the bus system for our departure time, but we arrived an hour early—just in case. At a little kiosk by the street, we paid for our tickets, sat on a bench near a park of green grass and trees and gathered our bags around us. Conversation seemed forced, and when the bus for Pleiku finally came, we were near the last to place our bags in the storage compartment.

I smiled at H'Don. "It will be okay, I will find another school, and we are still the closest of sisters."

She looked down and said in a low voice, "I know."

Not long after we settled into our seats, the wheels began to move toward Pleiku, and Qui Nhon City slowly faded into the countryside.

## *Pleiku*

I woke up suddenly when the bus made a quick stop. The sun had gone under, and the light was fading. "We are coming into Pleiku," said the driver.

H'Don was still asleep. I shook her. "We're here," I said. "It's Pleiku."

She looked out of the window. "But it's dark," she said.

"I know. When we stop, just get off the bus and act like you know where you're going."

We had no idea what to do next and didn't expect to be so late. "When does the next bus leave for Cheo Reo?" I quietly asked the bus driver.

"Tomorrow morning." He finished taking all of the suitcases from the bus.

There were no huts, no house for sleep, and we did not know the city. We started walking down the street toward a taxi, but I didn't know what we would tell him. Thoughts rushed through my mind. Then the name of a school—a Catholic school—came to my memory. I asked the taxi driver, "How far is Phaolo School?"

"Not far!" He didn't seem too pleased to take us, but he gave us a price that we could afford, and we climbed into the taxi with our bags. H'Don looked at me in astonishment. I just nodded my head, and then I prayed.

It took about fifteen minutes until he stopped. "This is where you get out."

"Why do you not take us all the way to the school?" I asked.

"My taxi doesn't go all the way. This is the fare." There was nothing to do but to get out with our bags. We paid him what we had agreed at first and started walking. It was very dark.

"H'Tien, where are we going?" H'Don was anxious.

"I don't know. Keep walking."

We walked three more blocks and saw a large building ahead with a thick wall around it. *I pray, Dear God, I hope that is the school.*

Our pace quickened, even though the bags had become very heavy, and we were dragging more than carrying them.

"H'Don, we must change out of our white uniforms to our black pants and blouses."

"Where are we going to do that?" she stopped moving.

"Let's go in these bushes right here! We can do it." I looked around to see if anyone could notice us and then moved behind the shrubs. "Come on, it will be okay." I encouraged.

There was a lot of searching with our hands to find the right clothes, but we finally came out again dressed as Montagnards.

A gate to the building was close by, but when we arrived, no one was there. Our emotions were thin, our stomachs empty, and our arms tired from pulling our heavy loads. Just as I sat down on my suitcase, I saw a figure on the other side of the wall walking toward us. I stood up and got close to the gate.

"May I help you?" a lady asked. She did not have a habit on and had a different accent, so I didn't know if she was a nun, and this was a Catholic school.

"Oh yes! Is this the Phaolo School?"

"It is Thanh Phaolo [St. Peter's]. My name is Mary, and who might you be?" she answered in a kind voice.

My words seemed to roll out of my mouth so quickly that I don't think I took a breath. It is a wonder that she understood my explanation about where we had been and why we were going to Cheo Reo and why we needed a place to stay.

"If you will wait here, I'll go in and talk to the sisters about this." *Her name is Mary. God has blessed us.*

She appeared again in a short time with one of the nuns and a key to the gate. H'Don smiled for the first time that day.

Several nuns, dressed in habits that I remembered from school in Cheo Reo, gathered around us inside the door and wanted to hear our story. I told them a little, but they stopped me, saying that we must be hungry and tired, and they would hear the rest after we had something to eat. We put our things in a room down the hall. Our luggage suddenly seemed much lighter.

While we were eating and telling them about Trinh Vuong, the nun who was the head of the school asked, "Why did you not come to our school? We are so much closer."

"I will think about that for next year in eleventh grade," I answered as my mind raced to the possibilities. H'Don just smiled and did not say anything.

There were no students at Thanh Phaolo. They had been dismissed for the summer just as we had. But the nuns who were there were so kind to us. They not only gave us dinner and a nice place to sleep, but they also fed us breakfast and blessed us as we left to find the bus for Cheo Reo. "Come and visit us again! We would like for you to come back in the fall."

We left the gate in the direction they had given us for the bus stop. It was not very far. As I walked, I thought about their open friendship. We were hungry, and they fed us; we were tired, and they offered us shelter; we were lost, and they helped us find our way. I would miss them. I gave thanks to God.

## *Short Stop in Cheo Reo*

I awoke in the early evening as we rode past fields, houses, and buildings that mingled in the shadows of the setting sun. My happy thoughts returned as I anticipated our welcome from friends and family. Our first stop would be at Thanh Gia.

Sister Amanda was surprised and happy. She gave both of us big hugs, a place to put our things, and then food. Even H'Don began to smile and relax. She was home. We walked in the garden around the church and talked and talked.

"I am so proud of you two, and, H'Tien, you made it to your junior year." She hugged me again.

"But where should I go next year, Sister? H'Don wants to stay here. The nuns were so nice to us at Thanh Phaolo in Pleiku, but I am not sure that they have all of the high school grades."

Sister looked at H'Don, who shook her head. "I am not going back to school. I am not a very good student, and there is little happiness in the work."

Sister Amanda nodded. "Okay, then you must go to the public school, Thanh Gia, here. You need to keep up your education." She turned to me. "Pleiku has another Catholic high school, Minh Duc. I know the principal there, Father Nam. I will see what I can do. He should be glad to have you. If H'Don will not go, would you like to have some other company?

"There are two girls here who will be going to Minh Duc in the fall. They are Huong Ksor and H'Pun Ksor. I will speak to them, and you can meet them soon. They are a little younger, but I don't think that it will matter."

Their names were a good sign, the same as mine, and it would be helpful to already have friends at a new school.

## *Family Reunion*

The reunion in my village with my family was pleasant. There was little arguing about school and education, as my cousins— H'Kong, Buk, H'Plip, and H'Nhim—had been in Cheo Reo taking classes during the year. There was an unspoken distance between Ama, Ami, and myself. They only knew farming. Ama had been in the army, and he understood life within the edges of his own village. Life outside was complicated. And I felt driven to be more—to be somewhere else, to experience new challenges. Education was my way out, I thought. I would return to Pleiku.

We did not know what was going on when the war in Vietnam started or what it was about or how bad it was. There was a bridge that joined the area of our village to Cheo Reo. The Republican army let us cross back and forth over the river. But the Viet Cong began to question everyone walking across and to kill people in villages on the other side of Cheo Reo. People from three villages moved over to be near us and separated themselves into small refugee camps around our village. I still could not imagine that it would touch me. I was fifteen. Surely no one would bother children. But when the river was almost dry, I waded under the bridge to keep from being stopped.

# Pleiku, Father Tai, and Minh Duc High School

## *Alone Among Friends*

In Pleiku with Father Tai, I met the girls Huong, a Vietnamese, and H'Pun, a Montagnard, at a house where nuns-in-training lived. It was not a school, but different people came to the house to teach the postulants and to have devotions. The nuns lived across the street in a convent and wore different habits than I was used to—more blue than black.

It was the summer of 1974. We ate all of our meals at the convent but slept at the house with the postulants. Sometimes we would go for a walk or to a movie, and on Sundays, we would go to a small church, which was only walking distance.

Father Tai even came to the house where we stayed to give a special blessing to the young nuns-to-be before their exams. They were all in their senior year of high school.

Father Tai often brought to the house people who were strangers to me, but they all needed a place to stay for a night or two. We tried to be friendly to everyone and knew that Father Tai was offering much-needed shelter to travelers. The long rectangular guest house was comfortable enough and had space to sleep about twenty people. There was a well outside for washing and cooking, one bathroom, but no kitchen. The most challenging time was when Father Tai asked a family of six to stay for a week. But it was free for us, and school would begin soon.

The three of us stayed there for a month until Father Tai found another place for us while we went to school. Our new house was a combination of living space and a place where religious groups could gather to learn and to worship. The house was called Tabitha, named after a group that met there, and another group was called Maranatha. They both met once a month for Gospel readings, discussions, and teachings about faith. Both were Christians but with different cultures and different churches. It didn't matter to them, and they got along well as they sang and studied and prayed together.

The Tabitha house was very close to a village, but Huong, H'Pun, and I didn't know anyone from there, and were not sure how to make friends. There was often caution in the voices of our countrymen, because people in the North Vietnamese government were around in many places, and it was difficult to decide who to trust, who would tell the truth. Even our own Montagnard villagers could not always be trusted. The government would pay for information about activities and possible rumblings of discontent. I listened to the talk but did not understand.

I watched numerous Montagnards pass by our house and could hear different tribal dialects as they walked the road, but I was uncertain about making friends with any of them. I was there to go to Minh-Duc High School, not to get into trouble with anyone.

## *Minh Duc High School*

The school was different from any that I had attended before. The sixth to eighth grades met in the morning, and the ninth to twelfth grades began at noon. H'Pun and Huong attended morning classes, so I was left alone to find my way. On the first day, I allowed a lot of time for walking, but it took almost two hours, and I got there just in time to register for classes.

When I went into my first third-floor senior class, I hoped to see other Montagnards, but there were none to help me feel comfortable. I could see that I probably did not fit into any group, but I tried to be friendly.

H'Yoanh age 16 school photo

New clothes were not possible, so I dressed in what I had and tried to keep clean. On Mondays, Tuesdays, and Wednesdays, I wore my long white skirt and white tunic top from Qui Nhon. On Thursdays and Fridays, I wore my usual white T-shirt and long black skirt. No one could really identify me by my clothes, and I don't think that anyone tried. The students spoke Vietnamese, which I could speak enough and which I understood, but I had to listen carefully and speak slowly. My stuttering, although it had improved, was in my favor.

H'Pun and Huong began to learn the guitar in school and practiced a lot in the afternoons and did not seem to worry about their lessons. When I got home, I usually was alone. The Minh Duc classes were not easy for me, so I studied late into the night and got up early to finish.

The girls did not have much money either. Father Tai brought a bag of rice around every now and then, but it was difficult to find wood to burn, and there was little charcoal for a fire.

A choyote vine grew up over his roof, but it was so high we could not climb up to pick any of it. Sometimes, at night, I could hear the neighbors next to us ease along the edge of the roof and steal the choyotes that hung close enough for them to reach. They didn't talk to us or share any of their food, but once I saw them selling the choyotes in the village market.

Father Tai lived at the Chuet Village, but sometimes he would stay in another place for a month, ministering to different groups of people. I guess that he thought we could handle everything. He did not realize how little we had, and I did not know how to earn money in Pleiku. We boiled a small amount of rice every day, but hunger became normal.

Father Tai told me that I could use his oil on the top shelf of a cabinet, but I did not bother any of his things or any of the supplies that belonged to the groups that met there, and I did not tell Huong and H'Pun. Their thinking was unlike mine.

One day when I came home, Huong said, "Go in and eat noodles!"

I was surprised. "How? I have no money. Where did you get the noodles?"

"Just eat, H'Tien! I have money. It's free to you," Huong encouraged.

I was hungry. I did, and it was good, but the next time I hesitated. She still did not tell me where she got the money to buy the food—or to take the guitar and mandolin lessons.

One morning I decided to find out what might be going on with the girls and the food. I opened Father Tai's cabinet, and the top two shelves were empty. I asked H'Pun, the youngest, what happened.

"We took it to the market and sold it so that we would have money to buy other things," she said. "Father Tai didn't need it."

I felt ashamed for what had happened, but I had no way to repay him for the items. Huong and H'Pun and I did not have many conversations together after that. Every day was the same for me—boring and lonesome—and I became afraid to be in the house by myself. The girls began to come home late at night with men who talked loud and made gestures at me. I often locked myself in the tiny toilet, covered the hole, and sat on the shelf around the opening to get away and to work on my studies.

One night, when I was alone, someone threw gravel through the front window. I was so scared that I could barely talk. But I slowly peeked around the edge of the opening and said, "Who is there?"

There was no answer. Then three men showed themselves at the bottom of the steps and asked, "Won't you let us in your house?"

I immediately replied, "No!" My heart was pounding, and I was shaking all over. The three looked like my countrymen, and I recognized one as someone I had often seen at the restaurant across the street from the house, but I did not let them in.

The next day, I stopped by the restaurant and asked the owner who was the familiar-looking man.

She became angry and told me, "He comes by the store often, looking for a job. He says that he has no money and wants to borrow money to buy cigarettes, beer, and food, and he always takes something. I keep a list of what he owes me. I don't like him hanging around."

What she said did not make me feel confident, especially when they came by the next evening, but this time they introduced themselves. One, whose last name was Ksor, the same as mine, was called Chue. I let them in because of his last name—and because they were my countrymen, whom I longed to see.

One of the three revealed to me, "We have been watching you every day, and we want to be brothers to you."

I didn't say anything, not even my name, but they had brought me sweet potatoes and vegetables and seemed determined to help me. I tried to show respect because they were adults and Montagnards, but I asked, "How do you think you can help me?"

"We try to find work, making repairs on houses or doing electrical work, but we want to be your friend and will share what we have with you. We will keep you company so that no one will harm you."

I said, "Thank you, but you cannot come here every day. Someone will tell Father Tai, and I will get in trouble. He will not like for me to have men in the house."

"Where is Father Tai?" they asked.

I was silent. They already knew that I was alone most of the time. And they did dress with nice clothes, and the one with my last name of Ksor was a brother to me in the Montagnard tradition. But they did not know my name at the time. I just answered them with, "I don't know. You need to leave because I go to school, and I have a lot of work to do."

They left, but two days later, they came for more conversation. I met them outside the house this time. They wanted to know more about me. My brain had been working on the man who seemed familiar to me, and when I saw him again, I remembered the connection. When they asked if I knew any of them, I looked at the oldest one and said, "I think that your name is Dai Kpa. You graduated from Hawaii University and probably are my brother-in-law."

He stood, looking stunned. "Why do you say that?"

"Your wife, H'Ring Ksor, with the last name as me, was my teacher and my Montagnard sister in the fifth grade."

"You are right that she is a teacher. She still teaches in Cheo Reo at Thanh Gia Elementary. I will ask her if she remembers you. What is your given name?"

I hesitated; then I almost whispered, "H'Tien."

"How are you paying for your school?"

"I am not sure. I just go to school, and they let me go to class. I think that Father Tai and his friends are helping the school in some way so that I can attend. I saved a little money from working in the village, and Father Tai brings rice every couple of months for us to cook. My two roommates sometimes come with money and food from their friends, but they are not here very often." I felt that I had already said too much.

Dai Kpa looked at me and shook his head. He said again that he would help me, but I did not know what that meant.

The next morning, one of the three men came to the house and brought scholarship money for me. "We want you to have this to save you worry about your school and about eating. We know that you do not have enough food to help you learn. It is two thousand dong and is only for you, not for the two girls with you. Use it well!"

"But where did you get so much money?" I remembered how many long, hard months it had taken me to earn that amount. I do not think that I blinked but stared at the gift.

"I brought this from Dai Kpa."

The older man in my group of new friends wanted to show me his house, so one morning before school I went with him in a *tuk-tuk* to his home near the outskirts of the city. It was a small wooden house with a thatched roof and three rooms.

"H'Tien, I want you to marry me so that I can care for you," he said very straightforwardly. "You can continue your school, but you will be safe here with me."

I looked down at the floor, out the window, and up at him. He was about my father's age and seemed to have a kind heart. I hardly knew what to say.

"You are a beautiful young woman and very smart, and we could be happy."

I regained my voice and said, "My mother wants me to stay in school and not to marry someone right now." It was all that I could think of at the moment.

"But I will take you to your mother and ask permission to marry," he pleaded.

I spoke with respect, "No, sir! I thank you for your kindness, but I cannot marry you. If you come to my village, you may speak of me as your sister."

Two months after I had received the scholarship from Dai Kpa, I shared fifty dong each with H'Pun and Huong. They had been good to me, bringing me food and being my friends. They were amazed and wanted to know where I had gotten the money. All I said was that a friend had given it to me and that I wanted to share some of it with them. I never told them about Dai Kpa, and I kept the money deep down inside of my pants, day and night, and only took out what I might need at any time. I thanked God every day for my new brothers and for the Montagnard community who cared for one another.

## Headless Chicken

Four months before the new Vietnam government took over Pleiku, Father Tai invited me, H'Pun, and Huong to his house in Chuet Village for a meal. When we arrived, he told us that he also had asked some of his old friends to come over, and he wanted us to cook for everyone.

"I'll be glad to cook, but what kind of food do you want us to fix?" I inquired.

His explanation was short: "There is a chicken nesting behind our house. I want you to catch the bird, cut off its head, and drain the blood from the neck into a bowl. Dip the chicken in a pot of boiling water and remove the feathers. Do you know how to cook it after that?" I just nodded my head and stared from the pot to the backyard. "I'll be back at five o'clock with my old friends."

"Oh my gosh, just where is the chicken, and how do I get its head off?" I said out loud.

H'Pun responded, "I don't know anything about killing chickens. He told me to pickle the turnip greens." And she left for the garden.

Huong was not any help either. She looked much busier than needed, getting water for boiling the rice and searching cabinets for fish sauce ingredients. She looked at me as I started to speak and said bluntly, "I don't kill chickens, H'Tien. Don't even ask me!"

*According to Father Tai, I need to have boiling water, which means wood and a fire under the pot. Building a fire and boiling water is not a problem. I've done that many times. Maybe this will not be too hard.*

There was one very dull large knife on a shelf near the stove. I took it and went into the yard to search for the chicken. Just like Father Tai said, the chicken was on a nest in a wooden box up on a platform near the back door. But the chicken was a rooster and had no intention of being boiled or eaten. I reached my hand in the nest and was immediately pecked. I jerked my hand out and stared at the eyes of the rooster. "You have to come with me," I said. "We need you." His red comb turned side to side each time I tried to grab his neck or his head. He pecked harder and squawked louder. He won—for a while.

I went to the house next door and talked to a man about my problem. He frowned but then laughed. "Let me come and help you." He brought a heavy string with him. We approached the rooster, who immediately broadcast his displeasure at my return. The man grabbed the rooster by the feet, turned him upside down, and tied the string around his legs. It looked so easy.

"Okay! Thank you." I reached for the rooster. "Let me try now." He handed the flapping bird to me, and with great trouble, I laid him on the ground, standing with the string holding his feet, and grabbed his wiggling neck with one hand and the knife with the other. It never stopped jumping. I cut its neck, but I didn't see any blood to put in the bowl that Father Tai had told me to use.

I put my arms around the flapping chicken and took him into the house, where the water was almost boiling. *It should be hot enough for him now,* I thought. I struggled to get the string off and dumped him into the steam.

I was not prepared for what happened. That rooster jumped and flapped out of the pot and splashed water on me and all over the house as he ran out the nearest opening and into the village.

"Oh help!" I screamed, but no one heard me. All I knew was that dinner had just flown out the door, and I was responsible.

From the window, I could see it running under the next house and across the road, its neck hanging to one side. I jumped from the steps and ran to its direction, yelling for help from anyone who could hear me.

The man next door came out again and followed me, and soon we had a parade of villagers chasing the chicken. I was horrified to think that he would get away, and I would be disgraced. But one of the young villagers caught him and brought him to me without so much squawking. My new friend got his own knife and finished the neck job.

I thanked everyone over and over, and the villagers laughed at the zigzag race. My smile disappeared when I reached the stove and found that the water had boiled out, the bottom of the pot was burned, and I knew that I had to start over. I had given up on getting the blood from the neck in a bowl, especially since a lot of it was on me. I held the rooster's body under one arm while I gathered more wood and lit the fire again. The slightly jumping body lay on the floor beside the stove, while I filled the pot with water. My helpful friend had told me how to get the bird ready to cook. So after steam rose from the pot, I picked up the chicken and dipped it in the hot water for a few minutes, took it out, pulled off the feathers, cut it open and into pieces, and removed the inside parts, which made my own stomach squirm and my eyes squint.

H'Pun and Huong had laughed at the chicken chase but had stayed away from the kitchen afterward. However, they did not have any trouble eating the meal once it was on the table, seasoned and roasted. Father Tai was very pleased with the dinner and all of our cooking, although he and his friends had brought extra food when they returned at five o'clock. I think that they must have known about chicken chases and feather pulling, but I didn't offer any explanation of the afternoon's events. I just vowed that there would never be a knife sharp enough for me to cut chicken necks again, and I have kept that promise.

# ESCALATION OF FEAR

## *February 1975*

In February 1975, army trucks throughout the cities and villages had noticeably increased, and with them, there was more dust and more noise and more stares from the citizens. The trucks carried lots of men and were loaded down with things that were invisible under the thick green tarps. Cars and trucks passed by our school so often that sometimes it was difficult to hear. When the teacher was not in the room, we stood up and looked out of the windows to gaze at the parade of vehicles. But we only watched, and if anyone spoke, the words were mumbled or whispered.

I never heard fighting or gunshots, and we did not have a radio or TV, so I had no idea why all of the activity and why people didn't talk. Dai Kpa and his friends had not come by in a while. I noticed that a movie theatre near where I stayed advertised the movie showing that week: *Tinh Mua Dong*. But there were no crowds, and all was quiet on the street except for the roaring engines.

The school stayed open, but every morning someone else was absent, and the classes grew smaller. I asked a friend if she had heard anything, but she didn't answer, and the teachers would not discuss any subject other than the one in our classroom. Within the next week, we had our first outward sign of something very bad happening. I heard that the war in our country was over, but the killing was closer to me.

My awareness began in Pleiku with the army convoys and the secret stares. Then news came from Ban Me Thuot, a close-by village where, a neighbor told me, the Viet Cong brought a big gun, and they shot and killed villagers and injured many more.

That week, Father Tai arrived in his car and parked as close to our door as possible. The girls were at the house with me. The road was empty, and he was very serious—not in his happy smile. "Pack all of your things quickly. You cannot stay here any longer. Don't ask questions—just pack!"

The three of us just stood there looking at him for a few moments, not believing what he was saying. "Girls, you must pack now. Hurry! We are going to Chuet Village in my car."

We jumped into action, as though we had been shocked by a rod, not just told by words. My heart began to beat faster, and it was as if hot flushes ran through my body. What was happening that would cause this sudden change? Since I had heard about the killings in Ban Me Thuot, I suspected that we might be in the same danger. I did not think that I had many belongings but found it to be a little difficult to stuff everything that I owned into one suitcase and a backpack. Even so, I think that we were packed in the car in less than thirty minutes.

The Vietnamese woman at the store across the street had seen us putting things into the car and ran over to Father Tai screaming that the girls owed her money. His eyes widened, and he said, "How could that happen? How much do they owe?" She told him, and he found the money to pay her from his pocket.

I looked at H'Pun and Huong. Huong shrugged her shoulders. "It couldn't be that much." But she didn't offer to pay any of it. We had no time to argue.

Soon we were on the road to Chuet, the car seeming to be very overloaded, but only with luggage, not with conversation. The place where he drove us was the house where he often went to worship. The house looked comfortable and felt safe inside— better than Maranatha House. In the first few weeks, there were fewer trucks in this village and no gunfire.


I made new friends and helped Father Tai wherever I could. Huong and H'Pun only joined in when the children in the neighborhood came to see us and to play games and sing songs. Every night, we took our blankets to the small kitchen and slept on bamboo beds. The sticky rice diet was a little hard to get used to, but it was steady food. We just did not grow that kind of rice at home.

After the first week, Huong Ksor left the house and the village. And in the second week, H'Pun left. They did not tell Father Tai that they were going, or where. They did not even leave me a note. Father Tai's eyes showed his disappointment, but he smiled a slow smile to me.

Soon after, Father said to me, "H'Tien, stay here and be safe. I must go and see about others in the villages around us. There is lots of sadness." He left, and I was alone again.

I looked out of the window and saw the children laughing and running, but I soon lost the desire to join them. We got along well when we were playing, but visiting the families was difficult as they spoke another dialect. I knew that they did not understand me, and now there was no one to translate what I said. So I withdrew into the house and often cried at night. I missed my own village, especially my family.

In the mornings, I could hide from my situation in my bed, but I knew that I needed to start a fire and heat water for the day. I never knew who might come by. Also, there was the sweet milk the priest's nephew brought from the army camp. I don't remember how he got it, but he left it there for me, and it was unthinkable to let it spoil. I drank it when I was very hungry.

Father Tai liked to make me feel good about myself and comfortable in my surroundings. Once when he came back for a day, he said to me, "H'Tien, we need teachers here in the village. You could be a good one for the little children."

I took a deep breath. "Father, thank you for thinking that I could do the job, but I have family in Cheo Reo. I like it here, and you and your friends have been so kind to me, but when we feel that it is safe, I must return to my home village. Ama and Ami need me to help them with the farming when I am not in school."

He said that he understood, but my heart beat in two directions for this man who had given me so much.

## *First Encounter with the Viet Cong*

In March, one morning after Father Tai left, barking dogs woke me early. They barked constantly. I decided that more sleep was not possible, so I got up and lit the fire to boil water. The barking mixed with the roar of trucks and cars on the road, and the sound of men talking came closer to the house. The language was Vietnamese, but there was a different accent. When I crept quietly to the wall and peeked through the bamboo, I saw several men sitting around in the courtyard of Father Tai's house, smoking and laughing in voices that they did not want to hide. They wore green Viet Cong uniforms and camouflage branches attached to their helmets. The green army bags that they carried were bulging. As I looked past them, I saw uniformed men at the doors of other houses on the road.

I stood frozen, my thoughts racing back to my bed where I could cover myself with my blanket to be invisible. My head told me that the man coming toward the door could not see me, but my shaking body said that no matter what I did, I was caught in a net.

"You in there, open the door. I know that somebody is there because there is smoke coming out." The man yelled louder, "Open up the door! I don't want to knock it down. You do not have to be scared." All of the men laughed. "We won't jump on your..." he mumbled. And the men laughed again.

My shaking hand reached to open the door, and we stood man to child. The surprise was his. A second man burst through the door past the first soldier and ran to the back of the house yelling at me, "Where are the other people from here? What is your name?" He grabbed Father Tai's South Vietnam flag from the wall, the president's picture, and any other thing he could see associated with South Vietnam. He held out his hand in front of my face, "Where is your ID card?" I just stared at him and shook my head. "Do you have one?" Again, I shook my head. "Can't you speak?" My lips seemed glued together. He left the house with an armload of Father Tai's possessions, and I could not stop him.

The first soldier spoke to me in a softer voice, "What is your name?" I stayed wrapped in my arms. My large eyes had cut off the sound from my throat. He went to his pack and brought back a piece of paper and a pen. From the courtyard his friends were calling for him to hurry on.

"Tomorrow my group will go to Saigon to get the head of President Thieu." He wrote his name, Liem, and his tank number on the paper and said in a little above a whisper, "Write me a letter and come to see me. Here is my address." And he handed me the paper.

I nodded in silence, my eyes never blinking, and took the paper. He went out to his group and laughed with a voice that had no humor for me.

I remained motionless and could see, through the open door, soldiers up and down the road, carrying guns from houses to their trucks and throwing Father Tai's neighbors' possessions into fires that they had set along the edge of the road. My body leaned into the door as it slowly swung shut, separating the outside horror from a terrified young girl inside, all alone.

I stayed in the back room, only going to the kitchen to find something to eat. It was the longest day of my life. I did not go anywhere, talk to my neighbors, or leave the house. I just listened to the noises and sat in my own silence, made a cocoon of my blanket, and curled into a fetal position. By evening, I heard less commotion and once peered through the bamboo to see that the soldiers were abandoning the neighborhood as the fires burned down. In their place, an eerie procession of older villagers, wrapped in blankets, slowly walked in and out of the shadows of dusk, speechless and stunned.

The next day, I froze when the door opened. The voice brought tears to my eyes. It was Father Tai. "H'Tien, it's me. Don't be afraid! Everything will be okay." He put some crackers on the table by the kitchen. "It is just beginning for us. We must be smart and stay calm."

I did not understand, but I put my arms around his waist and began to cry. All of the tension of the last few days melted down my face and onto his robe. I knew how to fit in at the orphanage, I could make my way in the fields with the cattle, I was determined in pursuing my education and strong at school, but all of this was something new, and I sensed that the life I had known was about to unravel.

Father Tai gently stood me straight in front of him and pulled a large bunch of papers from beneath his robe. "Put these in the burn container and set them on fire! Be swift because we do not know when the Viet Cong on the street might follow me to this house. Some of them leave, and others come, but they watch everyone and take what they want, and"—he sighed—"they kill if you don't cooperate."

I could not move for a moment, but then I lit the match and watched the smoke rise from the charred papers.

He went to the same wall where I had peered out through the cracks between the bamboo slats and saw that his small car was gone. He bowed his head, crossed himself, and murmured a prayer, looking heavenward only to say, "Amen."

Two days later, the car appeared at the house next door. It had a flat tire and smelled of guns and sweat. This time, Father Tai offered God a grateful prayer—grateful that only a tire was flat.


During the next month, the village became more settled and quiet. The VC patrolled the streets in their green uniforms, and most carried large guns, but when their conversations were overheard, their talk was cheerful about not having previous year-long duties in the jungle.

However, they began to call meetings in the evenings where all the villagers were required to attend. They told us that there was a new Communist government coming and that there would be better times for the people. They wanted to know how each of us could contribute, and they formed a "freedom ring" for the country. They were "proud of themselves for reaching out to the villagers" to help them in the new economy, but all—Montagnards and Vietnamese—were very frightened about these events and what was to come.

## *Rapid Return to Cheo Reo*

Three weeks passed, and early one morning, Father Tai arrived at the house in a rush. He told me that I must return to Cheo Reo immediately. Again, I packed quickly, and he took me to a parking place hidden behind some shops. People were climbing into a truck with a cover over it.

"H'Tien, you will be taken home. I must stay here."

I picked up my belongings and then put them back down. *How can I leave this kind man?* We hugged and told each other how much we would be missed, and he gave me a blessing. I thanked him for giving me good fortune and safety and care. Our parting was hesitant; I wept as we let go of each other. I was leaving part of my young life behind; he was moving into the unknown shadows of life and death.

Someone lifted my suitcase and backpack into the truck bed, and I put one foot on a step and was pulled up by a man standing on the edge. I did not know who was driving or, if for sure, we were going to Cheo Reo. Everything spun around me but slowed when I saw Farther Phan standing along the left-hand side of the truck. I put my belongings down next to him, and we smiled at each other. He held both of my hands for a moment. There was strength in friendship. When I turned to look out the back of the truck, I saw Father Tai standing with tears on his face, the tension of the past months seeping from the inside of both of us.

Some in the truck stood, and others sat on the floor, huddled together, rocking and bouncing back and forth over the bumpy, dusty road. I gave what money I had left to Father Phan to keep for me. He said that he had a safe pocket under his robe.

We moved slowly. The driver stopped often, inquiring about someone who was missing, or he was flagged down by a lone person walking along the road who needed help. I had left Pleiku at the onset of danger and was traveling toward my home where I might find everything turned upside down. On the ride, I was told about villagers who had gone back and forth, from hamlet to hamlet, from town to town, looking for their relatives and friends. They returned with information that some had been killed by guns or starved to death. Others were gone with no trace; still others were in hiding from the army.

My excitement soon turned into a sober realization that the village I had left no longer included a safe haven for anyone, not my friends nor my family nor my countrymen, especially not the Montagnards.


There was little traffic. After several hours of riding, I made my way around men, women and children to the back of the truck where I could peek through the edges of the canvas flap drawn across the back to keep us in hiding. I watched the scenery and tried to identify anything familiar. The signs that designated the villages had been removed. The houses often looked the same, and when I saw the fields where I had worked in my younger days, I knew that we were passing nearby my home. I yelled back over the noise to Father Phan, "Please stop!"

Father Phan beat on the top of the truck above the driver, and the truck slowed down. "What do you want?" the driver yelled from his window.

"Stop the truck! Someone wants to get off. This is her village." Father Phan made his way to the back as I was jumping down and handed me my backpack and luggage. I thanked him and smiled and said that I hoped that he would come to see us.

I wondered to myself, "Did I forget something? I can't remember." The roar of the engine muffled my words, and the truck disappeared in the dust that tailed its wheels.

I waved, and it was then that I thought about the two hundred dong that I had entrusted to Father Phan. It was gone, and so was he.

I felt as though the place where I stood belonged somewhere else, and I was dropped there to die. All was quiet—no laughing children, no barking dogs, no smoke from houses, no outstretched arms. Nothing!

I looked from one house to another and, in the distance, saw the steps that I knew led to mine. I hesitated, not sure if I should go there now, and wondered what I might find. Slowly, I swung my backpack over my shoulder and dragged my suitcase down the road. I walked up the ramp to the front door and found that it opened easily. The silence made me step back, even though I saw some familiar things. I slowly placed my luggage on the floor inside the door; then I went back outside to look around.

My long white dress—my school uniform—did not allow me to walk easily, so I tucked it up around my waist and eased along the path to our gardens and rice fields, about one hundred yards from the house. They were green, and I was hopeful that someone was tending them.

When I neared the garden, I heard a woman's voice crying and moaning, and then I saw Ami, sitting under a small tree, rocking back and forth, her arms wrapped around her knees and her head bent over. I moved in hesitant steps, fearing that a family member had passed away. Ama chopped tobacco in the garden and only looked up when I was almost in front of him.

He stood there unbelieving and threw his hoe down. "Here she is, she's here," he managed in an exhilarated voice.

Then Ami saw me. The moaning stopped, and the crying began again, this time in much larger waves, accompanied by gasps of words. "Oh, H'Tien, I have cried and cried; I cannot eat or sleep. We heard that you went with Farther Tai in his car and that you both died. I cannot believe that you are here in front of me."

"What are you saying?" I began to cry. "No, I am here, and Father Tai was alive this morning when I left him. Father Phan and I came this way in a truck with lots of other people. They let me out here in the village." I wiped my face and the tears from Ami's cheeks. "I put my things in the house, but I can't tell if anyone lives in the village anymore."

Ama came over to hug me, tears brimming from his eyes. He began in a whisper and then found his regular voice. "The village stays quiet because we are not sure what is happening on any day. People are being kidnapped and killed if they disagree with the new government, and the army of the government steals anything that it wants. We just try to stay away and not see the army when they come here."

I sighed deeply, sat down with them, and talked about the changes in all of our lives.

As the sun began to move shadows across the village, I was surprised to hear Ami say that we must go to the small storage building in the field behind our house for the night, that they were hiding there. But some neighbors had seen me and came to rejoice that I was not dead. They said it must be a miracle.

I answered questions that they asked about my school, about Pleiku, and about what I had seen of the army and what they were doing to frighten people, especially the Montagnards. But in Pleiku, my experiences were limited, and theirs had been more openly hostile. They helped me to understand that our country was no longer a happy, safe place and that our countrymen, our tribal villagers, were now living under a very threatening, brutal government.

# Life in the Village After Pleiku

Parents hid their children anywhere for safety. In the fields most families had storage houses built up on tall tree-trunk stilts, where ladders provided entrance and safety when pulled up after all of the family were inside. Harvested grain and corn and hay also were kept there. We had a smaller house where we cooked and washed early in the mornings before any soldiers roamed through the village. The authorities did not often take time to come to the fields. Our family lived in the field house for many weeks and gradually became used to the dust and heat. No one knew whom to trust. We just took care of ourselves.

Moving to the fields and barns seemed safer to the villagers who were trying to avoid diseases that the Viet Cong were spreading throughout the countryside. We thought that no contact was the best way to prevent sickness. But about a month after I returned, and our family had moved to the shed in the fields, I became sick with malaria. We couldn't blame it on the VC, but they were like the mosquitoes that invaded our homes, and we couldn't just swat them from our property. It took me a month to feel better. The medicine that Ami gave me at least kept me from dying.

In the mornings as I began to recover, I walked through the gardens to see my uncle Mtuat Ksor and his family. My uncle was a security guard in the city and the village. He was my mother's brother. I began to look after his children so that his wife could help him in the fields. He was the only uncle that I had now, and I had missed him very much.

One evening, I asked him and his wife if I could stay overnight with them. The children encouraged me so that I could play with them until bedtime. The next morning we arose early so that my uncle could manage work before the heat. I led the children through their chores and prepared lunch to take to the gardens.

As I went from the house down the path, I saw three men moving toward my uncle. I sent the children back inside, and I kept walking in the direction of the men. As I approached, I could tell that there was much conversation between the men and Mtuat. All four started through the garden where I was walking. "Where are you going?" I addressed my uncle.

"He has forgotten his classes at the correctional center where he works," one of the men said to me.

"Uncle Mtuat, don't go with them," I pleaded in a whisper. "I have never heard you speak about classes. How do you know where they are taking you?"

The men told me to move along, that they had business. I watched them take him to a truck, and my heart ached as my body shook. I ran to his house, told the children to stay there, and as soon as I saw their mother hurrying our way, I ran to our gardens to tell Ami. She had never heard of classes at the correctional center either. We all waited for word from him, but there was none. I went back to stay the night with the children.

At noon the next day, my uncle's wife went to the place where she thought he was to take him some food, but he was not there, and no one claimed that they knew where he was or even who he was. We prayed, but our prayers went unanswered.

Several days later, a friend of mine came to our house to tell me that he had news of Uncle Mtuat. He kept looking at the ground, and I kept asking him questions. "Where is he? Is he alive?"

"No!" came the unwilling reply.

"But where, how did it happen? I can't believe it. Tell me! Tell me everything!"

"H'Tien, it is very difficult."

"But I have to know." I shook him hard.

"I heard from a friend in another village that they made your uncle dig a hole, and when it was deep enough, they told him to take off all of his clothes except his short pants and lie down in the hole. After he did, they shot him and filled the hole back up with the dirt. I am so sorry to tell you this."

I screamed, "Nooooo! How could anyone do that? What could he have done wrong?" I could hardly breathe. I could not digest his words. I was stunned. I ran through the gardens and through the fields, convulsing and retching.

Being totally in despair, I stumbled back to our house to tell Ami. I found her weeping and realized that she already knew. His wife had been told, and I prayed that they left out the details from the children.

Innocence was destroyed.

# A VILLAGE SUBDUED

## *Compulsory Afternoon Classes*

In early spring of 1975, the North Vietnamese soldiers came to the houses and gardens, and they talked to the older villagers. "Where are your young people? We know that you have some here. Tell them not to hide, not to be scared. The new government needs them. Come to our meetings! Everyone in the village must come to our meetings every afternoon and learn how our new government is going to help them. We expect to see the young ones here, along with their parents."

They secured the confidence of numerous villagers and paid the men to organize groups for different kinds of training. The elderly were the main attendants at the first gatherings, and the village leaders kept a list of families for the government so that they knew what young people were missing. Children's names were called, and parents were questioned about their absence.

I came to protect Ami and Ama. I could hardly believe that the required meetings were right in front of our house. I didn't like the army but did not dare show it on my face. At night, my dreams were filled with bitterness, not forgiveness, and my uncle's death left blood on all of their hands.

We were told that it was our duty to choose a specific job that would help the whole village, and if we did not, they would give us one. They told Ami that she was to teach everyone how to be clean and to be healthy. She was so shy that she could hardly speak loud enough for anyone to hear. They raised their voices to her and mocked her efforts, until I stood in front of her.

"I'll do her job," I said. And I whispered to her, "Just say one word!" But she couldn't, and she went back into the house. There was no voice in front of so many people.

I turned sharply toward the leader and said, "If you want to have a healthy life, wash your hands before you eat." The villagers cheered.

The village leader glared at me, but my body and face did not change, and he turned and walked down the road. I expected bad luck from my behavior, and at that point, I did not care.

At the meeting the next afternoon, the leader said to me, "We don't want your ami; she's too old. We want you to teach the villagers. You know how to handle health and to be clean."

"No! My father was in the army, and even though he has died, I don't have to go. Maybe my friend H'Blin will do it!" I signaled toward her house across the road.

That afternoon, they went to H'Blin's house and told her that she would go to different villages with me and help me teach cleanliness. My defiant attitude had not gotten me in trouble, but neither had it saved me from obeying their orders. At least now there would be two of us—two who were best friends.

And so with great hesitation, we did as they told us. The village started filling up again, and the young people down by the river and in the fields came out to hear about the good news and the good government. Hammering could be heard throughout the villages as houses were repaired after so much neglect, and dogs again barked in the streets.

As demanded by the village leader, the next week, H'Blin and I rode her bicycle to another village named Robai and lived for seven days in the place where they told us to stay, but near the end of that week, we ran out of the food they had given us. I went to one of the army officers to ask for help, and he curtly said, "The food bus has not arrived, and I don't know when it will come. You will just have to wait."

But we couldn't wait. An old man in the village was supposed to look after our food supply. We were told where he lived, and we went to his communal house and asked where he kept his food. A woman at the door said that it was in his room on the left. He was not there, but I could see warm coals under a pot, so I took off the lid and looked inside. There was a chicken wing and a drumstick, with rice that he probably had saved for his dinner, and I took some of the rice and the chicken outside to H'Blin, and we ate it together and waited for the old man.

He came home before we finished and asked why we were there eating. I said that we had taken some of his cooked food because we had none and were very hungry, and he was supposed to keep us supplied with food. Instead of being angry, he went out somewhere and brought in more food and gave us rice and fish to cook for ourselves.

The "sanitation" job was boring, and the villagers did not seem to care that we were there. So I offered the old man a suggestion. "If I can find someone else to do our job, will you let us go free?"

He laughed. "Well, that may not be too easy, but you can try."

We left in the morning on H'Blin's bicycle, and I told her to stop at the next village. We parked the bike near where there were some girls talking. "Just laugh and act kind of silly," I told H'Blin. We did and went up to a girl whom I knew a little bit. Her name was H'Moai Ksor (a sister). I said, "I know of a really good job for you in the next village. You just have to teach people how to be clean. Everyone has to have a job, and this one is easy. All you have to do is take seven days of rice, food, and a blanket next week and go to the meetings held in the afternoon in the village."

"No one has told me to do that. I wouldn't know where to go."

I laughed again. "Oh, all you have to do is show up at the meeting in Robai Village at four in the afternoon, and there is an old man waiting to show you where to go. He has a room where you can stay and everything. I'm glad to find you so quickly, because I chose you. He is expecting you to come. It's easy."

"Well, okay, if you are sure. I'll get a friend to go with me."

"Of course, that's no problem."

She looked so naive. But we left before she could change her mind, and we were free. It was the first time we had laughed in many weeks, and we let the happy feeling roll with us back to the old man's place. We slept well, and when we saw him in the morning, I said, "We did it," and called him Uncle.

"Did what?" he questioned.

"Her name is H'Moai Ksor, and she is coming next week from the village down the road to take our places. She will probably have a friend with her."

Before we left the next day, on a blackboard that we found in the old man's house, I drew a picture of a man wearing a uniform, a helmet, and a backpack. In a note beside it, I wrote, "Thank you, sweet Uncle!"

He walked in and looked up in surprise. "Who did that?" he demanded.

H'Blin pointed to me. I pointed to her. We saw the beginning of a smile, but he erased the drawing from the blackboard, shook his head, and waved us out of the house.

H'Blin and I rode home singing some of the songs that we would teach in our own village where we would sign up the next week to instruct classes of dance and music.

I think that I was young and old at the same time—maybe naive like my "sister" H'Moai Ksor, who was now teaching cleanliness. Most days I felt the danger cowering inside as well as outside, but at sixteen, I was headstrong and defiant.

I did not understand everything that was happening, as the schools had tried to protect us, but stark realities, such as my uncle's unspeakable death and the bombing of Father Nguyen's bus, remained as scars on my unsophisticated life. And they were only the beginning.

But back in my own village, each afternoon, a little before four o'clock, the government-paid village leader rang a large metal bell three times to call all of the children from the fields and homes. They participated in social classes until the evening meal. Older children were assigned to teach music and dance. And several times in the months ahead, all village teams were compelled to compete in festivals to see whose team was the best. We tried hard, but our village rarely won.

I taught dance. I did not have a choice to say no. The security people told me what I was to do, and at first, I did not openly question their authority. They did not like that I taught dance in the Vietnamese style and to music that I learned from the nuns in school. I was not acquainted with any new government music and dance customs, but they still would not let me quit.

The security criticized my "not-so-good" teaching, and I got tired of being questioned. Twice I just did not show up, and they were angry with me and yelled at me the next day. And twice I said to them, my eyes glaring at their faces, "I did not have my dinner yet, and I was hungry." They were not pleased but walked away, maybe because they were outnumbered by villagers and did not carry intimidating guns.

# BOLD DEFIANCE—THE
# FIRST TIME

## *May 1975*

The major conversation in the village was of how soldiers ordered people, especially Montagnards and South Vietnamese, to move out of their homes, farther away from the cities. There were already quite a few settlements around our village. Government officials' instructions were often to kill villagers who opposed them. I realized that it was no longer safe to live in or near our surroundings, and I also knew that Ami and Ama would never leave.

H'Blin felt the same way that I did. We discussed it every day and made plans to leave our homes whenever we could find a way out. Some of our countrymen had quietly disappeared from the village, but we did not know where they went. It was whispered that they had slipped deeper into the jungles of the Central Highlands for safety. We also listened to rumors that a big boat on the Ayun River, about two hours' walk from the village, was coming to rescue whoever wanted to "disappear." It sounded exciting to us—a real adventure—and I hated teaching dance. We decided that we would be in the next group to escape.

There was no specific talk around the village about a boat, but we were aware of a lot of mumbling and signaling, especially among our friends. One morning we saw more than the usual group of people moving back and forth along the road and around the houses in the village. "Tomorrow night," I heard. "River...boat... jungle...shots...signal...safe...at ten...field by river."

My cousin Ji Ko appeared at my house. Ami was in the yard. "Where is H'Tien?"

"She and H'Blin are in the house."

He went in, and Ami followed. "H'Tien, do you and H'Blin want to come with us? We are going tomorrow night. Someone is meeting us at the river."

"Go where?" Ami asked.

"We are going away from the village for a while," he replied.

H'Blin and I said, "Yes, we'll talk to you later."

Ami stared at us, looking puzzled, and all I could say was, "It's a trip."

Ji Ko left in a hurry. We did not see him again that day, but we went outside, listened, and watched. People seemed more relaxed in the streets because, at that time, our village had no soldiers inspecting us, and we were more peaceful than usual. It was the perfect opportunity to organize a gathering.

I knew that Ami would not understand and would think that we were just going for a short stay. After all, I had gone away for long periods of time and always returned. She gave me twenty dong to buy something on the way, and I thanked her.

H'Blin and I packed a few belongings in our backpacks (mine was one that Ama had used in the army). Her parents did not like what they had heard and warned us that this sounded like more than just camping for a while. But we covered our ears. At sixteen, we knew more than they did.


The next evening, we sat in front of H'Blin's house, whispering about the rumors. We were determined to be part of the plan, but we had not thought through exactly what it would mean to join a group at the river boat, if there really was one.

The sun set through waves of orange, yellow, and purple. A haze floated on top as if to hold up the tinted pink clouds moving slowly through the darkening sky. From the front steps of H'Blin's house, we stared across the fields and gardens, held close to our thoughts, and locked hands, quivering and glancing at each other in our innocence and our uncertainties: Where were we going? How far was it? Who would be there? Would the signal be clear?

We were inside her house at ten o'clock when we heard the unmistakable three shots being fired from a distance. It was the sign for the leaders in each of the villages and surrounding areas to gather their groups and start toward the river. We hugged her parents (I had already said good-bye to Ami and Ama) and went into the road with our packs.

We were nervous but soon saw dark silhouettes emerge from shadows few at a time, all going in the same direction—toward the river—and we joined them. We passed several gardens and fields and became aware that each group had a leader. Any conversation was below a whisper. The quietness was what I imagined in a village of ghosts, but it just added to the excitement.

Most of the "spirits" seemed to be young people. Maybe the older villagers were afraid or just too tired to try this adventure. But after I had walked in the dark for well over an hour, my legs ached, and my eyes kept closing from tiredness, and then I fell in a hole. Several people pulled me out and let me rest a few minutes, but after they determined that I had not broken anything, they continued on their way.

H'Blin stayed with me, but she began to sound frightened. "Come on, H'Tien, we'll be left behind, and we're not sure where we are going. You have to keep walking."

"Let's go back!" I said.

"We don't know the way. We're too far from home." She sounded hopeless.

My tears brimmed over, and I said, "I think that it must be from the malaria. I get tired quicker." But I heard her desperation. I saw concerned people passing us on the road and knew if they could do it, I could do it. So I stood uneasily and ordered one foot in front of the other. My body hurt all over, and I shivered. I was stupid for not bringing a jacket.

After we waded across the river near the fields of our village, I looked for the boat, but there was no boat, and no one stopped walking. I had kept my pack from getting wet, but my clothes clung to me, which made the chill worse. We had to keep up with the group, and I had not brought extra clothing. *What else have I not brought? And where are we going anyway?*

It was 1:00 a.m. We reached the deep waters of the Ayun River—no boat was waiting. There were more than two hundred in our community of believers. Our leaders tried to be positive, but we were tired and hungry and cold. On the dry ground, some with blankets slept along the banks. H'Blin and I had nothing for comfort, and the snoring and fitful sleepers kept my burning eyes from closing. Clouds drifted apart, revealing a half moon, and I tried to count the stars, but the shivering of my body kept interrupting the numbers.

I must have fallen asleep briefly, because the dream that I had startled me awake. Ami was calling me, "Where are you? Are you okay?" Her voice was loud and clear.

I jumped up and blurted out, "Where am I? What am I doing here?" I stumbled over H'Blin next to me and shook her. My body seemed stiff and bound, but I found my cousin Ji Ko and said, "Get up! We need to go back—no boat. The time, what time is it? We are in big trouble."

My voice shocked many awake. My cousin began to shake those near him and any leaders whom he could see. "We must hurry back to the village before the sun rises. Everybody, gather your things up!"

I saw our leader, who knew the way, took H'Blin's hand, and we followed behind him, walking as quickly as we could in the dark, often not knowing where our feet were stepping. I glanced behind me and saw in the dim moonlight a large group of people resembling an animal herd running like prey from a hungry tiger—all rushing for their lives. Concentration replaced conversation.

There was just the faintest light on the horizon when we arrived at H'Blin's house at 5:00 a.m. Some of the "escapees" had already reached their villages. Her parents, surprised and a bit frightened, let us in, and we promised to explain everything later. The bamboo floor welcomed our muddy, aching bodies, and blankets covered our cold disappointment as I whispered to H'Blin, "Thank God we are okay!"

In the late morning, Ami heard that we were back and came to H'Blin's to inquire. When our parents saw what was under the blankets, they sent us to the stream to clean ourselves before we ate or talked to them. In the water, H'Blin and I washed and splashed and laughed at our looks. At first, we were so glad to be home safely, but while walking back to her house, we realized how dangerous the night before had been and wondered what went wrong.

Over the next three months, we found out that Y-Toan Nie had betrayed all of us and had lied about the rescue boat to freedom. We did not know what happened to him, but I do know that no one from our villages ever mentioned that night: the boat, the misdirected escape—nothing. It never happened.

# TOUGH DEFIANCE—THE SECOND TIME

## *August 1975*

For months, H'Blin and I thought and talked on the next plan of action. We listened. We listened for any scrap of information that might tell us of another attempt at leaving our village. Then, in August, we heard through friends that another group of our countrymen was planning to quietly slip away into the jungles. H'Blin and I were sure that we would be with them. The previous three months had not been pleasant in the nearby villages—prison for no reason, mysterious disappearances, murders, food taken from families, compulsory education for all Vietnamese and Montagnards. Rumors of betrayed friends undermined any trust between families. The village meetings and lessons, and farming continued, but life surrounding what we had known grew smaller and more restrained.

H'Blin and I had matured through our experiences. The word *survival* had come up often in our conversations. The months had given us more time to scheme and to think about another secret mission with its thrill and with its inherent dangers. We were sure neither of our families knew we were even considering another venture into the unknown. We told no one.

Word symbols began to be passed around quietly, designating times, places, and dates. I collected items that I now understood would be helpful on such a journey and scattered them in different places so as not to raise questions. But I could not find Ama's army backpack.

On a night close to time, I confronted Ami and Ama, "Who took my army bag?"

Ami was quick to answer, "Not me!

I looked at Ama. "You must have taken it. I know it was yours, but I need it." Panic crept up into my mouth. "Where is it?" I demanded to know.

"H'Tien, I have been watching you, and I know what you are planning. It is very dangerous for you to leave from us. You are too young, and you do not have experience. Where is it you want to go? Is it like last time when you thought that there was a boat?"

"I need to go to school in Ban Me Thuot," I lied.

"Why? You need to stay here with us. It is too dangerous. Are you planning to go again at night? Why would you go to school at night?"

"I don't know," is all I could say.

There was an awkward silence. My mind flew to Ama's reasoning. He had become suspicious that there might be another time, another disappearance, but he had said nothing. He had just taken the backpack—his attempt to stop me; his worry was real. It was the first conversation we had had in several years.

Ami did not understand either. She said, "Where are you going—to join the army? It will be very difficult for you—no food, no drink, no clothes, no one to look after you if you become sick, and no medicine. Not one person will care about you. And if you come back, they will kill you or take all of us to prison. Don't go!"

I stood up. "I will go to Thailand." I took a deep breath. "I'm not coming back."

It was a very difficult moment for Ami, Ama, and me. We three stood motionless, staring off in different directions, not daring to look directly at one another. Only the coals in the firebox flickered life into the room. I slowly turned and left the house.

*How could they know so much about life in the jungle? When had they lived there? It can't be worse than staying here and being killed—or...what do they know?*

What was lacking in their personal experience, they knew in their hearts from years of listening. I already had left the village many times, I had the education, and I was old enough to make my own way. But I knew nothing.

The next day, I found the army backpack in the field storage house where my ama had hidden it, and I began to pack the things that I planned to take with me. My clothes included a long white skirt and tunic blouse (my school uniform), two pairs of stylish black pants, several T-shirts, a notebook, pen and pencil, a spoon and bowl, toothbrush, toothpaste, socks and underwear, a hairbrush, and a photo album with my dad's picture—items needed by a "practical" teenager.

We were young. We had no fear. Nothing mattered except that we join our Montagnard friends and leave the village. We only thought that it would be daring and responsible to get away from the security guards telling us what to do and from the Viet Cong taking our villages. We did not think much of the risks ahead for us.

A friend stopped by H'Blin's house. "Two nights!" he told her privately.

The next day, H'Blin and I rushed back and forth from her house to mine, our excitement putting aside any apprehension that we might have had. Her mother prepared some food and rice and placed a blanket inside her bag with her clothes.

At my house, Ama observed me from a distance as I tried to decide on the final things to take. I dressed in my stylish black pants and black shirt and braided my hair that hung to my waist. I had almost finished packing when Ama slowly walked over to me and laid a blanket beside my backpack. In little more than a whisper, he said, "This is not too heavy and might help to keep you warm."

I reached for the blanket and touched his hand. "Thank you!"

I tied down the flap on the backpack securely and lifted it to test its heaviness. It only felt like a medium burden, at the time. My room suddenly became bright, lit through the window by a glowing full moon. It shined down on the empty space that I had created as it slowly arose to watch over our journey. I considered it a good omen.

Ama and Ami stood in the next room watching me. When I walked toward them, I could feel and see their sadness. I was sad too and wished that it might be different. But they had no power over the government, and I did not want the government to have power over me. A brother and a sister watched quietly from across the room. I did not know what they suspected was happening, for I had not spoken to them of leaving. From outside, I heard someone calling my name.

Ami and Ama followed me and my backpack to the door and down the steps. H'blin's mother hurried after her with a banana. "Take this, you'll get hungry." Her voice was weak.

I turned to my ami and ama and put my arms around them one at a time. We could not speak. I lifted my load to my back and helped H'Blin with hers. We stared back for a moment at our homes and our families; then we locked arms and walked toward our new life.

On the border of our village, we joined up with three young men who carried loaded backpacks. Two were from a village near us and seemed a little surprised to see H'Blin and me. In low voices, we assured them that we were ready to go and were committed to the journey.

One young man suddenly spoke, "I forgot my toothbrush and toothpaste."

"We'll get some more, don't worry," I said

"No, I'll go back and meet you later."

Our dark shadows crossed the moonlight that flickered in and out as we passed by trees along the road. A car that looked like security went past us. As the dust whipped up behind the wheels, we stepped off the main way and took a more hidden path. I looked back to see if our friend was following behind, but the dust from the car was settling, and there was no movement in the distance. He did not return, and we never saw him again.

"Where are we going tonight?" I asked.

"To Ama Hang in my village," one of the young men said. "Our plan is to travel by night and sleep during the day as long as we can." Few other words were spoken between us, except that H'Blin and I sometimes whispered thoughts and often held hands.

We arrived in the village about midnight. His house was very small, but it was a shelter. We dragged ourselves into every corner and slept on beds made from large bamboo trees. Our thin blankets were of little help, but we did not wake up until we smelled food late in the morning. Our new friend said that his mother-in-law had made lunch for us. My rumbling stomach became quiet after just two bites.

"What is your name?" I asked the mother-in-law. "The food is wonderful. We were so hungry."

"I am called Ami H'Crem."

"My name is H'Tien, and this is H'Blin. Do you have a garden?"

"Yes, it's behind my house." She smiled.

"Could we help you while we stay here today? We know about farming, and we would enjoy being outside."

"Of course if you like," she said.

First, we cleared the kitchen after our meal. Before we went to the garden, her son-in-law spoke in a serious, insistent voice, "Don't use your real names anymore in this village or any other that we may pass in case anyone comes by to ask questions."

I was caught off guard by his tone of voice and a little embarrassed. I looked at H'Blin, and we both answered at the same time, "Okay!" I was already using a nickname, but we would decide on something new later.

We spent the afternoon in the garden pulling weeds and picking vegetables for the evening meal. The sun brightened our spirits and kept the apprehension away. But Ami H'Crem's face was very sad. She would miss her daughter, H'Chrem, and it reminded us of our families whom we already missed and loved very much.

I did not realize it then, but it would be a long time before I could make decisions on my own. I was now with a group who depended on one another.

We helped Ami H'Crem fix the meal in the small house and thanked her many times for the food and for being so kind to us. But when we sat around the fire stove to eat, conversation was absent. The sadness took my appetite, but I ate enough to begin the trip.

We all napped until midnight when H'Blin woke me and told me we were almost ready to leave. At first, I didn't know what she meant, and then I saw where I was. I folded my blanket and zipped it into my backpack.

"H'Blin, I am so happy that you are my very best friend. Whatever happens, that will always be true." I had given her a pair of black pants just like ones that I had, and we put them on before we again expressed our thanks to Ami H'Crem and said good-bye to her tearful eyes.

## *Long Walk to the Jungle*

This night was not like the last. Clouds shadowed the moon and made it easier for us to walk unnoticed but more difficult for our footsteps. The Htrol Mountain was our destination. –"Two hours," one of the men had said.

*Not long*, I thought.

We had become four men and three women, seven young people who would grow up very fast. H'Chrem walked behind Ka, her husband, H'Blin and I behind them, and the three other guys followed. There was no breath to talk as we walked very fast. "We must hurry," one of the men said as we started out. "A large group is waiting for us. If we had gone first, we would be waiting for them."

There was a clean path to follow, but it lasted less than an hour. Already my eyelids began to droop from sleepiness, but my legs were keeping pace. Sometimes I had a difficult time seeing H'Chrem in front of me, and my feet fumbled on the unbroken pathway, but I only looked back at H'Blin a couple of times. We knew each other so well that just being together gave us strength.

As I looked up to make sure that I was not lagging too far behind H'Chrem, I noticed something different. The only sounds came from my footsteps, lungs working overtime, and bushes scratching at my hands: no village noise, no barking dogs, no crying babies, no words—only human determination that echoed in the silence.

The clouds began to drift apart, allowing light from the moon to weave in and out onto our path, as a breeze cooled my damp face. I glanced out at the end of the fields that we had crossed and the thick forest in front of us. As we grew closer, an owl gave a periodic hoot as if to say, "Come, follow me!" Or maybe it was a warning. Nighttime insects played their instruments louder and faster. I imagined my steps intruding on their homes—or their welcome music a cover for our rhythmic breathing. The combination was comforting and scary at the same time. *Sorry, bugs. We have to keep moving; we cannot stop. Our own homes have been stepped on; our orchestra has stopped playing.*

Suddenly, I almost ran into H'Chrem. She had stopped, and Ka was right in front of her. I signaled to H'Blin to stop. We heard talking.

A voice directed our way said, "Who is there?"

Ka immediately replied, "It is four men and three girls. We are a group of seven."

"We have been waiting for you," came the reply. "What took you so long?"

"We have walked as fast as we could. I know that we must keep moving, but we need a short rest."

"Then have a short one," a man's voice inched closer through the darkness.

I let my pack slide off my shoulders onto the ground. It did not have far to go as it hung below my hips when I walked, which made me seem even shorter. My aching legs responded little to the rubbing motion of my sweating hands.

Ka introduced all of us by name. The man, apparently another group leader, seemed just as surprised to see three girls as we were to see him, and as our eyes adjusted through the moonlight, a very large group of people came into focus. *How strange, they are all men.*

But the man called out for H'Mio Ksor to come stand by him. A girl about my age stepped out from the shadows. "Now we have four girls. They will walk in the middle of us. Including the new group, our count is now eighty."

*There is another girl. That has to be good.*

Then I thought of the two hundred people who had gathered three months earlier when we met at the river. I rubbed my legs again and remembered the shivering, the night, the betrayal. *Is this another trick, another lie?* The giant black "rock" that rose above the forest in front of us had to be Htrol Mountain. *Are we really going there? I can't imagine climbing it tonight.* But this group looked ready, and I knew that our cover of darkness wouldn't last.

My doubts no longer mattered. What seemed like thirty seconds passed, and words from our new leader directed us to organize our line and to start moving toward the outline above the trees. "No talking, just walking," he said in a muted tone as voices passed it around to the others. "Let's go!"

An adrenalin rush swept through my body as someone helped me with my pack, and a feeling of security calmed my anxiety. We were really on our way: no river, no boat, no turning back—just moving forward in single file. Someone near me dared use a match to see what time it was—3:00 a.m., two more hours of trudging along silently through unknown grasses and bushes and roots before dawn lifted the darkness. *I will make it. I know I can;*

*H'Blin will make it. The new girl—with my last name—is following her. I don't think she saw me smile. I will get to know her later.*

My view of my own strength was blown away. Within an hour, the pressure of my heavy pack and the long journey made me wobble, and I stumbled more often. A man I had not noticed before must have been watching. He did not slow down as he came up behind me and said, "I'll take your pack for a while. This is a rough trip."

"I'll be all right. It's just that my legs keep bending funny, but thank you."

"No, let me take your pack. I assure you that I can do it."

There was no argument left in me. "Thank you. I really do mean thank you. I think that I'll be better tomorrow." There was only a slight pause as he put his arms around my pack, clutching it like a child, and backed away from me. I could not see him clearly, but his face was familiar.

My body left me, along with the bag. I was floating over the path. When I glimpsed back, H'Blin was plodding steadily, her head looking down at the feet in front of her, her breathing labored. But there was nothing I could do to relieve her burden. Our leader must have realized how difficult it was for a lot of us who were not yet used to the strenuous trek. He stopped before dawn and ordered us to make camp in what appeared to be a protected area in the forest and, I prayed, would be free of creatures. Night noises had become our companions, but it was time for them to curl up under their own covers in the trees.

My backpack angel returned my belongings and said again that he was glad to help. He could not see my watery eyes, but I asked his name. "Rmah Anot," he answered. "Your father and mine were brothers." He turned and disappeared into the woods. Then I remembered seeing him a couple of times during our younger days.

*This is a sign that all will be well.*

H'Blin and I moved our packs near trees that seemed to raise the fewest roots. We made a rest stop behind some bushes, pulled out our blankets, introduced ourselves to H'Mio, and huddled together.

"I am so hungry," I whispered to H'Blin. "Do we dare eat something?"

She unzipped a side pocket in her bag. "I have a bit of cooked rice that we can share. It will be enough for a few hours."

The moon was very low and barely peeked through the forest walls. But when it slid under the earth, and the morning sky crept out of the horizon, there was only the sound of snoring rising from the forest floor.

About noon, I heard low voices nearby and lowered the top of my blanket enough to see around me. I smelled smoke and food, but only my eyes moved while I observed the scene: people lying on the ground, small fires burning, guns—lots of guns—lots of men, lots of my countrymen. I raised my head and saw that H'Blin was still next to me but was also just waking up, and H'Mio was sitting on the ground close to us. Even though I remembered from the night before that there were eighty in our group, the sight of so many in this strange place was startling.

I looked down at myself when I unfolded the blanket and saw that my hands had scratches laced by blood, my black pants had small rips, and my feet were streaked with dirt. Every time I moved, a muscle objected. "What do we do now?" I whispered to H'Blin.

"I'm not sure, but we need something to eat. Get out some rice, and I'll look for some wood for a fire, or maybe someone will let us use one that is lit."

I unzipped my backpack. "Do you want to cook with us, H'Mio?" I asked.

"Yes, thank you! My stomach aches as much as my body."

And we stayed hungry for the next week but were able to collect wild berries and fruits from around our campsites. H'Blin, H'Mio, and I learned to cook enough for two meals each time we stopped, but water for cooking was as scarce as our rice. Soon we accepted anything others offered to us.

One night we passed near a village, strangely quiet except for barking dogs.

"Can't we go in and ask them for food?" I pleaded. The answer was a definite no.

Our leader trusted no one, and for eight days and seven nights, we marched and slept, ate little, and felt our weariness become routine. The flat fields gave our legs a rest, the mountain trails dared our determination, and the streams and rivers welcomed our inexperienced bodies but challenged dry packs and weapons.

My shoes (light canvas flats) tore apart; I walked barefooted. My black pants became jungle-stylish, and my arms and legs resembled the vines that had tried to capture me. I cried a lot and told H'Blin how much I missed our village.

H'Blin tried to comfort me but said, "It's over now, forget about it."

I knew she was right, but I kept remembering Ami's words: *No house, no food, no medicine, no one to look after you.* They stung because I had dismissed them. She cared.

## Toward Ban Me Thuot

Our destination was Ban Me Thuot City, the Central Highlands capital for the Montagnards. Knowing there was a definite place made me a focus. My legs became stronger, I walked faster, but I could feel my body getting weaker. There was barely enough food. It was impossible to ignore the weight on my back that caused my skin to blister and my eyes to run over.

*H'Blin was right. This is not a meaningless adventure taken by frivolous people. This is a life-or-death journey taken by our countrymen, by me, by H'Blin, by persecuted Montagnards.* It began to sink in. *These are good people, brave people, people with resolve to defend our freedom. I chose to leave my village. No one made me come. I need to dry my tears.*

I began to listen more, to stand taller when I could, to realize that the jungle rules were very important: fill your water bottle at every stream; do not share water; do not talk, just walk; listen for screaming birds. Sudden screams mean your enemy could be in front: stop, listen, wait, watch for a signal to go ahead, or to duck and hide. But hiding a large group was not easy, and covering tracks at night was nearly impossible. We had to keep on the move.


There was not much left of the moon. Clouds made streaks across the sky, light moisture fell, and then heavy rain began to pound us, but I could see that we had come to a rice field, and I smelled fruit and vegetables, maybe corn. I noticed that figures hurried toward the trees on the left, and I hoped for a field house but saw none. H'Blin and I stumbled to the trees on the right and swung our loads from our backs to the ground under some branches that had not yet filtered the water. I eased my body down beside my pack, rested my head on top, and soon sleep drifted over my longings for food.

Someone shook me awake and said that we should collect vegetables from the garden about fifty yards in front of us before the dim light of dawn intruded on our cover. Empty gray clouds hovered over the fields, dampness penetrated everything, and drops of rain rolled down leaves and mixed with dirt that oozed between my toes. We could smell the freshness of fruit trees, but collecting their blessings would have to wait.

I followed the others, unsteady in my walk, but gained strength as I touched the dripping bounty of vegetables and wrapped them lovingly in my shirt. I picked a cucumber and guided it toward my mouth. I closed my eyes and let my body welcome each bite with a quivering dance. Had any food ever tasted more sacred?

Surely there was a village, but our scouts had not found one in sight. Besides the cucumbers, the garden had pumpkins, corn, and eggplant. We carried them in containers or shirts or jackets, and ears of corn were stuffed into backpacks. We kept our voices muffled as we hurried between rows, not knowing how we would be received if the farmers were closer than we knew. The aroma of bananas and mangos and papayas was nearby, but our leaders instructed us to leave the fruit until daylight and the rain had completely ceased and after we could send scouts to check the area more carefully.

H'Blin and I returned to the wooded area away from the fields and sat on our bed of leaves. We pulled our blankets over our heads and wrapped our bodies like cocoons, leaving just enough room for our hands to bring our good fortunes to our mouths, which savored each raw morsel. There was no dry wood and no desire to make the smoke alert any possible lurking enemy.

As the dark of night faded to gray, a scout went out to check past the garden that we had gleaned during the night. It must have been a good distance from the next settlement as he returned and reported no sign of activity. Someone said that the field and garden probably belonged to Buon Ho Village, Ban Me Thuot City, or a Rhade tribe. Others were sure that it belonged to the parents of one of the men in our group. I just thought of all that we took, what hard work my family did in our gardens, and how angry we would have been if someone had raided our fields and stolen from us. I was sorry, but my stomach had no regrets.

By evening, light rain began to fall again. Our scout said that the rain must have kept the farmers away from the fields, so we left early, collected fruit from the trees, and visited another garden on the other side of the rice paddies, taking less but gathering more vegetables. There were few places along the paths that were not slippery, and I often lost my balance, caking mud on my pants and dropping my wayward pack. But each step was a dedication to freedom.

## *Closer to Danger*

Through conversations during the day, I heard that we were near Ban Me Thuot, the village that was almost destroyed by the Viet Cong a few years earlier. Villagers had been used as human shields, and death was a way of life for the Montagnards. I was too young to remember; I shuddered thinking that we were going there. *How can I complain about my shoes and my stylish pants and my shrinking body? I am alive, and I plan to stay that way.*

Next I was told that plans had changed, and Buon Ho Village was our destination. It was the eighth day, and traveling during daylight was considered fairly safe. The rains had stopped, but the ground remained muddied. Even so, the noises in our stomachs were much less.

As though an echo floated across the valley, guitar music drifted above the fields, followed by a fine layer of smoke, and the appearance of six men in army uniforms. I stopped and crouched down but heard voices in front of us saying, "Welcome! How many are you?"

"We number eighty—seventy-six men and four girls. One couple is married."

We reached the main camp, and there were smiles and handshakes all around. Our packs slid off easily and looked like stumps under the overhanging trees. H'Blin, H'Mio, and half of our group went into a large hut, while others looked for rest stops and enjoyed the undemanding sounds from the guitar.

I removed myself from the gathering and took a moment to dream that I was back in school around my many young friends. But the sight of this long-haired tribe and the sound of an unfamiliar dialect were stark reminders of our long journey and of my newly chosen life. Tiredness and loneliness abruptly overwhelmed me, and I eased into some tall grasses, away from the hut, where I sat and shook and wrapped my arms around my body, my hands almost touching—rocking back and forth and releasing low-pitched moans of sadness.

When my swaying finally ceased, the moan became a sigh, the water on my face streaked down into my lap, and the air held together the rest of me. *What are you thinking? You are a big girl now. You decided to take this journey. Why do you question the importance of saving your own life? The others have left their homes and their families. Stop whining, stop the tears, be the strong person you know you are. Get out of yourself, help the others, help H'Blin and H'Mio. You know you can do it. God knows I can do it. God, I know I can do it—with your help.*

I opened my eyes, and in the distance I could see H'Blin looking for me. *I can't let her down.* I got up and left my pack in the grass.

As I passed the garden next to the hut, I picked two cucumbers and waved to H'Blin. "I'm coming." My step quickened with a purpose.

## *Developing Acceptance*

I concentrated on the words being spoken by the leaders in the hut, understanding little of their Rhade dialect but hearing the message of "dangerous journey for all of us." H'Blin was a better interpreter, and I knew that she would help me as my ear became accustomed to their dialect. As the discussions became longer, the air grew thicker, and faces and bodies began to blur. It was easy to slip out past the last row of tribesmen without being noticed.

Outside I sat by a downed tree and leaned into a deep sleep. From a dream, I was being asked by Ama to come and eat, but when the words drifted into reality, I heard my name called from the direction of the hut. "H'Tien, H'Tien, where are you?" And again, I heard it clearly. I did not answer but stood and walked toward the voice.

The man standing there introduced himself as Y-Ngoan Nie and said, "I saw you in the hut and know your name. You are so quiet—maybe because you come with such a large group. We are all friends here. I am the leader of this Rhade tribe, and you can ask me anything that you don't understand."

I nodded my head and said thank you. His voice was kind, and I was unsure of some of his words, but I understood enough to be grateful. He walked toward the garden, and I went inside the hut to find H'Blin.

She and H'Mio were stirring a big pot of corn that was cooking over a fire. We had ran out of rice two days earlier, and corn was our only substitute. "I don't think that I can," I said, my face in a deep frown.

H'Blin and H'Mio agreed. "There will be something else."

I had eaten corn on the trail, but my stomach rebelled. It had made traveling very difficult.

As she stirred, H'Blin told me that at the end of the meeting, Y-Ngoan instructed us to use nicknames to hide our identities and our villages. We recalled H'Chrem's husband telling us the same, but we had not taken him seriously—until now. At first it was fun, giggling through various sounds and recalling names of people we liked and didn't like, but when reality sank in, we chose names that would be easy to remember and to speak. H'Blin chose H'Bloanh (rhymes with H'Yoanh, my name at birth); I kept H'Tien (the nickname that I had been called by the nuns when I was little; it rhymed with H'Nhien, the name that H'Mio decided was perfect for her). The names fit us well, but actually using them proved to be awkward and inconsistent at best.

Smiling had been away from my face for so long that when it settled on my mouth, I realized how different I felt all over. A few hours after our arrival, we heard that we would stay in that same area for several days. Some even danced to jubilant guitar playing. One of our members had family in a village near our camp—a mother and a brother. The family and friends brought food and clothes and shoes and rice and happiness to all of us. I nodded and smiled often and said thank you in my tribe's Jarai dialect, and even though I stuttered, I knew that they understood.

## *Formation of New Leaders*

But the next morning, the village people met with our group leaders and said that it was not only too dangerous for a group our size to stay but also there was not enough food to support our numbers. The news silenced the air. Our leader, Y-Ngoan Nie, was in a squatting position, in front of the hut, and drew a wheel round and round in the dirt with a short stick. He made marks in the circle, and those who were nearby watched but did not speak immediately.

Conversation came slowly and quietly at first but soon reminded me of the Tower of Babel that I had read about in the Bible. Y-Ngoan Nie stood up. He commanded attention, and everyone stopped. His body was confident, and his mouth spoke with well-formed thoughts as he began.

"We must divide again. Our count is now 117. The group that has just joined us must turn back and find new areas." There were whispering and mumbling sounds from every direction. Y-Ngoan's voice became forceful. "It will be best for you to become smaller in numbers so that you will not be easily spotted by the Viet Cong. It will be up to you to decide how you will separate and where you will go. The girls can stay with us." I reached for H'Blin's hand beside me. "Each group should have a leader and messengers who are willing to return to Cheo Reo and other villages to show our countrymen the way to escape deep into the Highlands. We also need information about the army and their maneuvers—and we need rice and ammunition. The ones who have been here for a while already have scouts doing the same for us. As you know, it is extremely dangerous, but death looks us in the face anywhere we decide to live—and we all have chosen to live free and to fight against the VC. Our group will move out soon also."

Y-Nguan Nie was a strong, bold speaker, and no one argued with his leadership. But after a profound silence, the men sounded like they were playing a game of street ball as they attempted to divide the seventy-seven who had to find their own ways. H'Chrem and Ka were counted in, and I was sad to see them go. My own relief was like having my backpack lifted from my shoulders. I didn't want to move out of this campsite, but I knew too that I did not want to return to my village.

A few days earlier, I finally had recalled why the leader's name of the group that would retrace their steps was familiar to me. He was Y-Toan Nie, the very one who had deceived us about the boat-to-freedom on our first try to escape our village. I was uncomfortable around him and glad that he was leaving us. My mouth was closed about the failed river trip, but thoughts about the traitor still lingered in my mind.

Y-Nguan came to the three of us and said, "A woman, H'Tlon Nie, is with a group somewhere out here, and when we reach her, you will stay with her, and she will help to keep you safe. She ranks high in the army and is strong and determined and kind."

## *Rebel Cousins*

Muttering filtered through the discussions as all of us checked our bags. Suddenly, Y-Toan Nie appeared next to H'Blin, H'Mio, and me and said, "You three girls must come with us. If we go back without you, your parents will blame us, and there will be suspicion."

"No, please! We stay," H'Blin and H'Mio said together. They did not move.

"We stay together." I backed away from the group.

Rmah Anot, who had carried my pack on the trail to the camp, came toward me and picked up my pack. Even though we were cousins (his father and mine were brothers), and he cared for me, I did not want to go with him.

Then the level of arguing grew louder as tension was strung body to mouth. "H'Tien, you come with us," Rmah Anot demanded.

"No, I can't." I recoiled from his grasp.

He took my pack and made his way through the others who were starting down the trail that we had made the week before. I put my hands to my face and sat down where he had left me. When I looked up, I could see H'Blin and H'Mio standing near their bags, not moving in any direction, and others walking away from the scene. *Why does there have to be fighting over us? We have come too far to go back. The men must feel awful, but I am not going. What about my things? Rmah Anot has my things.*

After the group left from our hearing, the sky began to darken. Y-Nguan Nie came to where I was still sitting. "It is okay for you to stay, H'Tien."

"But Rmah Anot took my backpack." Tears still ran from my eyes.

Somehow his presence was like a turning time in my strength. I stood up and straightened my clothes. "But I will go after him and take back my things."

"Night is coming. Do you think that you can find your way?"

I took a half breath, looked toward the trail, took two steps, and turned back to him. "I can do it. I know I can. I'm staying with H'Blin." And I took a deep breath to give myself confidence as I walked.

It was not totally dark, so I could follow their steps. Seventy-seven people can make a wide path. The gate to the first field was easy to go through, but as I crossed the field, darkness was all around. Without my pack, my steps went better, and I could hear voices from a distance, but my feet were just feeling their way along. Every breath was a prayer to God to make me strong and sure. I hoped that someone would stand up against anyone who might try to hurt me. Then I came to the third gate and the third field, and I could see silhouettes moving ahead of me.

I reached the last man in line who jumped off the path when he heard my voice.

"Please stop!" I begged. "I need to get my backpack from Rmah." My words were direct and steady.

He quickly sent a message through the men to stop walking because there was a problem. From the exchange of words, I saw Rmah come toward me, with two packs on his back.

"So you are coming with us now!" he said with a bit of sarcasm.

"No, I am staying here, and I need my belongings."

"You cannot stay, H'Tien. You need to go back. Your family needs you. Why do you want to live out here?"

"It is too hard to live there. I am here, and I am staying, and I want my pack."

Rmah raised his voice and his gun. "I want to kill you."

"Then go ahead if you can." Anger boiled up inside me.

Rmah hit me in the shoulder with the end of his AK rifle. It pushed me back, but I stepped forward again, ignoring the pain. He jerked me forward by the hand. "You are so hardheaded."

Suddenly their leader, Y-Khut, appeared and grabbed Rmah's arm and demanded, "What is going on? Where are the other girls?"

"They are not coming," I said firmly. "We are all staying with a woman in Hu. I don't want to make anyone mad. I just want my things."

He came close to Rmah's face. "Give her the pack! We have a long way to go, and this is no place to fight and not worth the time. A much larger enemy waits for us." He jerked the pack from Rmah's shoulder and put it in front of me.

"Thank you! I'm sorry for this, but I thank you."

Rmah turned angrily and marched out of sight.

"Do you know the way back?" Y-Khut asked.

"Yes, I'll make it. Thank you!" They all turned toward their mission, and I stood in the field listening to their voices disappear.

In the camp, I had overheard some in this group talking about what would happen to them now. They knew that Y-Khut would lead them only halfway back toward their villages. He already had repeated Y-Ngoan Nie's instructions about dividing into smaller units, finding new leaders, and either returning to their villages or taking alternative paths to hide in the jungle, always covering their tracks. (I never saw any of them again.)

I slowly became aware of the chill, the sounds of night, the solitary figure in the endless dark, the shoulder that felt broken, the heavy pack. I turned in the direction of my new home, stooped down to painfully strap the load to my back, and moved one foot and then another. *Don't think, stop the tears, you won this battle, one step at a time, be strong!*

My repetitious thoughts encouraged me as I struggled along the slippery path, but through the second field, I fell hard twice, and defeat crept through my tormented body. *Don't lie there! Get up! You can do it! Tears won't make it better. God, lift me up!*

Time did not matter. Each step mattered. I remembered that the third field was the largest, but I knew that I had been in it a long time, and suddenly I heard gunshots.

"Help, it's me. Please don't shoot me!

"Are you by yourself?" came the voice near the sound.

"Yes, it's H'Tien." I crouched down on the ground.

Before I dared to stand up, I heard H'Blin and H'Mio calling my name and coming toward me. Unexpectedly, a memory wrapped itself around me of the night when the door opened at

Thanh Gia School, and Sister Helen stood there in her nightgown, rescuing me from a frightening night of walking alone from the dance competition.

All three of us cried and talked and laughed at the same time. Y-Nguan met us at the gate. "You made it. Good. You deserve to rest."

And I did. The three of us did in a haystack that kept us warm and with blankets that kept the sharpest straw from pricking our bodies. I awoke once during the night, feeling confused and dreaming that the dew on the hay was really water in a river. The damp air penetrated my sore body, and I shook from the chill or from lack of food or from the realization that I was stronger in spirit. I pulled more straw over my body and the blanket over my head and slept through part of the morning.

Y-Nguan Nie's kind voice greeted us after we awoke. "You are the first girls to come to the jungle. It will be a real challenge for you, as you have seen. We are all trying to stay alive and to fight the enemy when necessary. Sometimes our camps must change quickly, so you must be ready to pack and move on short notice, which may be often. We will be a close community, a family, and we must help one another. Right now, I want you to move your things into the hut on the other side of the garden field. I will talk to you later."

The hut was small, but there were ears of corn hanging from the ceiling to dry and to create seeds for the next season's planting. The shelter, the corn, the thought of a fire raised our spirits. H'Blin and H'Mio gathered wood, and I found a pan in H'Blin's pack that we could use for cooking.

The smell and the sound of the popped corn delighted three girls who had not eaten all day. We talked and laughed some about our adventures and about the people around us. I did not tell them all that had happened to me the night before—not about the angry talk or the strike of the AK rifle. I hid the bruise. As H'Blin had said, "it is over now, forget about it."

## *Chilling Reality*

Abruptly, gunshots came from the field near the first gate closest to us. We were stunned and crawled to the opening of the hut, saw no one, and started running toward the campsite. Y-Nguan came in our direction. "Over here!" He pointed to a growth of bushes. "Stay down flat!"

Gunfire went over us, and I put my hands over my head and cried for Ami. I thought that my heart would beat out of my body, which shook uncontrollably. We three were huddled so close that we breathed together.

It stopped as suddenly as it started. Y-Nguan Nie called to us, "Where are you?" We peeped through the bushes and then stood up. "Come over here by the haystack. We have to make plans." He put his arm around me. "Were you scared?"

There was one long *yes* from three terrified small girls.

"The Viet Cong have followed us and now know where our camp is. We must move immediately. I just pray that the other group saw them first and was able to go around them. No one in our camp was injured, but pack your things, make the camp look as unused as possible, and get ready to march."

Hurried preparations began. Forty bodies scurrying in different directions looked like a disturbed anthill.

We quickly followed the routine and were soon on our way before dark, the last men in the group covering our tracks and hoping that the next rain would finish the job.

I don't remember how much time passed before I began to feel dizzy, maybe a few hours. My popcorn dinner failed me, and my irregular sleep and emotional tension irritated my weakened body so that it could no longer hold up my pack. The path in front of me became blurred, so I told the men behind me to go ahead, that I was tired and had to sleep.

The next thing I heard was running water and the voice of Y-Nguan asking if I was feeling better. H'Blin had something soft that she was trying to feed me, and H'Mio brought me cool water to drink and a damp cloth for my face.

I sat up and looked around, not knowing where I was and thinking that I should be walking with my backpack. But not far from where I was sitting, there was a stream, and I saw members of our group sleeping or cooking or bringing fruit from somewhere in the forest.

Y-Nguan sat down beside me and said, "I have to go now to be with another group.

Y-Lem will be in charge and will look after you well. We want you three girls to stay together.

We pray that someday we will not have to run and hide and we will see one another again."

He put his hand on my shoulder for a second, stood upright, strapped on his backpack, and slipped away into the heavy growth of the jungle before my stunned mouth could speak.

I lay back down to absorb what I had just heard. He had been so kind, and we trusted him without question. And I needed to apologize for the trouble I had caused everyone.

H'Blin said, "You fainted, and two men made a blanket hammock and carried you."

My eyes closed. My mind whirled in thoughts of fragile friendships, of a stable place, of safety for those closest to us, of assurance of food and water, of survival—which might escape our grasp for a while, for maybe months or even a year. I had no idea how very long that would be.

# GAINING STRENGTH WITH NEW LEADERS

## Y-Lem

H'Blin and H'Mio helped me up and walked with me to the stream to bathe and to test my strength. I lay down on a large flat rock that was submerged in the shallow water and let the soft current gently lift and sway my limp body. I unbraided my long hair and watched it float around me like waving rice noodles in a pot of simmering water. There was no soap, just like my days in school at Thanh Gia, but we were much cleaner than we had been in days. When the three of us stood along the bank of the stream and looked at one another, our laughter began small and then shook us as our clothes clung to our frail thin figures, and we realized that we looked almost naked. As I peeled my blouse away from my shoulders and wrung out my hair to cover my bruise, I felt my limbs respond to the stimulation from the cleansing of body and of soul.

On our way back into camp, Y-Lem met us, along with Y-Vin and Chanh (a Vietnamese). "I see that you have been in the stream and look refreshed, but I know that you are very tired. You can rest well in my tent for tonight. There is room for all three of you." Y-Lem handed us three cooked sweet potatoes and three bamboo bottles (about twenty inches long) filled with rainwater from two days earlier. We thanked him several times.

We ate our potatoes while watching the sky turn orange and purple and wondered why it took the sun so long to reach the earth. Inside the tent the ground was dry, but falling asleep was difficult for me when my stomach was not very full, and the mosquitoes were having a banquet on my blood. I pulled my blanket up over my head, with only a small place to breathe, and I listened to the sounds of the night.

Conversation on the other side of the tent became heated: "How will we take care of the girls? Not easy for us!"

"Will they be able to fight?"

"Leave them here!"

"No, that is a stupid idea. They will come with us wherever we go."

"Okay, okay! I'm just joking." And they laughed.

Finally, sleep overtook the muttering outside and the buzzing inside, and I only awoke for a moment when the chill made me move closer to H'Blin.

We camped there for two nights.

## Y-Vin

Y-Lem called to me, "Wake up and pack your things. We need to move out."

H'Blin and H'Mio were already up. My mind was not yet with my body, but I got to my feet and pulled my blanket behind me from the tent. Despite the cover, the mosquitoes had found a way to cause me to itch all over.

Y-Vin's voice sounded urgent. "Come on, girls, finish your packs!" We did. There was no breakfast.

The mosquitoes still sang around our heads and sucked blood from any exposed skin. My stomach was getting used to being empty, leaving my mind to work hard to strengthen my body.

Fog had settled over the fields and drifted into the edges of the jungle. Large meadows connected the forests and made walking easier, but they gave no protection for our safety. The mist was a blessing, and I prayed to God that it would stay for a good part of the day. Danger was everywhere. The fog began to rise, and we made our way into the dense woods. We were like stalked animals, weaving through the shelter of trees but erasing our steps and dodging vines that grabbed our legs, slapped us in the face, and snagged our packs.

Y-Lem signaled for us to stop and passed the word back that it would be safe to build a small fire to cook some food.

Not knowing when we would have another chance, H'Blin, H'Mio, and I fixed enough small meals to last at least two full days. We roasted corn in the shucks. In banana and palm leaves, we wrapped cooked vegetables that we had picked from gardens along the field trails; we gathered jungle fruit wherever we could. The preparations gave us renewed energy.

It was much better than the days when we searched decaying logs for grub worms, centipedes, and other crawling things, and had to skin the snakes that the men killed. At those times our desire to eat died in the cooking pot, but I cut everything in tiny pieces, closed my eyes, and let the slimy bits slide down my throat with as little chewing as possible.


As we covered the ashes from the fire, the smoke drifted upward and flattened out to mingle with the fog, securing our safety for a little longer.

Our group continued to feel our way through the untouched jungle and to rearrange the growth to its original appearance as we left it behind. Daylight filtered through the tops of the trees but lost much of its power as the slender beams stretched to the floor of the forest. Even so, we made our way as fast as the undergrowth allowed.

Y-Lem allowed time to rest and was especially kind to us girls, but it seemed that I was usually dragging back at the end, and even H'Mio and H'Blin began to complain to me about being too slow. My determination had increased, but my body still lacked the strength needed to be near the front of the line. I could not understand it, but then I thought again of the malaria that I had had the year before. There had been no time for a full recovery. At least, by traveling in the jungle during the day, we did not have to use extra effort stumbling over roots and fallen branches with only glowing mushrooms to light our way. But we never stopped for long.

Our small group, now ten, had traveled five straight days, and suddenly the smell of cooking drifted into the edge of the forest. We all seemed to freeze in our steps at once as we noticed that the trees were shorter and the light stronger, and we lowered ourselves to the ground, hoping to be invisible.

Y-Lem whispered to Y-Vin, "Go up and see who might be there." He crawled back to prepare us. "If we are not near the place called Connection Communication, we must go in a different direction immediately."

## *Klut Siu*

On the ground with my pack, I moved my fingers quietly over the numerous swellings where the mosquitoes had dined. I only had a few moments of satisfying scratching before Y-Vin returned with friends from another group. The tension release from the rest of us was like air escaping from a balloon. Y-Lem asked about a man named Klut Siu.

"Yes, he is with us. I'll take you to him. We are not far. It is safe for now."

We followed the messenger through a field of corn and vegetables, and my stomach turned with excitement. I even saw a rice field in the distance.

Klut Siu and his son, Kan Nay, were camped in another forest in a very old hut hidden by tall grasses. As we approached his area, men came from different directions to welcome us with smiles and open hands. But they hesitated when they saw H'Blin, H'Mio, and me. Then they looked at Y-Lem and said, "What is this, these girls? We haven't had girls in the jungle. How did they come?"

Y-Lem sounded weary. "The same way that we did, and they are staying. They are one of us. And I leave them with Klut Siu in charge."

I looked at him in surprise. "Where are you going?" I asked.

"I leave you now, in very good hands. I must go to help other groups."

"But..." I stopped. This was the way that it had been, and would be, on a journey that was unthinkable back during restless nights and long, unsettled days in my village.

We said thank you and good-bye and watched Y-Lem disappear into a part of the jungle that was new to us.

Klut Siu was a timid and gentle man from the Jarai tribe. He treated us like his own family and was very protective. We called him Wa (another name for *uncle*), and he provided us with sweet potatoes—lots of sweet potatoes—roasted or boiled or grilled. They were easily taken from the gardens near the villages. He told us of the communities in the area, but we were permitted to go out only at night and not near the villages. During the day, while the fields were being tended, we hid quietly.

We heard that some of the villagers in the area were with the United Struggle Front for the Oppressed Races (FULRO). Their work with the new Vietnamese government—to refrain from persecuting the ethnic groups in Cambodia and Vietnam—was very dangerous. I was almost seventeen, but I did not understand it all. I listened and knew that we, my countrymen (the groups who were my companions and those I had met along the way), literally were running to save our lives. And I began to realize that I would never again see many of them, but I buried that thought deep down inside.

In the evenings, after the farmers left the fields, H'Blin, H'Mio, and Kan Nay went out to the edge of the jungle to find food or water or just to see what was there. They did not like having me come along, because they said that I was too slow. Sometimes I went anyway.

My stomach was tired of eating roasted sweet potatoes and vegetables that we pillaged. Sometimes I thought that the waves of emptiness and potatoes rushed through me screaming for just a bowl of rice. Sometimes the "exploding" noises that came from our bodies were the evening's entertainment. We tried to smother our laughter, but we already recognized that our privacy and our attitudes toward appropriate behavior had diminished.

Very early one morning, the mosquitoes were feasting, the birds were calling across the canopy, and I slipped away from our hut and went to the rice paddies with one of my two T-shirts. The air was damp, and the new sprouts of rice grass retained the heavy mist that had settled over the fields. In recent days, there had been little water—not for drinking, not for cooking, not for bathing. I just wanted to lie down on top of the rice, but I spread out my T-shirt and brushed it across the top of the grass until it was wet. Then I rubbed my face with the cool moisture and repeated the process until my whole body had been wiped at least once. It was especially difficult for girls to keep clean. At certain times, we made pads from any clothing we could find and rinsed them out the best we could when we had water. It was never pleasant, but there was no choice, and our cycles were not going to disappear.

When it did rain, collecting water was only slightly successful. The tents had holes, and the pots we put out to catch the drops were small.

Late one evening, when I was looking for food, I found a puddle on the trail I was following. I had my bamboo water carrier with me and was able to scoop up enough to fill it. I knew that the water was only good for cooking, but I laughed all the way back to the girls who were equally excited about our good fortune. We immediately started a fire and boiled some vegetables and roots that we had dug up two days earlier. The meal was hot and warmed the empty spaces inside.

## Colonel Paul Yuh

During our last days of trekking, I had prayed hard for some rest, for not having to run each night, staggering over rough pathways. Joyfully we had been in this camp about two weeks when a warning call signaled that someone was approaching. My heart beat faster than my running feet, as I crouched down behind some thick bushes. But our visitor was a friend of Uncle Klut—a colonel.

Wa called us out of hiding, "Come and meet Colonel Paul Yuh! He has heard about you. Come, come!"

We had not given much thought to our appearances for a long time and were shy about showing ourselves. The colonel just stared at us and said, "You three look no different from three monkeys." And he laughed.

Then he said to Wa, "I want to take these girls to a creek near my place where I live with my wife and where she has a garden. I'll return them safely."

The three of us held hands tightly, wondering if this could be true. The colonel saw us begin to smile; we looked at Uncle Klut, who nodded his head. "Come now, we go!" he said in a gentle, commanding voice.

We followed him for an hour or more near the edge of the jungle and then crossed a field to some tall trees that bordered a small but deep creek, where the colonel left us for some privacy. We just stood there for a moment looking back and forth from the creek to one another and then hurriedly began to take off our clothes. When I looked down at my body and looked over at H'Blin and H'Mio, I saw that the three of us had bites all over that we had scratched into sores, and, even worse, there were land leeches clinging to our legs and backs. I shivered at the sight and covered my mouth to keep in the scream. The slimy bloodsuckers were smaller than water leeches, but we did not compare sizes as we pulled them away from our skin and quickly danced into the water to drown the worms and to wash the festering mosquito bites. Our gasps turned into squeals when the warmth of the sun gave way to the cold stream water.

I sat down and inched my way along to check the depth. H'Blin and H'Mio could swim but stayed beside me until I was comfortable; then they left and paddled into the deeper parts. We let our hair flow in the water and our bodies relax with the cleansing of dirt and sweat and scabs. Soon we didn't care about the temperature. The leeches dropped off, our bodies adjusted, and we stayed in the creek until we were wrinkled and the colonel's wife came for us.

"You girls must get out. You have a long hike back to your camp before dark."

We had scrubbed our clothes in the creek and had laid them out to dry, but they were still damp and felt wonderfully cool against our clean bodies.

Colonel Yuh came to see us several times, and we went to the creek twice more. He spoke to Wa about separating "the girls," but Uncle Klut said a strong no. We were so happy, because we did not want to leave Wa and stay with someone we didn't know.

## *Banana Gardens*

After we had been with Uncle Klut for a month, he became very nervous and uncomfortable. He paced a lot, not sitting or standing still. Sometimes he became angry with us, including his son, Kan Nay. For two days, we had heard dogs barking in the distance. Wa said that it could be good news and that the villagers were allowed to move freely back and forth to their fields without being afraid. Or it could be bad news, that there were few people left in the villages.

We had already learned that our leaders relied on their senses, so it was no surprise that we left the next day.

The barking dogs reminded me of home and of Ama and Ami. I tried not to think of them, but my mind could not clear them away. I prayed that they were okay, and I wished that I could send them a message that I was still alive.

We moved to a new place called Banana Garden. Wa had heard that it was a safe haven—for now. It was easy to see from a distance because of the rows and rows of tall banana fruits that towered over smaller vegetation—a perfect protective covering.

The sun seemed to be racing us for a hiding place. Wa directed us to hurry our steps so that we could reach the grove first. It was dusk when we found a sheltered clearing.

At the same time, H'Blin and I saw a spot that looked soft and comfortable in the dim light. We motioned for H'Mio to come with us, but she said that the green grass was more for her, and on that she dropped her pack there and spread her blanket. Wa and Kan settled behind some low bushes nearby. We had not marched with our packs for four weeks, so we welcomed the night soon after we had a quick meal.

In the early morning as we folded our blankets, I saw a big hole at the side of the cleared spot that was our bed. When I looked down in it, I saw part of a traditional burial blanket and a skeleton with ten bony fingers lying limp in the dirt.

"Oh my gosh, H'Blin, look at that! We slept on top of a grave." I covered my face and walked away but returned and stared at the bony fingers. "I wonder if it will bring us bad luck. It's so scary—and so sad."

"Let's cover it over!" H'Blin whispered as she dug into the surrounding dirt with her hands and raked it over toward the opening. We all began to fill the hole, and soon the remains became hidden again beneath the earth and banana leaves and branches that offered a veil of protection. After we finished, we were silent. I prayed for the fallen person and for all of the people who had already been killed in the battle that was now mine, that was now ours, that was for the survival of the Montagnards. It was more real to me every day.

Uncle Klut continued to pace. We suggested that he go home to his wife and her garden, but he said that he must stay close to his friends who were waiting for their families to find them and to bring them food. *How could that ever happen?*

The bananas hung from the trees like temptation—always in eyesight, but often out of reach. Only a few men, with large knives and bare feet that gripped the sharp edges, dared climb the rough trunks to the top, and when they dropped the heavy banana stalks; others caught them in blankets to keep them from smashing on the ground. If Colonel Yuh had just been right, and we were three monkeys, we could easily have had plenty of fruit for everyone.

## *Buon Chuortlara—H'Tlon Nie*

After a week at the Banana Garden, Klut Siu's pacing finally stopped. A messenger found us and said that we should go to Buon Chuortlara where there was a gathering of different forces from FULRO. It was two days' journey from the garden through more jungle and fields, and the only directions were to follow the afternoon sun. That left me with a lot of uncertainty, but Uncle Klut was a seasoned tribesman and knew how to use that guiding light without hesitation.

When we arrived, I was surprised to see Colonel Paul Yuh, who greeted us well, and also other high-ranking officers in the Montagnard army, including General Y-Ichok Nie, second in command. Walking with the officers was H'Tlon Nie, the woman whom Y-Nguan Nie (from our first group) had told the three of us to locate—and I had no idea how we did or where we were.

H'Tlon Nie was beautiful and light skinned with a little extra weight. Her walk commanded respect, and her mouth was strong, yet reassuring. "I have heard about you girls," she said when we were introduced. "Welcome! Come and let us talk!" And she motioned for Klut Siu, Kan Nay, and the three of us to join her.

There were more men there than I remember had been in my home village. They walked in small groups, sat by tents, cooked around fires, and stared at us. Some of our previous shyness had left us as we stared back at this unbelievable sight, acknowledging any greeting with a nod. I heard what I thought were many different accents and tribal dialects. I was not afraid, but I was glad that we were walking beside H'Tlon Nie.

The camp looked stable but temporary. Tents were mainly lean-tos made of heavy dark plastic or lightweight canvas tarps—easier for transporting quickly. In some places, I saw only packs beside blankets around a fire pit. H'Tlon's "tent" had not much more privacy, but we sat on the ground where she directed and talked about our travels, our hunger, the people she knew, and the leeches. She gave us water and some fruit that tasted like sweet honey and warned us not to eat too much or too fast—our stomachs needed to adjust.

We three girls told her that our names—H'Tien, H'Bloanh, and H'Nhien—were not our real names, but we tried to use them every time we were not together or with an unfamiliar group.

"But you must use them *all* of the time now for your own protection. Then you will not slip when it is important. Remember that you are shielding your families too. H'Tien, you stay here. I want to talk to you, and I will take H'Bloanh and H'Nhien to Paul Yuh for a walk around the camp. Klut Siu and Kan Nay, there are several good places to settle your tents, maybe with a familiar tribe. You will find the men here to be welcoming."

There was something in her eyes that drew me to her confidence. It was that feeling that I had had many times in my short life—from Sister Helen, from my papa, from Father Tai, from Y-Nguan. There was a connection, a spirit, angels—something that bound me to earth but beyond my understanding.

When H'Tlon sat down with me, she said, "H'Tien, you are to stay with me. I cannot take all three of you, but the other girls will be cared for." I only hesitated for a moment. "You may call me Aunt." There was silence. She was old enough to be my mother.

"I would like to call you my big sister." A smile formed on her face, and she agreed. "May I see H'Blin and H'Mio—I mean, H'Bloanh and H'Nhien? Where will they go?"

"There is a commander who has agreed for them to be with his group. They will be as safe as we are. You can see them as long as our camp is together, but this is not like the village that you came from. Often we must travel in small numbers so that we may not be detected by the Viet Cong. It is not worth their time to follow only a few."

Even though we seemed to have an immediate bond, I was surprised to be under her protection. Maybe she had heard about my background or about my determination to get an education. Her own education showed through her spoken words.

H'Tlon emptied my pack and sorted through the remnants of two months on the run. It was worse than I thought, but we did not find any leeches or fungus. To better prepare me to endure life in the jungle, she repacked my sack with survival items. For emergencies, she laid out in a separate pile a package of salt, a cup of rice, a green bottle of clean water to drink, a small pot for cooking, matches for a fire, and a sharp knife. She put my worn blanket in the bottom and gave me a fresh small blanket to use on our next move. She found pants and a shirt that were too big but manageable, a small bar of soap, and clean strips of cloth to use when needed.

I could hardly believe what she was doing. I hugged her. "My new big sister, I am so happy. Thank you, thank you! I'll take care of all of it."

"Remember, H'Tien, keep your backpack ready at all times. If we have to move, it will be very fast, and we leave nothing behind."

I liked having this friend and being close to her good heart. I felt safe with her, but being safe and being responsible for one's own safety were very different. Later I was to realize that, through her guidance, I was being toughened for the journeys of endless wandering and urgent escapes.

For now, for the time that we were together, I had food to eat—rice, fish, meat, good vegetables, yucca leaves and roots, and hot peppers—not always sweet potatoes. The Montagnards who still lived in the Highlands had gardens and fields, and they raised pigs, chickens, goats, cows, and buffalo. They were very generous to all refugees, but they were always in danger if the Viet Cong ever suspected them of helping us.

Although my new life was good, I missed H'Bloanh and H'Nhien, especially not knowing where they were or if they were okay. Our last moments together had been tearful, but their group moved out with little warning, and they had run quickly to find me. "We'll always be close sisters," I said. "I love you and will pray to God for us to see one another again." And they were gone.

H'Tlon spoke to me of crossing the Mekong River to safety in Thailand and China. "This is what keeps me strong. I want you to come with me." She held me close and then stared into an imaginary space for several minutes. I didn't know how far that was, but I always agreed to be by her side.

In school, we had read about Thailand and a little about China, but I never thought of going there. From where we stood that day, in front of our tent, I was certain that it was a much better place and maybe not as far as I thought, but I wasn't even sure whether or not we were still in Vietnam or in Cambodia. The Central Highlands was very large, and Montagnard tribes had lived mainly in four cities in Vietnam for centuries. I could not even estimate how many were living there now.

H'Tlon and I had little time to just sit and talk and for me to ask her all of the questions that were on my mind. There was food to gather, cooking and washing to do, and others to help, especially new groups that found our camp. It was a good time because we did not have to run every night. But even that came to an abrupt end late one evening. She rushed toward me at our tent and said, "H'Tien, hurry and pack and make our camp look untouched! We have had a message from a scout that VC troops have been spotted a few miles away."

It was so sudden that I stood in place, unbelieving. A storm sounded in the distance, and H'Tlon's voice cracked through the air at me. "Hurry! We don't have much time. You know what to do."

She started taking down the covering of our "house," and I began to load our belongings into our packs, mixing clean and dirty clothes, rolling up blankets, stacking bowls, filling the fire pit with dirt and covering it with leaves. Our stay of four months seemed so short.

H'Tlon commanded authority, and ten others from the camp asked to go with her. It was a small enough group that it didn't take long for the twelve of us to be making our way in one direction, while others finished "neutralizing" our campsite and setting a path for themselves. Rain was coming closer and would wash all evidence back into the jungle floor.

# Marching, Mushrooms, and Messengers

The march was not different from the ones with Y-Nguan and Y-Lem that brought me to H'Tlon. But as we vanished into the forest, the darkness came on us with urgency, and night smothered our pathway. The trees kept the rain above us for a while and gave us time to gather glow mushrooms for light. Between flashes of lightning, we cut elephant ear leaves to cover our heads and backpacks from the water that eventually seeped through the canopy.

I was fascinated by the mushrooms months earlier, the first time that I hiked in the dark. Attached to logs and trees, they constantly glowed like fairy lanterns, guiding us through the blackness that was a hell on this earth. We attached them to our backpacks, and the person behind us could see the moving body in front and know that they were still with the group. I learned quickly to keep up because when a hiker allowed the glow to get out of sight, he or she was lost and alone, except for the person behind them, and a new group would instantly be created. That was so scary to me that I often reached out to touch the pack in front to reassure myself.

As the rain got heavier, we stopped at the edge of a garden field to pick up more fallen banana leaves that we could see when the lighting struck through the sky. They were only effective as umbrellas when rain was light. The storm would not quit until the water had reached our skin, covered our feet in mud, and taken the last of our energy. But H'Tlon had been in the area before and knew that a hut was close by. Distant lightning threw off just enough light for us to see what looked like a giant mushroom (not glowing) just to the left of our path.

The hut was dryer than we were, but not all twelve of us could fit under the shelter. Even so, by then the rain was only dripping from the trees, and hardly any words were spoken as we pulled damp blankets from our packs, wrapped our shivering bodies like mummies, and fell asleep on the damp ground. I murmured a prayer that the snakes and scorpions and crawling creatures were away night hunting.

When the morning jungle came alive, I opened one eye and peered around the hut to find that my big sister was already out looking for food. As the sky lightened, I could see that this hut was so well hidden that a person could almost walk into it before they saw it. I later learned that the hut was a meeting place for some of the scouts and communication runners. Messages and directions were relayed through many different points of contact.

It was there that a soldier from the resistance army came with a message for H'Tlon.

She was startled and asked, "Is there a problem back in the village, or are you giving warning of what is ahead?"

"Neither," replied the soldier. "This is from Colonel Paul Yuh. He has ordered us to bring H'Tien back to him before you continue on your way."

My sister's voice became very stern, "*No, she came with me.*"

The soldier was just as nonmoving, "*No!* Colonel Yuh *demands* that she return to be with H'Bloanh and H'Nhien." In a calmer voice, he said, "The girls are not to be separated. Those are his orders."

H'Tlon stood frozen in her thoughts; her jaw tightened. She looked at me, reached out, and wrapped me in her arms, and her voice said quietly, "You must go, my H'Tien. Colonel Yuh will look after you and the girls, and if I find a good, safe place, I will come back to get you. I'll let you go because I love you so much." Her tears rolled down onto my face, and I could not speak.

H'Tlon pointed to my things and motioned for me to pack up my damp, muddy blanket. I could not see clearly, but I stuffed it into my pack, which I carried toward the messenger and his small group, and we began our journey. I heard her call to me from a distance, "I love you, H'Tien."

I took a few steps more, dropped my pack, and ran back to her. We hugged again, and I whispered in her ear through a choked voice, "I love you, my sister." It was plain, straight, and without a stutter. I turned away and joined the soldiers for an hour of hiking before we had to camp until dark, the safest time to return to the village where Paul Yuh was waiting.

By the time we arrived at our destination, my clothes had dried, redampened from the trees and vines that we passed, and dried again as dawn crept out of the darkness. My eyelids began to feel the heaviness of my pack until a barking dog startled me. The village had to be close. A soldier turned to me and said, "We are not far. There we can rest."

My eyes focused not so much on the ground but looked for familiar sights. Two girls saw us first, and I found myself being hugged and kissed by H'Bloanh and H'Nhien. In the excitement of the moment, I forgot how much I missed H'Tlon and remembered how much I cared for my two friends.

Colonel Yuh came to greet us, put his arm around me, and said, "H'Tien, I made a promise to Y-Nguan that you three girls would stay together and that I would be responsible for your safety. I'm sorry that you had to leave H'Tlon, but she should not have taken you."

There were no words for me to say.

## *Pleasant Weeks—Tragic News*

After I left H'Tlon, a lot of things began to change, and I was allowed to stay in the village. There I matured, grew more responsible, and learned a lot about cooking for groups. Y-Khiem Eban's family let me stay with them in their longhouse, and my living conditions improved for several weeks. I had my own bamboo bed and was given new clothes and shoes—a treasured pair of sneakers. I took good care of them and still walked barefoot on most of my day trips to cook for nearby groups. A lot of the time the shoes stayed wrapped in a cloth in my backpack.

The Ebans' longhouse was at the edge of Buon Chuor Tara, a village where people were friendly, but not everyone was to be trusted. Even so, the Ebans and I and some of their friends made hikes to encampments where we could take food or needed supplies. On rare days, I was allowed to spend a whole day at the house. The relaxing time quieted my body and soul.

H'Bloanh and H'Nhien were not far away from me, and I saw them often, but our various jobs allowed little more than time for smiles and waves. I was glad for the promise to keep us together.


In that area, the Rhade dialect was spoken all around me and by those who came back and forth from other jungle camps, so I constantly practiced the dialect that I could not speak easily. I made new friends every day and tried to treat everyone with respect. By listening, I learned more of the language and about all that was happening in and around the village. That skill would be very important to me, especially while traveling with my next "family."

There were larger groups, including women, coming to our village—more than I had seen since we began our journey. Many Montagnards had fled the Viet Cong, and, with each team of travelers, reports arrived about the killings of our countrymen—farmers, shopkeepers, women, and children. After taking our farms and moving our people to useless land, they now were trying to erase our population and were continuing to destroy our culture.

After I had been with the Eban family about three weeks, a scout who had arrived that morning with eight Montagnard men and one woman came to me while I was washing clothes. He stared at the ground, shifted his feet, and finally looked straight at me. "H'Tien, I have some bad news for you. I have just come from one of our connection points and was told that H'Tlon and four others have been shot and killed by the Khmer Rouge."

I stood up and stared at him. "How can that be? I just saw her. You are mistaken."

He shook his head and said, "I'm very sorry."

I looked through him in disbelief. "She was always careful and only wanted to go across the Mekong River. They could not do that to her. How could they do that?" I sat down and put my hands to my face and rocked backward and forward, mumbling, "Why are they killing our people? I just don't understand."

The messenger put his hand on my shoulder and left me to my grief.

*Who are these people who go around killing for no reason? She was shot. How could someone shoot her? The Khmer Rouge, I think, is the Communist Party of Cambodia. It must be power they want. They want to kill all of us—but why? H'Tlon just wanted to make her dream— to cross the river. If I had been there, maybe I could have stopped them. Maybe I could...if I had been there, I would have been where she is now.*

# CAUTIOUS PROTECTION

### *Buon Hra*

Y-Khiem Eban met me coming from a day of washing clothes at a nearby camp. "H'Tien, a letter from Dam Per Quay has been sent from Buon Hra in the Ban Me Thuot area. He wants you to come to his camp. You must leave tonight with a group that is moving toward Buon Khit."

"Who is that? How can I get everything ready by then, and how far is it? Isn't Dam Per Quay that general who leads the whole army? What does he want with me?"

"H'Bloanh is there. She may have told him where you are and that you two should be together."

It seemed impossible that I could be on the trail after such a hard day, but I did what I was told. No one took whining seriously.

After I tied the laces on my treasured sneakers, Y-Khiem Eban helped me with my pack, and I gave one last hug and handshake to the Eban family, thanking them for their kindness and encouragement during the previous three weeks.

I noticed that the night was clear, and the stars had begun to show in the sky. There would be enough light to outline the person walking in front of each of us, and the leader already knew the path that he would follow. None of us realized that we would repeat this routine every night for a week before we found the Buon Hra region.


Twenty-four hours before we arrived, it was safe to travel during part of the day. Our breathing became heavier, and our leg muscles ached at the higher altitude, but we were allowed to rest more often as we inhaled the lighter air and basked in the beauty of the mountains all around us.

After clearing our identity with one of the scouts who guarded Buon Hra atop a mountain crest, we descended into a valley where the village was partially camouflaged under a banana grove and a jungle of tall ficus trees. Instead of going through the village, our leader led us to a camp some distance away, where we were greeted by Dam Per Quay, H'Bloanh, and H'Nhien—the two girls welcoming me with much joy.

The general held out his hand to each of us from the journey, and to me he asked, "How are you? You have come a long way." He was tall for a Montagnard, but his hair was cut short and neat, and his uniform was sharply pressed. Even his smile, under his mustache and over his small goatee, was kind and friendly but commanded attention.

I answered him, "I'm fine, thank you!" That was the most that would come out from my mouth at the time. I was awed by his presence, by the heavily guarded surroundings, and by the elation I felt at seeing my dearest friends.

"Show H'Tien to the house," he directed to H'Bloanh and H'Nhien, "and let her rest."

## *Abundance*

This camp was well connected. Food was abundant—all kinds of fruits, vegetables, and coffee as they ate breakfast. I had never had coffee. Every morning, relatives and friends came from the village and brought all sorts of supplies—rice, goody cake, salt, pepper, oil, garlic, onions, meat, fish—anything that a restaurant might have. It was a rich camp. I guessed that it was because of the general.

Dam Per Quay immediately asked me to call him Ama (Papa). H'Nhien already used that name. *Uncle* was good for me at first, but over the next days and months, I gave in to his wishes.

The day after we arrived, he asked me to cook for his commander, Y-Juel (second in command). Some of the food was new to me—fresh fish, cakes, coffee, and seasonings of salt and sugar. Y-Juel was nice and kind and did seem happy with my preparations, but I knew that I needed a lot of practice. I called him my brother.

"Did all of this food come from another country?" I asked him on the second day.

He laughed. "No, there are villagers most everywhere we go who want to do all that they can for the general and the army. They bring food as kind of an offering. I'm not sure where they get all of the supplies, but it is good for us."

It was like living in the city for as long as it lasted.

H'Bloanh had been at the camp for a while, so she was able to tell me names and explain personalities of the soldiers—about one hundred of them. A lot had families in another village, Buon Khit, maybe two miles from our location. Some were taller than most Montagnards whom I knew. They wore new uniforms and long hair and were respectful of us, but I did not have much to say as I was shy and uncertain and still stuttered.

The bamboo house where the general stayed was large enough to sleep the three of us, an older woman named H-We, and her husband. When the general was there, he smoked a pipe, and when he was happy, he sang. Not as tall as some of the other men (maybe about five feet six inches), he had very good body shape and spent lots of time hiking with groups of his soldiers to the mountain peaks, talking about best plans for the army. Because he wanted me to take care of his backpack, his washing, his cooking (ways that H'Bloanh taught me), and his coffee every morning, I heard conversations that others didn't. Most of it I kept to myself, not even telling H'Bloanh. I just listened with my mouth shut and served as directed.

I kept my belongings packed, as H'Tlon had taught me, but now was feeling more relaxed and settled in one place—until at the end of the week that we arrived when Dam Per Quay announced that the camp was moving to Yang Reh Mountain. He must have seen the total disappointment on my face.

He put his arm around my shoulder and said, "We must move. We are a large group, and our connections tell us that enemy spotter planes have come too close to this area. But tonight we will build a large fire in the camp and gather to remember fellow countrymen who have given their lives as a sacrifice."

I went in the house to repack my things, wondering how long we would march this time. Tears were not on my face, but sadness made my body move quietly. H'Bloanh and H'Nhien rushed into the room. They had heard.

## Farewell Fire

Before dusk, bamboo stems and tree branches were brought to the center of the camp where much chattering and excitement accompanied the making of the fire. I thought that someone must have killed a large animal, and it was to be roasted (like in my village). But I saw no carcass and saw others cooking their own dinners. People I had not seen before came to the camp from different directions, and the numbers grew large. H'Bloanh said that it was a welcome for the newest group, but it was much more than that.

As we sat around the flaming fire pit, Dam Per Quay stood up to speak, and all was silent except for the snapping of the burning wood and an occasional hoot of an owl.

"I am so grateful to all of you here and to God for our safety. We are one voice, one mind to come together as FULRO. We are the United Struggle Front for the Oppressed Races. We are the ones who are sacrificing our lives for the survival of our countrymen, our culture, and our very existence. Many have gone before us to stand up to the oppression and destruction by the Viet Cong and Cambodian forces of the Khmer Rouge who want to destroy us. We must not give up. Tonight, I ask Y-Hin Nie to praise those remembered tonight and to bless all of us gathered here and to ask that God will guard us on our journey."

Y-Hin Nie was a Christian Baptist. His prayer was one of joy for our safety and for guidance and persistence as we flee our enemy. He prayed for loyalty and peace among our people and for us to be always healthy. He asked God for safety and wisdom for our FULRO leaders of the Highlands, President Y-Bham Enuol, and our Vice President Kpa Koi. And he prayed for our friends and families who had already lost their lives in their determination to be free.

Dam Per Quay then named a long list of soldiers, mothers, children, parents, and grandparents whose souls encircled our lives. He asked for silence for five minutes so that others could be remembered in our hearts. Most I did not know, but my thoughts rested on my big sister H'Tlon, and my eyes clouded over.

As if a universal spirit surrounded us, the fire made a leap upward, creating starlike sparks in the dark sky, and music from a guitar began to reach into our collective center as we lifted our voices in song. We stood at attention and joined in singing our patriotic national anthem. It ignited our group to continue our music with happiness—singing in threes and fours and ones.

I heard someone call my name, but I could not believe it and hid behind some soldiers. Then the voices kept demanding, and encouraging applause grew louder. A soldier took my hand and led me to the center. "Come on, H'Tien, I've heard you singing on the trails and in camp. You have a good voice."

"But I don't know any songs, what to sing," I protested. It was very awkward for me. And then, I remembered a verse from my days in the Girl Scouts at Thanh Gia School. I cleared my nervous throat, looking for a first note and then began:

> Trong dem tam toi, co bao loi tran troi, trong dem toi co buo
> loi, troi tran, 365 ngay qua, toi da,365 ngay qua toi da
> Ah, ah, ah, ah, chang lam dyoc gi suot atem truong?
> suot dem truong suot dem truong voi tieng tho, dai.
> In the dark of the night, we ask what can we do.
> In the dark of the night, we ask what have we done.
> In the past full year, in the past full year.
> Ah, Ah, Ah, Ah, what have we achieved?
> All through the night, all through the night, all
>     through the night
> Only a sigh.

There was silence when I finished—and then lots of clapping. I smiled but was still shaking from my fear.

My jungle ama was kind and pleased and calmed my worry. "H'Tien, where did you learn that? My heart was touched by your words and your voice. You must teach us sometime."

I agreed, but after the music got louder, and Cambodian dances whirled around the fire, I went to the house arm in arm with H'Bloanh. We stopped at the door and looked back at the fire and up at a half moon standing guard over the mountains. The guitar strings seemed to reach out into the valley, and we felt safe. "Why do we have to leave this, H'Bloanh? I get so tired of running."

"So do I, but you know that the leaves will start falling from the trees soon, and all of the color will be gone along with the camouflage for our hiding. We must find a better place."


Most of the next day was spent clearing the camp of "living." We smoothed over cooking pits and covered numerous small areas with banana branches to leave the camp "abandoned," but we knew that we and others could use it again if necessary. The more that we moved, the more I realized the importance of this deceptive system. From the air, the camp would look just like a forgotten village.

Since planes had been reported nearby, we would travel before sunrise. I was happy to hear that the next place, Yang Reh Mountain, was only a day away. Because we would be going up more than across, we were advised to find strong walking sticks to help us keep our balance.

I had not noticed how much the leaves had begun to change colors, but when the sun searched for its hiding place behind the mountains, the valley looked like a sea of butter, and the ridges were washed in bright shades of gold, spotted with rocks reflecting the bloodred rays of the setting sun.

A longing made my body feel limp as I thought of Ami and Ama, of Sister Helen, of my village and friends, of Father Tai. I knew that they wondered if I lived, and I was anxious about their treatment by the Viet Cong. I felt guilty about leaving them, but in my youth, I thought that I was saving their lives by not staying in the village and irritating the Communists. I might have been shy, but my mouth could move in rapid words—and I longed to be free. This place in the Highlands was free, but it came with a price.

As the stars and moon were fading, I awoke and prepared my backpack as usual. I went to the nearby creek and refilled our water bottles in case we left in a hurry. I wanted to be ready. I could see from a distance that Yang Reh Mountain was very tall and that the hike would be difficult and that the bamboo stick that a friend had cut for me would be a good companion. Fruit was our breakfast, and then Ama said that it was time. As I pushed my last shirt into the pack, I looked around to be sure that nothing was left behind.

## *Comfort at Yang Reh*

Hiking up Yang Reh was an adventure that I looked forward to taking. Our group, maybe a hundred, moved out in single file as usual, with H'Bloanh in front of me and H'Nhien behind. Covering our tracks was left to the last few soldiers. The valley trek was steady, easy walking, but the climb began sooner than I thought. My walking stick and my sneakers brought me happiness. My long army pants and shirt protected me from the morning chill and the scratches of vines that constantly hung down around us and hugged us as we passed through the forests. But after a couple of hours, my legs ached, my breathing shortened, and my clothes became damp from my sweat. When we finally stopped for a break, I sat against my pack and welcomed the fall breezes to fan my face as I napped like a cat.

It seemed like only a second later, two words, "Let's go!" punctured my sleep.

I groaned to my feet, adjusted my pack again to my shoulders, and looked down at the green valley that we had left. It had become like a large carpet with quilted designs similar to those that I had seen on bed covers in the windows in Pleiku. In contrasts to the softness of the valley floor, the mountain was disguised by a mixture of palm and ficus trees, blazing hardwoods, jungle vegetation, and vines that stood guard over large boulders and rock formations.

Yawning seemed to help me stay awake. I started counting the number of times my mouth widened, and when I got to twenty-five, I quit. There was no break for a long time, and I became desperate for a rest stop. It was good that the trees and vines were thick near our path as I could not wait, so I asked H'Bloanh to cover me while I relieved myself. It was embarrassing, but there was no way to avoid these inconveniences. Although never comfortable for us, it became an unquestioned necessity on our marches.

Dam Per Quay must have heard the trail of heavy breathing when he allowed us to rest again. He called out, "Where is my daughter? Where is H'Tien?"

"I'm here." I walked up toward him.

"Are you okay? Let me take your pack."

"No, I'm fine." I did not want to look weak, but he took my pack anyway and gave it to one of the soldiers.

"Come and walk in front of me!" he ordered.

"Okay, thank you," I said while I rubbed my shoulders.

"There is a stream not far, and all of us will take a rest there."

Light crept up the mountain as we leaned against our backpacks and stretched out our legs. Some of the men jumped up as three soldiers quietly appeared in our path, but they were quickly identified as friends. They had come down from the camp to welcome us and had already met our guides. They were from the M'nong Lac Thien tribe and spoke Rhade as well as their tribal dialect.

My ama said that we would rest before the three-hour hike to the top. "Over there, Bu [a dear-to-heart nickname], is a place for you and the girls to rest." He pointed to a cave with a platform built inside the opening.

I reached the gaping black hole and immediately sat down but noticed that H'Bloanh and H'Nhien went to look for wood to burn for cooking. I could only stare at them, unable to move except to the ground, where my heavy eyelids closed off all activity and locked me into immediate sleep.

Ama shook me awake and said that the men had cut the heart from some small palm trees and had slaughtered some birds and a monkey for us to cook. H'Bloanh and H'Nhien were waking beside me, and all of us went to the fire to help. I wondered if the men ever slept much and if sometimes they must have dozed while walking on the trail. The monkey had been skinned, and the birds' feathers were plucked; then we cut them into pieces for the cooking pot. Often monkeys were roasted whole over a fire, but there was not enough time, so boiling was the best choice. I was not ungrateful; the birds I could nibble, but monkey meat was not on my diet.

Being with Ama was a big advantage because the whole group looked after him first, and even though each day we fed about twenty people in our immediate group, others had to search for themselves as well as for Dam Per Quay.

Fires for cooking were allowed to burn no longer than necessary for a meal, and when extinguished, the smoke was smothered properly with dirt. That day, no planes flew in the distance to stop our forward movement.

Near the top, our three guides led us into a clearing with two bamboo houses built on concrete bases—a square one on the left and one that was longer on the right.

"General, please take this one," one of the guides led Ama to the larger of the two. "It will be the best for your comfort. There is another group in other houses nearby."

"Thank you! This spot looks good. We will settle here for a while."

Dam Per Quay was a strong man, but he looked tired even though he did not have to carry his pack or cook his food. The burden of a leader must surely have taken as much energy as hiking. Everyone in our group and those whom we met seemed to be grateful for his leadership. In fact, we shared in that responsibility of protecting our people, preserving our culture, and saving our own lives.

Once the decision to stay was made, men rushed to cut wood for the hammock-bed they had brought for Ama. H'Nhien, H'Bloanh, and I looked for a flat rock or space that would sleep the three of us. The rocks were hard, but the ground was full of crawling things, and it seemed that this camp would be our home for some days to come.

H'Nhien went one way. "Over here, I think, is best!"

"No, over here!" called H'Bloanh. "It is part flat rock and good, solid earth—and has a cover."

When we reached H'Bloanh's chosen space, we all immediately agreed that the canvas tarp roof that someone had left was ideal for discouraging rain and too much sun.

We heard Dam Per Quay ask, "Are you girls finding a place to sleep?"

I met him and showed him our new home.

"Good, it is not too far from me. It is easy distance for you to go back and forth to cook."

We said, "Yes," put our things down, and went out with the men to gather wood.

This place that had been selected for our new home felt safer than all of the others over the last year of wandering. Yang Reh was tall, sturdy, peaceful, and sheltering. It was especially nice at night. We could leave the fires burning a little longer and enjoy the smoke from the smoldering ashes because it kept the forever-roving insects at a distance, but the mosquitoes were particularly bad. They buzzed in our faces, eyes, and ears; sucked blood; and left lumps of red that itched into the night and the day.

We were now experienced jungle combatants. The act of survival had become routine. No one had to remind us to keep our packs ready, to always have our water bottles filled to the top (when there was water), to immediately look for wood when we made our camp, to watch for fruit trees and fields of vegetables or rice as we marched, to hide on short notice, to hunt, to cook, and, in my case, to pray a lot and to sing to myself.

When we had rice, we boiled a large amount, filled a cup for each person, and made sure that there was enough for their packs for the following day. When the supply ran low, a few men went to village farms several miles away to collect food and supplies and to bring the latest news of the Viet Cong in South Vietnam and the Khmer Rouge in Cambodia.

A few days after we arrived, Ama asked H'Nhien to cook for another visiting leader, a kind man whose name was Y-Ngong Knul, the former secretary of agriculture in the South Vietnamese government. He was much older than Dam Per Quay, and we called him Awa, which means *great-uncle*. He and his son, Y-Dhun Nie Buondap, came often to our camp, and H'Nhien usually did the cooking when they were there.

I noticed that Y-Dhun's and H'Nhien's eyes met and stayed a lot on each other and that H'Nhien became giggly when we teased her about it. A year later, H'Nhien and Y-Dhun declared their love for each other, and she went to live with his family as his wife.

Before she left, we gathered ourselves for singing and dancing, laughter and tears, best wishes and joy for the two of them, and H'Bloanh and I adjusted that there was now only the two of us.

H'Bloanh was a much better cook than I was, but I watched her a lot and asked questions that sometimes were too many. She was quick, and I tried to keep up or get ahead. Sometimes I would get up very early and slip to the cooking stove to start the water but found that she had already been there and had gone back to sleep. Then I would go back to sleep, and she would get up before me and would have the morning meal done by the time my eyes reopened. She was closer than a sister and only became impatient with me if I complained.

By experimenting, she learned that if you boiled rice with the heart of palm fruit, the rice would last for a week. She showed me the method, and one day Ama said, "*Bu* (my daughter), I want you to cook for us tonight."

"Of course," I said, and then ran to H'Bloanh in a panic.

"Just cook like we have been doing and start with the rice meal first!"

I did, and I boiled low and stirred and put the lid on the pot and took it off and put it on, and the rice looked like soup, and the palm hearts stayed hard and smelled burned from the bottom. My distressed face brought H'Bloanh up from her resting place. She added more wood to make the fire hotter, and I stirred and boiled and stirred, and soup became the main part of our meal.

"This is good for my digestion." Ama smiled. "I should eat this every day."

It was his way of making me feel better, so I smiled, but my eyes watered. And later I asked H'Bloanh to let me do more of the cooking by myself. Only a few more scorched meals, and I mastered the "experiments" on my own.


The anxious feeling that we would be moving any day soon went to the back of our minds. There was much comfort here, and I thought of the happiness of summers in my village, often thinking of Ami and Ama back home. I prayed for them every day.

The mountain was pleasantly cool and cold at night. We "showered" when the sun was high in the sky, and the water from the mountain streams and caves came through the bamboo pipes like a waterfall that covered our bodies with refreshing ripples. Our "shivering dance of screams" made others laugh but was worth the invigorating run from the icy outpouring to a warm spot on our "sunning" rock not far away.

If I timed it right, on the days when it was my turn under the pipes, I could lay under the sun afterward and pretend that I had nothing to do and nowhere to go. I would hum songs with the birds, dance in my mind with the monkey swingers, listen to the insect orchestra, and give thanks that I was still alive. From the rocks, I could see the tops of trees and green grasses below, and my thoughts were not of running and war and running and guns and running and killing and running.

Other times were filled with many chores: sewing tears in soldiers' uniforms, washing clothes in the stream, gathering wood, preparing food that the men brought. The mountain water seemed pure, but we often boiled it for safe drinking, as I had learned years before in the Girl Scouts. Every morning I made coffee for Ama, and he called me his little *tic* (which meant deaf), but I was not deaf. I still stuttered and tried to make myself useful without speaking, but I loved to sing, especially on Sundays when my voice was steady and strong.

On Sundays, we gathered to honor God. We gave thanks for our safe place, for the food that we had to eat, for the water that we had to drink, for our friendships. We asked God to protect our families who were not with us, to help all of our group leaders, to stay with our soldiers who were always watching for the enemy, and for the safety of our brave leaders who agreed to meet with the Vietnam government to bring about peace. News of torture and executions brought much sadness to all of us, but on Sundays our music soothed our aching souls.

## *FULRO: United Struggle Front for the Oppressed Races*

Dam Per Quay was always busy giving directions and receiving messages about the successes and the defeats of our countrymen. I did not discuss any of it with him, but I listened and knew what his close commanders were saying.

Our army in the Central Highlands grew larger when Montagnard special forces and paramilitary groups from the South Vietnamese army joined FULRO. In order to make the union of tribes and ethnic groups stronger, FULRO adopted the word *Dega* to identify all as one group, but most of us referred to ourselves as Montagnards (French for mountain people).

FULRO asked the Communist government to recognize our people as the rightful citizens of the Central Highlands, to take their forces out of the Highlands, and to restore our right to rule ourselves. The government said they would do all of these things, but instead, they recruited our villagers as spies so that trusting our countrymen was often difficult. More citizens fled to the Highland jungles every day, and more survival groups and army forces formed throughout the mountains.

The government took over private property, forced villagers to labor for them, prohibited the speaking of any Dega language, taught obedience to the Communists in schools, let public health systems die, and abolished all tribal courts of law. When Ama used the word *genocide*, I understood.

# Separations and Reunions

A year later, H'Bloanh was sent to another camp to tend to a soldier who had a bad wound in his leg. Three men replaced her work in our camp, because they knew that I was much slower in my jobs. But I learned more about jungle food combinations and new ways that the men taught me, and soon I was getting compliments on the different tastes in our meals.

The camp where H'Bloanh went had several wounded soldiers. It seems that two of our groups mistook each other for the enemy and fired their guns on the trail somewhere near Yang Reh.

Dam Per Quay was extremely upset. He sent messages to the leaders: "You are so lucky that no one was killed. Train your troops better and be more careful when you are marching! With all of the groups of our countrymen in the resistance, we must not lose anyone to carelessness."

In 1977, Ama announced to our camp that we had been invited by Y-Khok Nie Krieng, one of the special forces leaders, to celebrate the anniversary of the beginning of the Montagnard revolution on September 20 at Buon Sut M'Drang. We began our journey a week before, as it was a very long way. My happiness spilled over when I saw H'Bloanh join us for the adventure. She had taken a break from nursing her wounded soldier, whose healing was still incomplete.

A few disappointed guards and scouts were assigned to stay in the Yang Reh camp, but the rest of us, including four girls from nearby villages, made our way back through the mountainous jungle as before, going from camp to camp and staying through the night at each one.

"That's Dam Per Quay. He's the general leading our troops in the jungle," I heard many people almost whisper in awe. Some cheered, and three fell to the ground in front of him; many shook our hands. "We have heard of you for a long time but have never seen you."

The attention made me feel uncomfortable and confused. Vietnamese were scattered throughout the camps, and I was not trusting them, even though they were considered part of our army. But I stayed close to Ama and watched him greet everyone with a pleasant smile.

News traveled fast, and when we reached Buon Sut M'Drang, the crowds overwhelmed me. Villagers and camps from all over the Highlands had come for the big celebration. A rich Vietnamese man brought us clothes, shoes, money, and food from Ban Me Thuot, and messages from Y-Khiem Eban's family where I had stayed before.

The party, in a huge field, lasted one night and one day. A cow was sacrificed, but I was joyful that I did not have to clean it or cook it. Security around the festivities was extremely tight, with lots of soldiers. I forgot about the jungle and the running and the camps and the guns and the killings.

When the great campfire was started, the music began. Some was from songs of the jungle, and groups danced to the beat. But many songs from the cities were new music, which were played loud on tapes, and boys and girls danced together. That was a new dancing way for me, and I kept close to Ama to see if he needed anything to drink, but a smile was all over me. H'Bloanh was much less shy and eased into a lot of the new dance steps, turning and clapping and moving quickly to the fast beats, always laughing and enjoying her freedom.

We celebrated into the nighttime and awoke a little later than usual, but Ama said that we must start back to Yang Reh. I hurried to make his coffee and to fix his backpack, because when Dam Per Quay said go, he meant *now*.

By the time that we began the trek, I glanced back at our numbers and knew that they had increased—mostly men and six more girls. Then I saw H'Nhien and her husband. I waved excitedly. H'Bloanh and I walked with Ama, but they came up beside us for a while. We hugged and laughed and took the party spirit back into the jungle overgrowth and enjoyed more visiting time in the first camp where we stopped for the night.

## *Being Family with Dam Per Quay*

I liked staying on Yang Reh Mountain. It felt safe, and we camped there for a few months. When H'Bloanh's soldier got well, she joined us again, and I had more smiles.

Among the men who escorted Dam Per Quay was Y-Niam Nie Buondap, a close, trusted friend. He gave assistance to a lot of people and was kind to me with his good heart. He trained me to be a better help to Ama and directed me in how to keep Ama's backpack ready for his convenience. When Y-Niam brought clothes for Ama, he showed me how to alter them, hemming pants and shirts to fit Ama's body. I could also make pants for myself from old uniforms, but they always hung on me like scarecrow clothes. I didn't look so much like a girl, but I was comfortable and blended with the soldiers.


Dam Per Quay was always good to me, but he was a very demanding leader. Not only did I have to have his things ready for immediate departures, but also the soldiers were always on alert for his sudden commands. Neither the soldiers nor the patrols questioned his power or authority over the Montagnards in the jungle. After all, he was the general. No one talked back, or he or she might be "missing" a few days later. I might have been his *bu*, but I knew to keep quiet.

Yang Reh became a home for me, But Dam Per Quay moved a lot from camp to camp, and I had to go when he ordered, but always under his protection. Two times we went to Buon Khit (a rich village in that region) for meetings with FULRO leaders. Dam Per Quay's wife and family lived there. He visited with them, but most of us camped away from Buon Khit, near the rice fields. It was harvest time, and the soldiers and guards, with families nearby, needed to help in the paddies. Their wives and children, left alone for many months, celebrated the men's return.

Y-Niam Buondap was with us, and I began to call him *Ayong* (brother). I felt that he protected me as well as my ama. The guns that he and Ama carried were R18s, shiny and smooth, but I had never seen them shoot anything or anybody, yet the guns made me feel safer. Also, when Ama went anywhere, loyal soldiers surrounded him—front and back—to shield him from snipers. Even though I did not have the same security, it was as safe as it could be.

## *Establishing a Provisional Government, 1977*

A small group of twenty soldiers accompanied Dam Per Quay to another conference with the Jarai tribe at Buon Hra. Buon Hra was a large area, and we stayed for a week while many army commanders came to meet with the president of the Highland forces.

Commanders were men who were appointed or elected by other ranking officers. They usually were good people—active, hardworking, and smart. They knew how to shoot and had good behavior.

I did not know why they met, but other leaders who had voices that could match Dam Per Quay's spent time together. Of the Jarai tribe, I remember Nay Rong, Nay Phun, Ksor De, and three others who stood up to Dam Per Quay.

During the gatherings, I sat quietly in the shadows, not speaking to anyone, waiting to bring them water or food, as my ama directed. In one meeting, conversation became heated, and I heard Dam Per Quay say, "We must fight."

And Nay Rong answered, "Don't do that! We need peace, not a war." Everyone spoke at the same time, but when it was over, "peace" won, and I moved quietly through the group offering water.

After the meeting was over, they shook hands and showed friendly smiles. I did not say a word, but I felt happy that there was no additional conflict.

Many leaders came to Buon Hra in the days that followed and celebrated the establishment of the Montagnards' first provisional government. They brought with them families, civilian countrymen, and musicians to join the festival.

Among them were three ladies—H'Lonh, H'Ngonh (H'Lonh's sister), and H'Juaih—who welcomed the guests and danced around the campfires. H'Lonh was especially good dancing the *ramvong* from Cambodia. I went back and forth cooking and boiling water for coffee and watching Ama watch H'Lonh. As his eyes rested on her, I watched his attitude change from enjoyment to irritation when she danced with other men.

I did not know if H'Lonh was an ex-girlfriend, but by the time the celebration ended, she moved in with him, and I was not comfortable with the arrangement. I worried about what that would mean for him and for me. Would I still take care of his food, his clothes, pack his backpack, bring him coffee in the morning? I also was concerned that he did not set a good example as the president of the Montagnard army.

# *Equal Leadership and Nam Pai*

(Testing Nam Pai - Courtesy of Dr. Gerald Cannon Hickey Collection)

Equal honor was between Ama and another man called N'Du. He belonged to the M'nong tribe in the An Lac region and spoke three dialects: Rhade, M'nong, and Kaho. With respect he addressed Dam Per Quay as *Ong Kra*, which means "High Chief," but translated from Jarai and Rhade dialects, it means "monkey man." I did not know all of the tribal dialects; however, I knew enough to wonder why they called him a bad name. Ama always smiled when his friend used that, but I only heard one other man say it to his face.

N'Du was another kind heart and seemed to have very large ears, as he brought Dam Per Quay much information about what was going on all over the mountains, especially from the M'nong and Kaho tribes. Ama listened to every word and sometimes took notes in a book that he kept.

I had respect for N'Du and called him Ama Par (a young *ama par* means "brother"). He loved Yang Reh as much as I did. Many times we talked of the spirit mountain of the Da Lat region. He was a clever man, had been to so many places, and Dam Per Quay trusted him and his judgment.

N'Du also brought us vegetables, dried fish and dried meat, useful personal supplies (clothes and shoes), and cheerful items for Ama (tobacco and wine). Rice wine was not easily obtained in the jungle, but *nam pai* was considered the best that could be found, and friends knew how to get the best for Dam Per Quay.

*Nam pai* took a long time to make. Corn, or rice, kernels were soaked overnight, pounded to remove the hard shell, and then boiled to make a mush. After the mush cooled, it was spread out on bamboo trays, sprinkled with a mixture of yeast and sugar and allowed to sit for three days and three nights so the corn could absorb the yeast mixture. Rice husks were added to the mush, and the three main ingredients were spooned into bamboo jugs or jars to ferment. Banana leaves, tied tightly around the tops (acting as lids), secured the mixture for a week or two or more. The type and strength of the wine were determined by the color of the banana leaves as they turned brown—the longer the stronger. The color in the jug ranged from light to reddish brown and was another visible test of strength and taste.

The banana leaf tops were removed, and the liquid was pressed out of the mush and strained into other containers. The mush that remained could be eaten, and additional sugar made it easier on the stomach. Water was poured through the mush; a new banana leaf was placed in the jug to keep the mush from escaping, and the mixture rested for at least fifteen minutes. Sometimes the wine was mixed with other liquids, and oftentimes the men would sip it slowly up through bamboo straws. Preferences varied with the desire for different experiences.

Nothing was wasted. The depleted mush was fed to the pigs.

# ADVENTURE TO DA LAT

O ver the next year, the days hurried into nights, into months. I became a part of the "family." I knew the people who came in and out of our camps, the men who protected us, the villagers who were generous, and those who did not seem trustable. I thanked God that I was cared for. I was my ama's Bu, and our jungle friends were my brothers and sisters.

Ama continued to joke with me, calling me Tic (deaf one). When he was happy, he joked with some of the men, saying, "Oh Ti, Oh Teo, come eat your dinner." (Those were nicknames for the men who moved as slow as a turtle.) I enjoyed the moments when he sincerely smiled, but most of the time, I remained a shadow, listening at the corners, hiding my stuttering voice, respecting his position.

I often sat on a stool by my rice soup that cooked over a wood fire in a pot that hung from a metal hook and listened to Ama and Ama Par tell stories to each other. Their dreams of going to Da Lat helped the cooking time to go faster.

Ama seemed unusually happy one morning. "I have decided that we should go to Da Lat to see the place where Y-Niam Buondap is from. We will leave next week."

"How far is it, and what will we need?" I asked.

"It is several days' walk and is in other beautiful mountains. I hear that it is very pleasant and maybe cooler than here."

Even though I did not think that any place could be nicer than Yang Reh, my excitement about going to Da Lat built each day. Da Lat City had a reputation of being a famous place in the center of the Highlands and a destination for tourists. I dreamed of seeing their big waterfall and of not having so many bugs and to sleep soundly at night without the heat.

When our day to depart finally came, there was much busyness in packing clothes and food into our backpacks. I already had most of Ama's needs in his pack and added snack food of leaf-wrapped sticky rice, dried meat, and extra water. I listened to the men laughing and talking together about not eating too much before the trek, so I didn't. It would prove to be a mistake.

Dam Per Quay, N'Du (Ama Par), and a number of soldiers walked ahead of us, and we, H'Bloanh and I, and many Yang Reh settlers were told to stay in the middle, while other soldiers and men walked behind us. We were a larger group than usual, about fifty in all, who had rushed through the afternoon to ready the camp and ourselves. Talk on the trail began in low, expectant voices that became lower when the sun set as we realized that we would hike through the night. Dam Per Quay allowed rest times but no stopping to set up camp.

As shadows overcame the light that seeped through the thick canopy of jungle leaves, we began to collect, from the trees and logs, the florescent mushrooms that would give us eyesight until another dawn. It had become routine for hiking in the dark. Again we attached the glowing mushrooms to the backpack of the person in front of us and carried some in our outstretched hands to form the width of our path. The light was not brilliant but steady, and the supply was generous.

One foot went in front of the other as we climbed up steep trails and down into valleys and up another mountain and down by the light of another day. My stomach rumbled from hunger, but I remembered from the soldiers' conversation at Yang Reh camp that I shouldn't eat too much. I lagged behind my group. Some called to me.

"Are you okay, H'Tien?"

"Yes, okay, I'm coming." But I was tired and wanted to sleep and eat and be in a quiet place. Even so, I kept it to myself. I did not want my friends to think that I was weak.

I walked along through the lower damp part of a mountain, my head watching the feet in front of me, when I heard what sounded like small fruit falling from the trees. Sudden yells came from everyone.

"Run, run fast! Hurry, hurry, *leeches!*"

The bloodsucking worms were all around us, smelling scratches and sweat and clinging to any skin they could find—up from the ground, down from vines and leaves. They were my worst nightmare. Nothing else in the jungle scared me more. I shrieked.

"What do I do? I hate leeches; I can't stand them crawling on me." I shook all over and jumped up and down. I took off my old shoes and socks and rolled up my pants and rubbed at my legs and feet and arms.

"What are you doing? Run, hurry, run!" said my friends, and they pushed me along the path.

Even with my stomach empty and my legs trembling, my eyes woke up, and I ran with the others and left the slimy, slippery dark bloodsuckers behind.

"Why do you wear your shoes around your neck instead of on your feet?" asked H'Bloanh.

"I didn't want those creatures nesting in my shoes. I love my shoes." And I laughed at how funny that sounded. "You do crazy things when you are frightened."

The traveling became routine again. I lost count of the mountains and the hours, and I became weaker. Insects in these mountains swarmed as much as the ones I remembered in the flatlands. Their looks were different but their bites were the same.

The sound of a stream rushed to my ears as we came to the top of a peak. Dam Per Quay let us rest, and I stumbled to the water and soaked myself while resting beside a big rock, drinking the coolness in and out of my body. I was so thirsty and could not seem to get enough.

Then we started again toward an abandoned rice field where the soil was no longer fertile. I said to H'Bloanh in front of me,

"This must be some of the land that the government has given to the mountain people who have farmed very little."

But as I looked at the dry, barren field, I realized that I could not see it clearly or the man in front of me—or was it H'Bloanh? The field moved; the person swayed and became two. *Where was Ama?* "Ama, Ama." He was up front somewhere. There was smoke all around, or mist or…

"I'm so thirsty. It's white and black all at once."

I heard Ama Par's voice. "Drink this!"

I drank and drank, and everything went dark.

H'Bloanh and H'Nhien were there when I woke up by a fire. I immediately felt the heat.

"What happened? Why are we here?" I tried to rise, but my body did not respond quickly.

"You fainted, and the men took turns carrying you in a hammock until we could find a place to camp for a few hours. I know that you won't like what has happened, but Dam Per Quay has been pushing us very hard, and we are all glad to have this break. I heard that you have not eaten much. That is not good. Why are you doing that?"

I hesitated and then quietly said to H'Bloanh, "At Yang Reh, they talked about not eating too much on the trail. Could they have been making that up?"

"Probably! Now eat this food, and eat a little more as we go along until your stomach gets back some strength. Dam Per Quay won't stop much longer. Get up and try to walk." H'Bloanh was gentle but firm.

"I am embarrassed. It's the second time this has happened to me, and I'm sorry for all of the trouble."

"Here, just eat this banana—a little at a time—and drink this water," another friend encouraged.

## *Arrival at Da Lat Village*

We hiked most of the week—up and down, around, and up and down. My hiking stick was my close, steady friend, and Dam Per Quay let us rest more often. The jungle path was quite dense, but from the top of one of the mountains we could see, through a clearing, a creek that looked like a dream from our best imaginations. No one waited for directions. We immediately began a cautious descent toward the water, so happy to refill our now-empty bottles. I sipped slowly at first and then drank my full bottle as we rested. The cool water woke up our faces and strengthened our bodies.

As I sat on a large rock by the creek, I noticed that a tree close by had been cut back and that there were bushes pushed away from the edge to make a narrow path at the water's edge. A slight breeze moved the leaves, and a familiar smell had all of us whispering and pointing down the path in its direction—smoke. There was smoke drifting from near the top of another hill. Backs straightened, chatter quickened, and our leaders moved us toward the gray column rising from the trees. Now I prayed for someone to invite us to stay for the night and offer us food—any kind of food.

Of course, our soldiers went ahead and found that two guards of another camp were cooking their meal. They were glad to see us and said that others had heard that we were coming and were waiting for us at the bottom.

I could not make out any village until we got much closer. Then I saw people standing near their houses (fifteen in all), sturdy shelters camouflaged with roofs and sides covered by tree branches but built with bamboo floors. It was in the Da Lat region—a large village and our destination.

After all of us had arrived, Dam Per Quay called for me to come. He introduced me as his daughter and pointed to a small house. "We are invited to stay in there, so you and H'Bloanh come and put your packs down."

I was the first to get there and was so happy to see the inside with sleeping mats and without bugs and spiders or snakes hanging from the roof. We even had a woodstove fire, which we could keep burning all night to keep away mosquitoes and to keep warm. The air felt wonderful—much cooler than places we usually stayed.

The Da Lat civilians brought us some of their jungle vegetables to cook: dry corn, nonflorescent mushrooms, leafy greens; there was no rice, but there was dried meat that made everything taste better.

Some of the Da Lat soldiers came in the evening to ask, "Do you need anything more?" They spoke in the Vietnamese language.

"No, thank you," Dam Per Quay answered. "We are so many, and you have been generous to us already."

The sun was barely hidden by the time that we all, including Dam Per Quay, fell asleep.


The next morning, later than usual, I awoke all curled up in my blanket, feeling very secure. I was afraid to go outside because there were tall trees everywhere, and I thought that I might lose my way. But I didn't need to think about it long.

Voices outside called to us, "Hey, girls, come out and fix the fire. We have birds for you to cook—lots of birds."

I went to the door, amazed at the number they brought. "Today will be a great meal day." I laughed and stepped back inside to hurry H'Bloanh.

Later in the morning, N'Du came to Dam Per Quay. "Ong Kra, General Nicolas and his soldiers will come to visit us here soon."

Ama answered him, saying, "We will welcome him. Stay here until they come and remain until they leave!"

In the early afternoon, a soldier appeared to announce that General Nicolas was arriving with a large escort. It was an impressive group. Ten soldiers led the way for General Nicolas, who was accompanied by six girls in traditional dress (with overfilled baskets on their backs) and twenty soldiers who completed the procession. The presentation was quite impressive; the general was striking, with his ponytail gathered neatly behind his neck, and all soldiers wore freshly pressed uniforms.

General Nicolas's girls brought their baskets to Ama and deliberately laid out each different gift: food, wine, a new shirt.

"Greetings, Ong Kra!" Nicolas shook Ama's hand. Ama ignored the particular salutation, but as old friends would, they spent the afternoon drinking wine together, laughing and talking for a long, long time, sometimes in low voices, occasionally loud and sharp. Our soldiers socialized with theirs, and conversations echoed from small and large shelters.

H'Bloanh and I only listened from a distance as we cooked a lot of the vegetables and meat that had been brought to us, but the interest in wine took importance over food. We finally had meals for ourselves and went to bed.


We slept late until one of our soldiers came to wake us and advise that we were packing to leave. We had not heard any word from Ama.

"But we are to stay here a week," I complained.

"No, Dam Per Quay says that we are to go."

N'Du came by our house to see if we were up and quietly explained what had happened, but we were to say nothing. "I had to tell Ong Kra that the villagers had rice, chickens, and much more to offer to him, but Nicholas took all of it and hid it in the mountains. The villagers thought that he had given the food to Dam Per Quay, and when the soldiers went to look for it, there was no food. Nicholas used all of the provisions for himself."

"That is why he couldn't sleep," I whispered. "I saw him walking in the night and asked if I could help, but he said, 'No, go back to your bed!' He spoke angrily."

"Yes, he is very angry, so we must pack up our things and return to Yang Reh as soon as possible. I will help where I can."

Dam Per Quay was already out waking the soldiers and all who came with us. I was very unhappy, and the soldiers had heavy-hearted faces and not very clear heads from the wine. But there was no arguing with Ama. We prepared quickly and returned—up the mountains, down the mountains, by the creeks and streams, through the leech forest—relying on the mushrooms to keep us together. I ate and I drank and I sang only a little, but I prayed a lot.

# DISAPPOINTMENT, UNCERTAINTY, CONSPIRACY, AND DEATH

I almost hugged the trees when we returned to Yang Reh, and in my happiness to be "home," I wrapped my arms around H'Bloanh first. At last I could feel safe surrounded by our own friends and soldiers.

At the end of a week, and many meetings with his leaders, Dam Per Quay said, "I must go to Buon Ea Tieu to see my mother and my two brothers. H'Tien, you will go with me."

My heart sank, and I could barely look at him.

"Only you and a few soldiers will go—maybe ten. We will leave tomorrow night."

My body complained and moaned, but my mouth remained shut, for it would not be useful for me to speak my thoughts.

We walked for two nights and part of three days. As we approached the village, Ama said, "Five of you men come with me. H'Tien, you stay behind with the rest. Over there is a thick bamboo forest where you can make a camp."

I stood frozen; the memory when I met with the snake near my village whirled around me. After Ama left, I sat at the edge of the bamboo grove and declared that I would be the guard. Dogs barked in the distance, and I recalled another night, years before, when Y-Toan Nie betrayed H'Blin and me at the boat. The flashbacks came fast through my mind. I wrapped my arms around my knees and rocked back and forth, putting the past behind, pushing painful thoughts away. *How long will this last? Where is my family? Why did H'Tlon have to die? Is Sister Helen still alive? What about Sister Amanda? I don't like hiking the jungles, but what if something happens to Ama? Who would protect me?*

The dogs in the distance began to bark continuously, and I knew that Ama and the soldiers were at the village. I prayed for their safety. I prayed into the night when they did not return. I prayed in between waking during a restless sleep.

Late the next morning, Ama and his guards found us in the forest and explained.

"I cannot leave my mother now. She has cried many times for me to stay, and my brothers, friends, and relatives have begged us to remain for a while. They have sacrificed a chicken and a pig for a celebration. They have not done so since my marriage in Buon Khit some years ago, after I escaped from a Viet Cong jail and went into the jungle. All of you, come, and we'll rest for a few days."

Nine weeks later, Ama's family roasted a dog for a farewell dinner for Dam Per Quay and our group. Our visit there had not been the "resting" time that he told us. He had met with leaders and high-ranking officers from many villages and camps. As I listened, I understood that the Viet Cong were infiltrating our villages and pressing close to our camps. Each soldier had a weapon, but our army was not a match for the armed VC. I knew that more moving and more running would be our life again.

## Dam Per Quay Leaves

The morning after the dinner of honor, I had our packs ready, and Ama motioned for me to come and sit beside him. He held both of my hands and said, "Bu, I must go to Da Lat, and I must go without you. I may be gone a long time, and it will be very dangerous for you to come. You will be watched over, until I return, by Y-Wo. He is a good person, and you can trust what he says."

I couldn't move, and my mouth stayed silent. Ama stood up and pulled me up beside him. He was not often a tender person toward me, but he wrapped caring arms around me and said that he hoped his trip would not last more than a few weeks.

He called to Y-Wo, "Take good care of H'Tien! I will send you a message when it is safe to meet again." Then he turned, lifted his pack, went outside, and motioned his soldiers to follow. They soon disappeared into the thickness of the trees, and I sat in the doorway, stunned and unbelieving, staring after the empty path and wondering what would become of me.

I watched the different leaders, with serious faces, take their groups from Buon Ea Tieu to begin their treks back to their own camps. And soon, Y-Wo came to me after he had finished supplying his own pack and said that it was time for us to go.

I had known Y-Wo for a while and easily began calling him a young brother. As Dam Per Quay had said, my new brother was good and kind. He told me that my ama was going back through Yang Reh to get more soldiers, but I could not understand why he left me there and did not take me to Yang Reh. No additional explanation was given.

Y-Wo guided me and our soldiers toward the flowing green rice fields that had not yet turned to a yellow, harvest color. When we camped, Y-Wo surprised me with a hammock  and some rice that he had brought from Buon Ea Tieu. The fresh breeze from the fields helped to soothe our disappointment.

Although I was very anxious for Dam Per Quay and all who traveled with him to Da Lat; those two restful weeks of pleasant mornings and cool day breezes were a welcome interruption to a life of uncertainties and daily tension. But soon Y-Wo received a message that we should be on the move again, back toward Ea Tieu area, to another camp—many travel days—where Y-Wer was in charge.

The Central Highlands were now full of Montagnard camps. We passed nearby or through several, stopping during the days and nights when we needed a break from the pit vipers, killer wasps, poisonous spiders, and the jungle floor. I constantly thought of Ama and his soldiers climbing the high mountains, rarely stopping, and although I missed him, I was glad that our hikes were not as long and as dangerous.

For most of one day, a humming sound reached my ears like a low drone from an airplane, but it never got closer or farther away. During a rest I asked, "Y-Wo, do you hear any unusual noise in the air that could be a huge swarm of bees? We seem to be circling around it."

He smiled and explained. " That is coming from the Dai Phat Thanh tower, which sends signals across the Highlands from its antenna close to Buon Ale-A, beside Buon Me Thuot City. Look over toward Ea Tieu, and you can see the light on top of it."

A spot of red, blinking on and off, reached toward the sky on a very tall pole. I had never seen anything like that before, and no one could explain exactly how it worked except that it helped send wireless communications from mountains to valleys. I prayed that it was reaching Ama in Da Lat and keeping him safe.

## *Ea Tieu—a Camp on an Island*

Y-Wer and Y-Ran's camp was like an island in the sky surrounded by rice fields. When we arrived, I was amazed at the number of people—maybe a hundred—who had joined together, but some were only passing through for a short stay.

From a distance, I heard someone say my name, and running across an opening was H'Nhien, calling to me, "I'm so glad to see you. Where have you been?"

For a moment, I could only stand with my arms around her before I could speak. "I have been assisting Dam Per Quay for a long time, but he had to go to Da Lat and couldn't take me, so Y-Wo is my protector until he returns. Are you here with your husband?"

"No, he has gone to Da Lat with Dam Per Quay."

I caught my breath, recalling what Ama had said: "You can't go because it is too dangerous." I patted her belly and immediately changed the subject to her growing family.

Y-Wo showed me where I should put my pack, and H'Nhien and I sat and talked a long time. She told me that H'Bloanh was in Buon Khit with a group and shared news of other friends.

Y-Wer's camp was positioned to allow soldiers to be watchful while many of us went down into the fields and gardens to gather vegetables and fruits. The villagers all around the area were very generous, and the Montagnards' friendship in the camp was welcoming. But with Dam Per Quay absent, the guards lacked attention to detail.

Very early on the third morning that I was there, four people from a nearby village came to the camp—three Montagnards (two women and one man) and one Vietnamese man whose name was Quang. He claimed himself to be from the Kpa Koi group and wanted to join up with us. H'Nhien and I were starting the morning meal over a fire near the leaders' house.

Y-Wer and Y-Ran welcomed our visitors, but as I listened to their conversation, I wondered how well they understood Quang's Vietnamese language. There was something in the way that Quang spoke and the way his body moved that made me question his sincerity. His eyes shifted from side to side as he talked, and he glanced around the campsite a lot during the discussion about the group's plans.

I buried some sweet potatoes in the ashes to finish cooking for the breakfast, wrapped a blanket around my shoulders, and went to the nearby stream to wash my face and to collect fresh water. As I rose up from filling the bottles, Quang appeared at my side and offered to help. I said that I could take care of everything myself and backed away from him.

He followed my moves. "Do you know that this group is living in a dream?" He paused. "I feel sorry for you. Why are you not in school?" I did not answer. He pointed to the stream. "Are you going to drink that dirty water?"

He kept talking. They were not bad questions, but too many. He had a fine face, was about fifty years old, and told me that he had three sons. I did think that he was concerned, but he was not like our people. He was too forceful. And why was he even talking to me? Finally, I said, "Why are you here?"

"Because I want to join your group. I want to help."

Our conversation stopped when we reached the fire where H'Nhien continued stirring a pot. She looked at me questioningly, but I didn't say anything. Who could I tell about my suspicions? Our leaders trusted him, but I saw him as someone inspecting our camp and asking for too much information.

The day passed quickly, and Quang joined us for the evening meal. He didn't eat much, as he said that he missed his family. Y-Wer and Y-Ran were understanding and spoke about their own families, and then to increase my fear, they gave him an R18 weapon for his protection.

I kept my eyes away from faces. I had not decided what to do, but their approving trust made me nervous. That night the snoring in the house was very loud, but my eyes only rested. Then the sound of someone walking past my sleeping place made me open my eyes to see Quang leaving with his R18 gun.

I lifted my head and said in a Vietnamese, "*Clui Quang, di dau vay?*" (Uncle, where are you going?)

He turned sharp in my direction and said, "I can't sleep. It's too cold."

I answered him by inviting him to stay near the fire, and I got up and brought more wood to make additional heat and to make enough light to awaken our group. Y-Wer called from his mat, "Is that you, Quang?"

Quang answered, "Yes, I'm here. I am warming by the fire."

Y-Wer settled back to sleep, and not a person moved the rest of the night.

Early in the second night, no one heard Quang get up to leave. We were all asleep soundly. But some of our soldiers returning from a nearby village with gifts of food saw Quang on the trail. They stopped and questioned him, and his first answers were not acceptable to the patrol.

I heard this when I awoke, aware of men in the house talking to Y-Wer and Y-Ran. The commander of the soldiers told Y-Wer and Y-Ran the details and said that he had directed ways to get better answers from Quang. Once the truth was revealed, Quang was "lost" in the jungle forever. Y-Tai's words stung, but he made it clear that we must all break up camp and move immediately.

Quang was a spy, paid by the Buon Thuot government run by the Viet Cong, to report back to them about our location and numbers. The VC was planning to surround us with one hundred or more soldiers and to kill our entire group. He not only had gained the trust of our leaders but also had deceived the Montagnards who had brought him to our camp. In the jungle, there was no second chance.

Packing was difficult in the dark, but we were practiced in being ready and alert, and everyone knew what to do with very little warning. H'Nhien and I were ready when Y-Wo came to get us.

By the early light of day, six of us, led by Y-Wo, were far into another part of the Highlands, exhausted but alive and thanking God for his protection and our safety. After a short rest, we moved through the cover of the jungle toward the Buon Khit region. Other groups from the camp made their own escape routes to avoid threatening danger.

The nightmare was over and seemed only a dream, but we all knew the guards failed to tightly secure the camp. That one mistake and misplaced trust could have cost all of us our lives. As the jungle had made me sensitive to sounds—to the habits of birds and monkeys and slithering snakes—I also was a quiet observer of the language of body movements and honest eyes. The next time that I was suspicious, I would not be just a listener.

## *Back to Buon Khit*

In the Buon Khit region, we joined others at a camp that was not too close to the village. Soldiers were more alert and stood guard in wide circles. We had come too close to not seeing another day.

When H'Bloanh heard that we were nearby, she came from the village to the camp. There was much rejoicing among the three of us, but it did not last long as there was no word from Dam Per Quay or H'Nhien's husband.

H'Bloanh sat by my side while I told her of our close escape from the Viet Cong, and she became serious with me when I finished. "We all need some direction that only Dam Per Quay can give us. I believe that we will be moving into Cambodia soon."

"He has been gone so long—two months now," I said.

"I know, and one of the civilians has heard from a relative who is with him in Da Lat. They have been in a difficult fight with the Viet Cong around An Lac, and there is no word about injuries or deaths. Y-Wer and Y-Ran must have heard this by now. God bless all of them!" H'Bloanh closed her eyes and bowed her head.

The information spread quickly around the camp: Dam Per Quay and his men were on their way and would travel through Yang Reh. Our leaders chose ten soldiers to go to Yang Reh to wait for the group and to lead them to us at Buon Khit. Yang Reh, between Buon Thuot and Da Lat, still offered safe passage for weary fighters.

## *Vivid Dream*

The night before Ama returned, I had a disturbing dream. In it Y-Niam, Ama's trusted friend, and someone whom I called brother at Yang Reh turned his back and kept walking away from me. I ran after him but never got close enough to touch him. He wore a red shirt, and as I begged him to stop, the red became smaller and smaller and soon disappeared in a mist.

I awoke early in the morning, remembered the vanishing figure, and pushed the negative dream to the back of my thoughts. Soon happiness overcame me when one of Dam Per Quay's soldiers arrived with the news that he was not far away. H'Nhien and I left our cooking and immediately ran out in the direction where the soldier had pointed. We first saw the guards, then Ama, and more of his soldiers, all slowly walking with weapons strapped over their sweat-stained uniforms.

My eyes were only on Ama. He looked up and smiled and didn't object when I took his heavy pack and put it on my shoulders. They all seemed to be in a world somewhere else.

A trusted friend walked with Dam Per Quay and gave me a hand with the pack, but another of the leaders was missing.

"Where is Y-Niam?" I asked in a voice that did not really want to know.

Ama hesitated, "He's gone."

"Gone where?" My dream of the night before suddenly made my stomach sink inward.

"He is gone. He died," that was all Ama said.

"Why?" Silence. I only heard footsteps on the path.

There was a stillness in the camp the rest of the day as news of the fighting and of the casualties spread through the hearts of friends and family. After he washed and dressed in clean clothes that I had readied for him, Ama sat against a tree and quietly smoked a cigar, alone in his thoughts. My few words of comfort for him and for me were swallowed up in our grief.

After the evening meal, Ama sent word for the camp to gather.

"We must pray for all who lost their lives as we fight for freedom, and tonight we must especially remember our brother, Y-Niam." He paused for some time and then added, "We were trapped after crossing a stream. Y-Niam stayed behind, shooting as though there were many of us. He distracted the Viet Cong long enough for our escape. They killed him. He saved our lives. He saved my life."

Like a magnet, the heavy silence drew us together, as did the strain from years of war, of running, of hunger, of exhaustion, of absence, of loss, of great sadness, of thankfulness. God's power sustained us. My dream haunted me. But as I thought about Y-Niam, his plain message comforted me: "Believe! I am safe, I feel no pain, I am free."

# BROKEN TRUST,
# NEW COMMITMENTS,
# SHATTERED SANCTUARY

## *Fresh Leaders, Old Faces*

Y-Dhun Nie Buondap, H'Nhien's husband, took the place of his cousin, Y-Niam, as the confidential guard of Dam Per Quay. After a few days' rest, Ama said, "We all will go to Yang Reh."

We remained on the mountain for two months, protected from VC troops by a group of soldiers who settled, with N'Du as leader, on the lower slopes.

Two weeks into our time there, Dam Per Quay and some of his guards went down to the base camp to see N'Du. I remained at the top and went to the stream to wash clothes. I was close enough to some of the soldiers who were washing pots to overhear their conversation about their experience in Da Lat.

At first I kept quiet and washed slowly so that I could hear more clearly although I pretended not to be paying attention. Their words stunned me.

"I was confused by Dam Per Quay's orders," said one of the soldiers. "Glad I was not the one to carry them out!" He stopped scrubbing his pan and stared at the water. "I didn't know three of the soldiers that he had killed, but the three of them, including Colonel Nicolas, had traveled with us."

My heart seemed to stop, and a sick flush rose to my face. Words flew out of my mouth, "Why would he do something like that?"

They abruptly stood up and turned my way. "We do not know for sure," one of the men said with hesitation in his voice. "We think that they didn't follow his directions and threatened him in some way. You must not say anything."

I sat back down and moved my hands over the clothes, frightened and dazed. "I cannot think of speaking those words."

## *Y-Si Nye at Yang Reh*

After the meeting in Buon Hra, where the provisional government was established, Dam Per Quay had named Y-Si Nie vice president in charge of Yang Reh. I had not thought about that for a long time. But now, at Yang Reh, something seemed familiar. *What is it about this man who is a stranger and yet very familiar? His face, his voice—he seems to be from somewhere deep in my memory.* After a few days, I recalled an incident that happened when I was visiting my ama and ami in Cheo Reo City in 1974, away from Mi Nu Trinh Vuong School in Qui Nhon.

Ama had invited a friend to come to the house to have some rice wine, and Ami sent me to the market for extra food. It was not a far trip; however, on the way home, my right pedal fell off my rusty bike. After trying to make the five-mile ride on one pedal, I gave up and started walking beside the bike.

A man in a white truck, going the opposite way, slowed down and asked if I needed help. He was not wearing a uniform, so I looked straight and kept walking faster for fear that he was one of the army in disguise. The truck turned around and followed me. There was nowhere for me to go off the road, and I wouldn't leave my bike.

"I see that your bicycle is broken. I can help you and take you home. Where do you live?" he spoke from his window.

I just kept walking and shook my head. He got out of his truck, took my bicycle, and put it in the back, but I walked as fast as I could, and he slowly followed. Finally I gave up and got into his truck; I couldn't lose my bike.

His continued to question me.

I spoke in the Jarai dialect, *"Hogot ih ci king to nha kao?"* (Why do you keep asking me that?)

He tried to give me his business card. I would not take it, but I did see his name.

About fifteen minutes later, his truck sputtered and ran out of gas.

I jumped out and went to the back where he had put my bicycle. My village was in eyesight. He got out of the truck and lifted my bike down to the ground.

It was the same motion that he used after a long day of hiking to Yang Reh when he helped me take off my backpack. Suddenly, the pieces fit together, and the name on his business card returned to me: Y-Si Nie.

Here he was in the Highlands of Vietnam as my jungle ama's vice president. We laughed together over the incident and wondered at the chance of meeting again under such circumstances. And after four years, I finally thanked him for the ride.

## *Guard Training*

Three nights a week, Y-Si Nie took his time training each of us in the camp to be a lookout guard. It was not too difficult. We just had to be alert to sounds and motions around us, and if we saw or heard anything unusual, we were to run fast back to the person on guard at the camp and give a warning, or if we could not identify the motion, we were to fire a shot in the air from the gun that Y-Si Nie trained us to use.

When I arrived down the mountain, about one hundred yards from our sleeping group for my first guard duty, I gave the identification whistle that we had been taught to do, and a recognition whistle was returned. H'Bloanh was on duty. She shoved a gun into my hands and said, "It has been quiet. Don't shoot anyone—or yourself!" In the dim light from a setting moon, I saw a slight smile. She turned and retraced my steps back to the camp. My first watch was short—from 12:00 midnight until 2:00 a.m., only two hours.

*What can be easier?*

I leaned back against a large rock and wrapped myself in the blanket I had brought to keep away the cold breeze. My ears were sharp listeners as I grew accustomed to the night sounds and adjusted my eyesight to the stars and the dark night. And I did well, probably every bit of ten minutes, before my eyes closed and sleep took over. I dreamed that I was falling, and when my head fell to one side, I awoke with a sudden jerk. Slowly I sat up, conscious of every sound and frozen in place for fear of what I might have missed. I only heard a few night insects and the rumbling of my stomach. Gradually I relaxed and decided that I could stay awake the rest of my patrol if I only had a little something to eat.

I had no watch to tell me the time, but I knew that I was a fast runner, so I hurried up the path to my shelter, fumbled around in my backpack, and came up with hands as empty as my stomach. When I looked at those empty hands, the thought of the gun that I had left on the ground by the rock shocked me. There was no longer any hunger, as my heart surged into that vacant space, while I raced back to my lookout. The gun was gone.

The sound of the guards' whistle alerted me to H'Rei's arrival. I answered her. She approached and said, "It's two o'clock. What do I do?"

I was ashamed to answer. "I left the gun here for a minute, and now it's gone."

We both looked over the area in the dark but found nothing. "I don't know what to say, but it was here when I ran back to the camp for a minute."

I did not have to see her face to know that she was unhappy to guard with no protection. I offered to stay with her, but she insisted that I return to camp. With heavy footsteps I went back to my shelter, totally covered myself with my blanket, and tossed and turned on my mat the rest of the night.


In the morning, Y-Si Nie called the guards for a meeting. I walked there with my eyes on the ground, expecting big trouble.

The words he said before he called my name were blurred, and when he said, "H'Tien, *never* leave your gun when you are on watch! The enemy can sneak up on us, take that weapon, and shoot all of us."

His words stung like my eyes, but I knew that I deserved everything that he said, and I felt all of the disapproval from my friends. I managed to speak, "I am very, very sorry, and I hope that I may be forgiven. I will not do it again. I'm so sorry."

"I know this was the first time that you were on guard, you can be forgiven, but you must take it more seriously."

"I promise," I murmured. "I promise! Thank you!"

After the meeting, he came over to me, his slim figure bent over as he looked down and reminded me again about the bicycle four years before. He teased me about speaking to him in Jarai, and we both managed to laugh at my shyness. Even though he was about Dam Per Quay's age, he had a kindness that Ama lacked, and I was especially grateful for his friendship in those moments.

## Dam Per Quay Returns to Yang Reh with H'Lonh

When Dam Per Quay returned to Yang Reh Mountain from Buon Hra, he brought with him the three women we had previously met there: H'Lonh, H'Ngonh, and H'Juaih. They were of the Rhade tribe. H'Lonh stayed with our group, and the other two camped with groups who needed them to help with cooking and washing.

As usual, I was glad to see Dam Per Quay, and I felt confident that he would protect me, but I also recognized that he now had someone else to care for. And I knew about General Nicholas but would never speak to him about the incident.

He and H'Lonh stayed in a shelter away from the center of our camp. I listened and observed to see exactly what part she would have in watching over him and in tending chores. He still called me his daughter and clearly wanted H'Lonh and me to be friends. That was not difficult as she was almost as shy as I was and wished to please Ama and her new family.

Cooking was something that she did well. I tried to help her with unfamiliar jungle foods around Yang Reh. We did not have gardens, but our men were good hunters, and we often had monkey brains, birds, large snakes, hearts of the palm tree, wild berries, or fruits found within a mile around us. H'Lonh soon became the main cook for our entire unit of ten.

It was an easier time for me. I slept with H'Bloanh and H'Nhien (her husband was away), and we had time to talk and laugh and sometimes dance while the guitars played.

I was no longer responsible for washing Dam Per Quay's clothes or making his coffee or packing his backpack. My freedom brought a lot of joy. H'Bloanh and I often hiked out to surrounding areas, up to the higher rocks, to gather wood for our fires or to explore the forests for new fruits. H'Lonh always smiled and thanked us when we returned.

Except for our shyness, H'Lonh and I were opposite in personality, but we became good friends. I helped her learn how to handle Dam Per Quay's various moods, and I called her sister. She was afraid to leave the camp and didn't mind the cooking and washing. She had not yet experienced the tougher side of jungle life—the almost-routine days of hiding, running, and sleeping on top of graves, and poisonous centipedes, scorpions, and black widows.

Yang Reh was a place that I held near to my heart. For four years, no matter how much we traveled back and forth, from danger to safety, from hunger to plenty, through tears and laughter, it was a haven between Buon Thuot and Da Lat.

And on Sundays, Y-Hin Nie preached the Gospel, and we sang praises to God, and we asked for help until the end, whenever and wherever that might be. It was lovely and serene—a refuge from the horrors of the inhumanity forced on the Montagnard culture. Our only desire was to live free and in harmony with our families and with the land. Evil seemed to disappear when the sun settled into the valleys below.

## *Final Day at Yang Reh Mountain*

The camp was quiet. Some of us were sleeping after our midday meal. Suddenly an enormous noise jolted us from our naps and shook the mountain so hard that my body throbbed as though thunder had rolled through my bones. The sound jerked me from my bamboo mat. I stood as silence penetrated the camp, trying to think. Yelling and pointing and running in lots of directions pushed me into motion.

I ran to Ama. He was already out and staring at his surroundings. N'Du rushed toward us, shouting, "Ong Kra, come with me quick. Hurry, hurry! The VC have launched a rocket on the mountain. No time to explain! H'Tien, Ong Kra, H'Lonh, come—there is a way out. Quick! Grab your packs!"

We were prepared in case this event suddenly happened, but when it did, it was such a shock that it took me a moment to put into practice the drill that I knew so well. It was N'Du who brought us to the reality that we were very much in danger, and immediate action could save our lives. I heard shouted directions and saw uniforms, guns, men, women, and packs all in a blur, but N'Du was steady in his insistence that speed was critical.

H'Bloanh and H'Nhien appeared from somewhere with their packs. H'Juaih and H'Ngonh followed a few minutes later. We did not speak, but fear held us together, and we began to follow N'Du as he had instructed. Yang Reh was our rock, our sanctuary, our joy in the face of our persecution. The intrusion on our mountain was a merciless violation of our tentative peace. But there had been only one rocket so far, and for an hour or more, hurried footsteps took fifty of us down the path of escape, away from our now-scarred sanctuary.

N'Du allowed a short rest. I turned to look upward as my heart shattered, and the tears flowed. I crossed myself and softly prayed out loud, "God, help us! Where do we go from here? I beg you to be with all of us!" God was my refuge, I knew. He was my strength, but I felt so weak.

Another rocket exploded on the mountain, and then another. Our peace was totally broken. *God, look over our soldiers and show them the way to safety.*

## Ordered to Da Lat

We heard that some of our group went to Buon Thuot. Dam Per Quay ordered N'Du to lead us to Da Lat. It was not an easy march, as we kept mostly in the dense forests. Some of the mountain paths took us up much higher than Yang Reh, and we stayed on the move more than we slept, but no one uttered a protest. The journey brought fresh memories of our earlier jungle years, only now the explosions that destroyed our mountain echoed in our saddened hearts, and the chatter of other times stayed in the past. *Dear God, is there another place?*

We, especially Ama, were fortunate to have N'Du. He was clever and sensitive to sounds of the nature around us and to the needs of the people he was leading. He taught us how to duckwalk across the pine-covered floor of the jungle so that we would not slip down or turn an ankle, and he knew plants that were good to eat in the areas that were new to us. He was a kind man—a strong man.

After days of walking, Da Lat was still in the distance. We approached from a new direction but passed a few fields and gardens where we picked fresh vegetables that we ate raw: pumpkin, hot peppers, sweet potatoes. Empty stomachs could only digest small amounts at a time, but each bite eased the rumblings. Fires for cooking were too dangerous and rest periods too short, but we relied on messages that security was ahead. So our large group of fifty kept hidden as we marched and complained little of our hardship.

# *Dam Rong District*

The people who owned the fields near Da Lat came out to meet us after two of our scouts went into their village to inquire about safety. The people of Chang Tor camp were very sweet and made us feel quite welcome. Their language was different, but I still remember the first words that they spoke: "*Niam sa?*" (How are you?). Their dialect had a rhythm that added a soft musical touch to my soul. Even though we were all strangers, they showed us their good hearts and immediately shared their food. It was cooked quite differently, but I ate it with thanksgiving for their kindness and their generosity.

We had ended up in the Dam Rong district where there were many regions and villages, and I was sure that we had stumbled on the best.

Dam Per Quay, H'Lonh, H'Juaih, and H'Ngonh were given a house for sleeping, and H'Bloanh, H'Nhien, and I had a small house all to ourselves. It was like the home that I had left behind years before, and I sat at the door, longing for news of my family, grateful for these wonderful, unselfish new friends.

The day after we arrived, H'Bloanh and I went with a villager into the jungle to search for food and to have our first lesson about unfamiliar wild vegetables. I only knew the bamboo shoots, but there were so many more wild vegetables and leaves that we gathered and later learned to cook properly so we won't get sick. The *nham biap* was a bush with especially tender and sweet red and yellow leaves (green ones were old). The bushes only grew in that area, and the leaves turned out to be a favorite of mine. She showed us the difference between good and poisonous mushrooms and how to select fresh ferns from along the stream, which ran by Chang Tor and other camps in the district.

"Always cut new wood instead of dead wood," she said. "It will burn longer and keep you warm all night." We needed her advice, because it was colder there than at Yang Reh.

"Thank you for all of your help," we both said to her. "We would be lost if we had tried to come alone," I added. "It will take us several hikes to remember the jungle signs. Thank you, we are happy to be with you in this place!"


Two weeks later, people from other villages came to bring gifts to Dam Per Quay and to see the strangers from far away. They brought chickens to slaughter, rice, bananas, dried fish, rice wine, and vegetables. Truly, each one was a treasured offering.

Two ministers came and led us in prayer services. They helped me feel more connected to God. I prayed every day, but sometimes I wondered if God heard me or if my prayers were correct. We had news that the new government was trying to take away the Catholic Church and to keep the Montagnards and Vietnamese from worshipping together. That was very sad to me, and I welcomed the touch of anyone from the Christian faith.

One evening, all of the guests assembled for a celebration party. Dam Per Quay thanked everyone for their love and respect and spoke of our appreciation. We ate and danced around a large fire to guitar music, while Dam Per Quay enjoyed the rice wine too much.


An additional fifty soldiers and followers put a real strain on the villagers at Chang Tor. Food for that many was becoming more difficult to find. The people were so kind that they apologized to Ama when they discussed the problem with him, but he understood. And the next day, he announced to our group that we would be moving in two days. Once he saw a problem, his decisions came quickly.

# COMMAND UNREST—
# VIOLATED TRUST

## Dang Jri Camp

Dang Jri was still in the Dam Rong district—only a day's hike—but a few stayed behind at Chang Tor with new friends and knew that they could join us later. Scouts again went ahead to warn the camp that we were coming, so another welcome by the camp's leader, Krajan Xuyen, was well prepared by the time we arrived in late evening.

Dang Jri was in another beautiful lowland setting in the center of the district with a stream running through the middle of the camp. Maybe that was the reason that there were so many more people in this camp. Their fields were nearby and well farmed, and although a challenge, they were better equipped to handle fifty more people, especially if one of them was Dam Per Quay.

Days after we were comfortably settled, a new woman, H'Ock, from Quang Duc came to the camp and seemed to find favor with Dam Per Quay late at night. He still lived with H'Lonh, but I knew, and probably others also, that he made his way between two places in the darkness. I thought that this would damage his reputation and anger some of the people, but I stayed silent.

Another officer, Colonel Knam, and his son Dack (about eighteen years of age) were living at the camp. The colonel had escaped from jail and had information for Dam Per Quay. They met late into the night, and I brought them water and coffee. I saw

Colonel Knam give Ama his wristwatch, but I didn't understand. The next day, Ama gave it to H'Lonh and said, "Keep it! It is a gift from Colonel Knam."

Something was not right with Dam Per Quay. It appeared to me that his life and his position were as a woven mat that was beginning to unravel.

I watched civilian families come often to visit the soldiers, and I heard a few of them say to Dam Per Quay, "Have you eaten the long banana yet?"

He always waved to them and said, "No, but I will."

I never asked him any questions, but as I listened, I understood that it was a reference to someone's long nose. And there was only one person who met that description, but I still didn't understand.

Two weeks later, I realized that I had not seen Knam or Dack around camp. I thought that they might have gone to Chang Tor, but I didn't mention it to Ama.

I had extra time in the afternoon and decided to go to the stream alone to catch some little crabs and shrimp for our dinner. I was not having any luck, so I began to fill my basket with fresh cinnamon fern as I walked along the bank. In the distance, I saw smoke coming from a small hut and went to see who was there. I didn't think about being afraid. As I approached, I saw Dack bent over the stream, washing a pan.

"What are you doing here?" I asked, surprised by the pale skin on his face.

"They keep us here."

"What do you mean? Who keeps you here?" I looked in the hut, and there was Colonel Knam on a mat, appearing very sick. He was so thin that his cheeks were drawn inward, which made his nose seem much longer. I gasped at his appearance and at the comments I had heard in the camp.

"I will go back and find you some medicine, but it is late, and I cannot return today."

"Thank you, H'Tien! I don't want to get you in trouble."

I left before he said more, but I kept repeating to myself, "Who, who, who wants them to stay? Why?" I could not sleep much that night, wondering what I could do for them.

The next morning, I asked Ama for something to help my headache. He gave me a pill, an Advil, which I hid for later, but I knew that I would need more than that. I would have to steal them. It was an ugly thought for me. Sister Helen taught me, "When you think about doing something bad, put your thumbs down. When you think about doing good, hold your thumbs up. It will help you guard against temptations."

I put my thumbs up and then down, and then up and finally down, saying to myself that I had a reasonable excuse. In the morning when I folded Ama's blanket, I took four more pills—two for Knam and two for Dack. I made on myself the sign of the cross and asked God to forgive me.

After lunch, I took my basket again to the stream and hurried out of sight toward the hut. When I arrived, I called out to them, "It's H'Tien. I'm here with some medicine." There was no answer. I looked in the door and saw that they both were too sick to move off their mats. I eased into the hut and handed Dack the pills; then I took two water bottles to the stream and filled them. My mind raced with thoughts. *What else can I do? It is awful to leave them here.*

"I must go. I don't know whether these pills will help, but I cannot get any more. I wish that I could stay and cook for you."

Dack nodded his head and whispered, "Thank you!"

I hurried back, picking ferns on the way so that no one would suspect what I had just done. I was pretty sure that Ama would not miss the four pills from the many that he had.

A week later, many leaders from different villages came to Dang Jri for a meeting that lasted into the late afternoon. I helped prepare their lunch. Knam and Dack were there but were thin and bent over with their illness. We only glanced at one another. It was the last time that I saw them. I did not know where they went, but I heard that someone killed them. It was hard to believe that anyone but the enemy could have done such a thing.

A month later, I got up the courage to ask Ama if he had seen Knam and Dack.

He said, "They went to China."

"When will we go to China?" I began to brighten.

"Later!" he said in a voice that put a stop to our conversation.

## *Moving Becomes Normal*

Dam Per Quay began to move more often, not always taking me with him. I don't know whether or not he sensed that I had observed more than he wanted and that I was becoming a danger to him. He still was good to me, but I felt his tension.

Chang Tor and Dang Jri camps were not too far apart, and I was moved with small groups back and forth, occasionally with Ama. But he traveled to numerous camps all over the Highlands and took H'lonh with him, especially to PC 8 Base in the Da Lat City.

In the Dang Jri camp, the people taught me their language while I learned their different customs. I could weave bamboo baskets and work the fields, harvest wheat, and plant crops to make money. Five pleasant months, with less tension, was my longest stay there.


The week before Ama left for PC 8, he sent N'Du to Quang Duc with H'Ock, his "companion," so that she could visit her family. That was what I was told. I missed my good friend. She helped me chop fresh wood and prayed the rosary every day. I did not fully understand her Quang Duc language, but we loved each other.

When I first met H'Ock, I gave her money to go into Quang Duc to buy needles and thread for me to sew and mend clothes. She came back with nothing and never returned the money. I let it go, but Ama knew about it and must have held it in his mind.

N'Du was gone for a month. When he returned, H'Ock and her friend H'Ot were not with him. He looked at the ground a lot and avoided talking to me. I did not ask where they were, as I thought they must have stayed to be with her family. But when Dam Per Quay returned two months later, I did ask, "Where is H'Ock, Ama?"

He answered quickly, "She drowned."

I gasped, "But how did that happen?"

"I don't know. The water, too strong. No one could save her. She's gone."

That was his final word. I was overwhelmed with surprise, and soon with tears. *How? Why?* "*She is gone. No one could save her.*" *She was a good swimmer. That's no answer.*

Later I told him that I missed her, and he said that he did too. I said that she was going to buy me needles and thread.

"H'Lonh will share with you. Don't worry!"

Days later, I met a friend, Y-Tong, in the forest, and we chopped fresh wood together. To make conversation, I asked, "Did you have a good time when you went to Quang Duc?"

"No," was his abrupt reply.

"I thought that it was supposed to be a nice camp."

"N'Du killed H'Ock and H'Ot with his gun. Dam Per Quay ordered him to."

He quickly walked farther into the forest. I let the wood fall to the ground and stood in unbelieving silence. My shallow breathing caused me to drop to my knees before I fainted. I covered my face and rocked back and forth. *Why? Dam Per Quay is not a man to murder people—is he? Why? Would he have killed*

*N'Du if he had not followed orders? What had they done? It couldn't be over needles and thread. Why?*

I needed to think. Y-Tong probably had told me too much. I put some of the wood in my basket and turned back toward my small house. The rest of the day went in slow motion. *I must not let anyone know what I heard, especially Dam Per Quay. The enemy seems to be closer all of the time. I must concentrate on the enemy.* My normally silent mouth was good for me, as no one questioned my silence. But I could not look at Dam Per Quay in the eyes. He did not seem to notice that my heart was in confusion.

## *Dang Rahong Camp*

It was evident that Dam Per Quay had come only for a short visit to Dang Jri, for he quickly had a meeting with camp leaders and said that his group must go to Dang Rahong camp. I listened as I passed out water and coffee. It seemed that most of the men there said that it was too dangerous, but Ama did not hear that. He listened only to himself. "We leave tomorrow." After the meeting, he told H'Lonh, H'Juaih, and me to be ready.

I packed slowly. Again, something was not right. Ama made quick decisions, but my confidence in him had been shaken, and my stomach was uneasy. The enemy was closer; we need not take unnecessary risks. I could not say no. I pushed that thought way down inside.

# SHADOWS OF DEATH

The next morning, N'Du and Dam Per Quay led the way for seven soldiers and the three of us behind them. Near the end of the day, we came to the top of a hill and could smell smoke from cigarettes. The enemy had been there not too long before. A little farther we found warm ashes and small scraps of food. Someone, maybe Dam Per Quay, said, "Stop!" But N'Du said to keep walking toward an abandoned field that he knew was about an hour away.

When we reached the field, there was a small hut where we could safely cook a little food. I put the dried corn that we had brought in some water and began to boil it for our meal.

One of the soldiers near Ama aimed his gun and said, "Look, there is a deer in the field!"

Ama reached toward the soldier and said, "Don't shoot! Don't shoot!"

It was a second too late as the gun fired, and the deer fell. But shots immediately came from the other side of the field toward us.

I left the boiling corn in my favorite pot that Y-Tlur Eban had given me long ago and started running. Ama shouted at me, "Don't leave the pot! Go back!" My immediate reaction was to do as I was told. I grabbed the pot and my pack and ran as the shots came closer to us. It was like a nightmare in quick motion.

N'Du didn't seem to know what to do. We were running, but N'Du and two soldiers stuck next to Dam Per Quay to protect him, and everyone else darted like animals down a small path that led to the hill we had previously climbed. On the left was a deep valley; on the right, swampy wetlands. Shots came from somewhere in front, and we all fell to the ground under the thin forest covering, dragging our packs and crawling through soggy, muddy undergrowth.

Bullets rained down from the tops of the trees, and I covered my head and moaned, "Oh God, help us! We're in trouble. I'm so scared." I heard two men cry out in pain, and I tried to dig deeper into the forest floor and cover myself with leaves.

The guns were quiet for several hours. Somewhere around midnight N'Du crept through the forest to each of us to say that the enemy had gone, and we should move. He had found the two men, our friends and scouts, dead.

I could not see myself, but after moving my hands across my body, I could imagine that I was not as clean as a water buffalo. We spoke in whispers and helped one another with our packs, asking all of the time, "Are you okay? Are you hurt anywhere?"

Our two friends were a very big loss. They were not only good men, but they also knew signs and trails and details that scouts should know. They were trusted by Dam Per Quay and had kept us safe many, many times.

As we strapped on our packs, I could not say the words that were on my heart: *Are we going to leave our two friends here without a burial?* There was no time to explain our lack of compassion.

When I got close enough to Ama, I could tell from his movements that he was shaken. His mouth did not speak; his walk was unsteady. N'Du was the one to set us in the direction of Chang Tor.

We arrived early morning. The Chang Tor people met us with lots of worried questions. The first words that I heard from Ama were, "Thank God we are okay!"

H'Lonh, H'Juaih, and I walked into the nearby stream in our clothes, while friends cleared a house for us to share with Dam Per Quay. The water was cool and washed away the mud, but not the scars of fear. I had never been that close to death. There was not much conversation, even when someone came to the stream to tell us that Dam Per Quay was calling a meeting for late in the afternoon. All I wanted to do was curl up under a fresh blanket and close my eyes away from the world. *Will this ever end? Will all of us die soon?*

Dam Per Quay was direct in what he said. He began by instructing the girls who cooked to transfer to other groups. I sat in silence, but my eyes darted from face to face as he called out names.

He told H'Bloanh that she would go with Y-Hin Nie to Cheo Reo, and H'Nhien would go back to Buon Me Thuot. He assigned others to different camps, as I waited for him to look at me. "H'Tien, you will stay in Chang Tor camp with Y-Tlur Eban, Nay Guh, Y-Drun Nie, and Y-Rin Arul." Then he reassigned his men and soldiers into different areas. Everyone tried not to react to his plans, because no one questioned Dam Per Quay.

Two days later, Ama left for Dang Jri with H'Lonh, H'Juaih, N'Du, and new soldiers. He had not glanced my way, but I ran to him as he lifted his pack. I stopped, hesitated, and said, "Ama, good-bye and thank you for everything."

He would not, or could not, show emotion in front of his soldiers, but he put his hand on my shoulder and said in a low voice, "I'll miss you. Take care of yourself." Then he turned and walked out away from the camp.

I could not believe that H'Bloanh was going to Pleiku. *How can she be safe there? Isn't it dangerous? Why is he sending her to the city?*
That afternoon we walked by the stream and talked about all of the things that we had experienced together and what it would mean to be separated. There were more tears than laughter. The next day, as she came to say good-bye, our voices cracked as we tried to smile.

I said in a low voice so that only she could hear, "H'Blin, I pray that God will bless you and keep you safe and that we will see each other again."

We hugged; she put her hand on my face, "Be good and may luck be with you!"

"And also with you!"

We waved good-bye until her hand disappeared into the trees.

And luck was with me; God had a plan. I had a new family; happiness healed my fear.

My new friends looked after me as though I was one of their children. Their Kaho dialect was easy for me to learn, and I enjoyed being myself without Dam Per Quay. I hoped that he was safe, and I prayed every day for H'Bloanh and H'Nhien. But I also thanked God for allowing me to be in the jungle with kind and caring people, and I thanked them by doing my best with the cooking, washing, cleaning, and sewing. For three months my ears would not listen to the bad news, my mouth sang peaceful songs, and my stuttering was less noticeable.

One afternoon, while washing clothes by the stream, a friend came to find me. "There is a soldier in the camp who says that Dam Per Quay is coming to visit his daughter. He asked where you were, and someone said his daughter is H'Tien. Are you that daughter?"

I stopped my washing and stood up. "Where is he?"

"He is coming in a day or two. You must be happy."

I was happy and surprised and knew that I must prepare nice things for him. I quickly finished washing clothes and brought them to the house to dry. The house was small, but I would have it clean and looking nice for him and have plenty of freshly cut wood to burn at night to keep him warm.

Ama had been such an important part of my life. I was grateful for his protection and friendship, and I put my doubts and disappointments down deep inside. We were in the jungle, fighting against an enemy that I understood only through gunshots.

He came two days later. I met him at the edge of Chang Tor. I could feel emotion—joy mixed with a little uncertainty—from both of us.

"Bu, how are you? I have missed you." His voice was gentle.

"I have missed you too. How are you?"

"I am tired. Our march from Da Lat has been long."

"Then come and rest in my house. It is nice, and I have prepared food for you."

By evening, we were able to talk together a little.

I asked, "Ama, have you any news of H'Bloanh? Is she safe? I miss her so much."

"No, I don't know about her. H'Nhien was not feeling well, and friends brought her to Dang Jri camp. I have not heard any other news of her."

He changed the subject and tried to joke with me. "H'Tien, let me ask you, what do you feed your pigs? They are getting so fat."

He made me feel embarrassed. "Who are the pigs? What pigs? I don't understand." He was being rude, but he and H'Lonh both laughed at me.

"I'm sure that he means that you are so thin." She shifted her eyes from me to him and smiled.

Dam Per Quay closed his eyes and said nothing. But I guessed that he was really talking about the men from the area who had long hair, cleft palates, and ears pierced with wooden buttons and large rings. He always favored neatness when possible.

He stayed a week. H'Lonh and I cooked, washed clothes, and cleaned for him and his soldiers. Ama seemed relaxed, and I was glad to see him, but I reserved my speaking to little things. I was, and would always be, grateful to him, but I would never fully trust him again after all that I knew.

At the end of the week, he did not tell me but asked me if I would like to go with him to Lieng Khang. H'Lonh and H'Juaih would go with us. I said, "Yes, okay." But I went to Y-Tlur to ask his permission and told him that I would come back. He agreed and said that he would find someone to take my place until I returned.

## *Lieng Khang*

Nothing looked familiar walking toward Lieng Khang. We climbed a mountain for a long time, and when we reached the top, there were still no houses, villages, fields, but only a small hut where a man and his wife lived. Her name was Ritor. She was a nurse for expectant young women. She told me that H'Nhien had come to her during her pregnancy and was brought back to her the day before she delivered a baby boy.

I did not know what to say. It was the first time that I had heard about the birth. I was happy for her, but now she would have to watch for herself and for a baby.

While I asked Ritor a lot of questions about H'Nhien and the baby, Ama settled into a hammock, and we stayed the night. Since the hut was very small, I rolled up in a blanket and slept on the ground. I had forgotten how hard that could be, but when I tried to get up in the morning, I remembered. My body was like a rock that would not roll, and my eyes felt like dried corn cobs.

Ama kept calling for me to get up and pack my bag. "We must go."

Even Y-No Buon Krong (who replaced Y-Niam Buondap, H'Nhien's husband's cousin) came over to encourage me. "Dam Per Quay is ready."

I was up by then but moving like a snail. We told Ritor good-bye and thanked her and started down the path. Ama looked back at me and stopped, then moved forward, then stopped—three times. Finally, he told everyone to stop, and he came back to me. "*Bu*, you can stay here with sister Ritor. Would you like that?"

I thought that my ears had betrayed me. Before he could change his speech, I said, "Yes I would."

At the moment, I could not understand his eyes, but I knew that they had become softer. "*Bu*, be good. Ama will see you." And he turned in the direction of Lieng Khang.

I went back to the hut and to the generosity of Ritor and her husband. We did not speak much, and I took the day to relax and to think about Ama's unusual actions. I had only had a glimpse of that gentle side when I first met him, and he had vowed to take care of me. But this kindness that he acknowledged to me in front of his soldiers was a surprise that stayed in my thoughts all through the day. *What happened? Why is he allowing me to stay behind? Will I see him again? God, tell me what to do.*

I stayed one night and returned to Chang Tor camp by myself.

# DELIVERED INTO DARK DESPAIR

One week later, Ama sent a message to Krajan Xuyen, the leader of the district, to go to Chang Tor and take me to Dang Jri camp. I did not know what to say when his men arrived, but I went wherever the leaders told me to go. I was at Dang Jri for a month, receiving no information from Ama. Then Krajan Xuyen took a day trip to Chang Tor for a meeting and returned saying that we would move to Quang Duc camp. I was sad, but he said that all of the girls would go with us, even though some of them had families at Chang Tor. We would stay at Quang Duc until further orders.

We never got to Quang Duc. After a week of walking, we camped in a place of many palm trees. Every time that we went to a new area, I learned new foods, dialects, and ways to look invisible. There were a few different types of fruits and greens to cook around our camp, yet we ate a lot of the hearts of the palms. They were delicious, but very difficult to cut down. And there was a most unpleasant result to camping at our new site—dry leeches.

A month and a half we lived among the palms with the nightmarish leeches all around. They were only afraid of fire and smoke and left us alone in the areas of our bodies that we covered with fruit soap, but it was an everyday battle. We made the soap from a fruit that we beat into liquid form with bamboo stalks and then smeared over our bodies. After it dried, it made a shield that the leeches would not touch.

Occasionally in the mornings I would find a leech attached to my face and had to learn not to scream in terror. At night, my face was wet from tears that often washed away the soap. I hated that place, the war, the enemy, the slimy worms, the hiding, the stealing from farms. And I had no close friend like H'Bloanh.

When I thought that I could not last another day, soldiers came from the leader of the district, looking for me. They said, "We have orders to bring H'Tien and the girls back to Dang Jri district." I was so happy that I cheered and ran to zip up my pack. It was another week of walking, but I would not protest. I just thanked God for my liberation.

Again, our destination camp was different. The men had long hair and spoke the Rhade dialect. "Who are these people, and where do they come from?" I asked our leader.

"They come from Buon Me Thuot. Their camp has been here for several months."

A few people sat around wooden bowls rounded out from tree trunks. I was glad to see H'Juen Nay and a girl whom I recognized from Da Lat, so I joined them. It was a joy, even after a long journey, to be pounding rice again.

H'Juen Nay smiled at me. "You remember pounding rice in the wood mill?"

And another one nearby asked, "Are you H'Tien?

I looked from one to another and said yes to both questions.

Another glanced my way. "Would you like to stay here?"

"It doesn't matter. The jungle is the jungle." I pounded the rice harder.

"Maybe you would like to go to Buon Me Thuot."

"Yes, I would if I am told to do so."

"Do you recognize me?" a long-haired man asked.

"No!" I replied and looked at him again. Still he was unfamiliar. I was glad for new conversation but tired of the questions.

My arms ached from the pounding, and the soreness from a week of walking seemed to rush over me at once. I left the group to settle my belongings. Across the shelters, hammocks, and small houses, I saw N'Du coming toward me. I moved quickly to his side and held out my hands. "How are you? Are you with Dam Per Quay? Is he here?"

"H'Tien, let's go down to the stream near the edge of the camp."

I did not like the way that his eyes avoided mine. I just hurried along beside him in silence.

We stopped, and he motioned for me to sit on a flat rock beside the water.

"This is difficult for you, for all of us, but I must tell you that your ama, Dam Per Quay, is dead."

I stared at him. "What do you mean?" I started to get up and then sat back into a heap, only to rise up and look at him with eyes too wide to cover my disbelief. "Where was he—an accident?" The knot in my stomach grew larger. I hesitated. "Did someone kill him?"

"H'Tien, I cannot tell you more. And I ask that you do not speak of this to anyone. It is not good to talk about it. But I knew that I had to be the one to inform you. I must go now; I can't tell you where, but maybe we will meet again soon." He vanished as if it were all a dream.

My body was rigid. I don't know how long I sat there, not trusting his words, but tears were spilling from my eyes. *My God! Oh my God! Is the enemy that close? Did someone in our army kill him? He wasn't good to everyone...and the people he had killed. I cannot think about that. He was good to me. The last time, he told me, "Bu, be good. Ama will see you." Did he think...? God, if I had been with him...* My thoughts froze, and my body began to shake. The tears would not stop, and my head spun with aches and shooting pain. *What has happened to H'Lonh and H'Juaih?*

I don't know how long I sat there, but the day became gray, and I finally uncoiled my shocked soul and went to the stream to wash. Avoiding conversation was not a problem. I just kept to myself until I could escape under my blanket, into the darkness of the night.

# GRIEF, JOY, PAIN, AND FAITH

## *Krajan Xuyen at Dang Jri Camp*

I saw the new faces around the camp for a week and then heard that they went back to Buon Me Thuot. I stayed and cooked for Krajan Xuyen. My duties were the same as in so many camps, and he did not complain about my cooking, so I continued my routine, with few words and a heavy heart.

I kept my voice pleasant, but my friends were few. No familiar faces showed up in the camp, none of Ama's faithful soldiers. The frustration grew and multiplied, and I could not even ask what happened to H'Lonh and H'Juaih. I longed to get away from Krajan Xuyen's jealous wife from the nearby village who made comments to others about me, so I was often teased about my relationship with Krajan Xuyen. It was very disagreeable.

Finally, his wife wrote to me and said that she was afraid that I would steal her husband. It was such a silly idea.

I replied to her letter:

> You do not need to worry about me and your husband. You should leave your village more often and visit him at his camp. Come and cook for him and be happy with him. I did not ask for that job.

The morning after she received my letter, she appeared in the camp wearing makeup, fancy clothes, and high heel shoes. It was the first time I had laughed in weeks. No one came to the jungle dressed like that, especially wobbling in high heel shoes and all dressed up. I wondered if she would break a foot walking in the dirt and across tree roots. But Krajan Xuyen liked it. They both smiled a lot more, and I had less cooking to do.

# H'Nhien and Her Baby

News traveled from camp to camp in the words of soldiers and their followers. I heard that H'Nhien had a baby boy and was only three days' march away. They told of her escape from the Viet Cong across a river when she was more than ten months pregnant. Gunshots followed her as she swam to the other side, but she was saved by God's grace. Her baby stayed protected in her body until, a day later, she was able to reach Ritor, who helped her with the delivery.

My heart filled with joy and great concern for H'Nhien. When I saw Krajan Xuyen, I asked permission to go to her to help with the baby. He refused until after the third request, and declaration that "I won't stay. I will come back." He looked defeated, and I filled my pack with everything that was mine.


H'Nhien and I hugged for so long that our tears of joy rolled down on each other's shoulders. Then she took me inside her small hut, introduced me to her baby boy, and showed me the tooth that he had when he was born. My whole body tingled when I held that new life. "He's beautiful, so cute. He looks like his name should be Jeremy."

H'Nhien smiled. "That is a good name."

"I heard that you were almost killed swimming away from the Viet Cong. How did you ever make it across the river?"

"I prayed. I prayed for me, but I prayed harder for the baby."


Little Jeremy was good, and we were able to spend a lot of time catching up on where we had been, and she told me the horrible details about Ama's death.

"First, they killed my husband, Y-Dhun Buondap, then Y-Blieng Nie, and then Y-Nhanh, Dam Per Quay's brother.

Finally they shot Dam Per Quay. It took place at Lieng Khang on October 2 [1978]. One of Dam Per Quay's guards, Y-No Buon Krong, escaped."

My body felt sick all over again, and my eyes could only look at the ground. "Who killed him? Why did they kill him?" I let that come out slowly as I raised my head to look at her.

"I cannot say."

"What happened to H'Lonh and H'Juiah?"

H'Nhien hesitated for too long. "You don't want to know."

"Yes, tell me everything."

She took a deep breath, waited a few moments, and looked at the ground when she spoke. "They were both tied to a flagpole and made to watch. The men took the clothes from the dead bodies and wore them around the camp. Since H'Lonh and H'Juiah were not of Dam Per Quay's family, they were let go." I don't know where they are now.

After all of the endless days and nights in the jungle, the years of respecting life, the shootings, the deceptions, the hunger, I had no tears. I went in the forest behind H'Nhien's hut and vomited up what emotion I had left in me.

## *No Going Back*

I stayed. In the response to the letter that I received from Krajan Xuyen, telling me to return to Dang Jri, I said, "I am helping H'Nhien. She needs me now."

I cut up my clothes and made new ones for little Jeremy. At first, he brought such joy into both of our lives, even though there was always a worry for his safety—and for ours. Babies were not a welcome addition to jungle life. They could cry when the enemy was near; they could slow a group down when traveling, and they kept the mothers from working in the camps. If a mother did not care for the baby properly, the baby might be tossed in a river to drown. That was not going to happen to Jeremy. His mother was able to provide milk, and I strapped Jeremy to my back in a sling while doing my duties. But H'Nhien had a lot of depression. She did not know why her husband was killed; she had responsibility for a new baby and often distanced herself from him in case he would suddenly be taken away. So we moved to a different site, thinking that the change would help her.

## *Dong Knoh Camp*

The three of us left Balmah camp and made our way to Dong Knoh, which was in the same area; however, we felt safer with the baby at Dong Knoh. There we met H'Bo Eban, who had just arrived from Dang Rahong, and who moved in with us.

We immediately offered our skills: I would cook for Tang Ang, and H'Bo would cook for other soldier groups, but we all would help with sewing and washing and gathering food for the almost one hundred inhabitants.

The people in the camp were kind and offered H'Nhien help with Jeremy. They were fascinated by the baby boy and gave us a small hut with enough room for two, maybe three, people. We put our packs there, wondering if night would bring us together to sleep like a new litter of kittens.

The men could see that the room was too tight, and in just one day, they built a small hut for H'Bo and me. It was separate from the others but across from Tang Ang, their leader. We both were afraid to live alone, so were very grateful to have a place together. When Tang Ang said, "Your house is finished. Take your packs there!" we left our chores and rushed from H'Nhien's, saying, "Thank you! Thank you!" to the men who had worked so quickly.

There was enough room to sleep and to place our belongings on a bamboo floor surrounded by bamboo walls. It did not matter to us that the house was cold and smelled damp. We got out our long knives and immediately went to the forest to cut wood for a fire.

Dull knives were not meant for chopping trees, especially tall ones, but they were all that we had. Our main concern was which wood burned the best. The trees were all unfamiliar. We agreed on a tall one that would provide lots of wood and started sawing and hacking on either side. The possibility of hacking each other was high, but somehow we safely reached close enough to the middle to imagine that we could push it over.

We strained and rocked and put our shoulders to the tree, and it slowly gave in and bent over to the ground. It took revenge on me, though, and on the way down, a branch stripped my long skirt and would not let go. I just stood there stunned for a moment until H'Bo and I both burst out laughing at the same time. After I finally got my breath and stopped clapping my hands, words came flying out of my mouth. "Run, get some pants for me! No one can see me like this! Hurry!" I watched her disappear quickly into the forest and returned to chopping firewood, trying first to release my skirt, which ended up with a hole too big to repair—more clothes for Jeremy.

After H'Bo and my pants found me again, we were able to cut as much wood as we could carry. It would last at least a few days—or so we thought.

The sun between the tree trunks followed us back to camp, hovered above the forest floor, and began to fade as we reached our new hut. We would build a fire, and the chilled air would become warm around our bamboo beds. Well, that was what we intended.

The wood was too green and sent up smoke the color of night. We blew and blew on the sparks, but the hut just filled with blackness. A few people came when they saw smoke and heard us coughing, but no one offered to help us. Even wrapped in my blanket, I shook from the cold. I had to build a fire. H'Bo curled up like a snail in a blanket shell and went to sleep, but I had a brighter idea.

I took ten different pieces of our chopped wood and went to ten different houses where their wood was stacked outside, leaving one log for each piece of wood that I took. When I came back to our house, I built a new fire with our neighbors' wood and put a piece of ours on top. I could almost see my smile in the light's reflection on the wall, and I soon drifted off into a comfortable, deep sleep, with hot coals from the dirt pit sending a warm message to my feet.

Before the sun could crawl up through the opening of our hut, H'Bo shook me awake; she said that she had already finished cooking and was going back to sleep for a while. Our fire had gone out, and the air was cold, but now I shivered from fear that Tang Ang would be very angry with me. I rushed to his house and saw that his fire was burning, his food was cooked, and five other men were asleep nearby.

"Tang Ang, I apologize to you for being late and for not having your morning meal ready. I promise to be of good help to you after this."

A slight smile crossed his face. "Go back to your sleep. I don't think that you have had time to finish it."

I did not expect that pleasant response. After a moment, I caught his smile and made it bigger on my face. "Thank you! You are a kind man." He must have been watching me when I collected wood and saw us struggle with the fire.

We stacked up rocks to hold some of the water in the nearby stream and washed clothes—with no soap—scrubbing items between stones and slapping them against rocks to get out the embedded mud. Sometimes we found dirty clothes in piles, and we cleaned everything together. Afterward, we spread the washed clothes on bushes and on the ground to dry under the sun, and when dried, soldiers had to search for their clothes among the pile.

The culture of these tribes was different from the other Jarai and Rhade tribes. Some customs were similar but not all. Tang Ang had already asked me to wash my hands in front of him in a bucket of water by his house. I was glad to respect his request, but I finally asked him about that and about other things that I should and should not do.

"Do not hang the clothes so that they swing backward and forward and show to everyone. Do not sit at the head of the bed." That was the most puzzling. I learned that the place where the head lay was almost sacred. The foot of the bed should be closest to the fire outside in front of the house so that the blanket could be folded back and the feet could stick out at the bottom to warm the rest of the body.

He never told me to wash or to sew his clothes. Soon after I arrived, I said, "Do you need help with anything?"

He said politely, "No, thank you!"

I did not ask him a second time. He did not talk much, and I was a little afraid of him. We just did not communicate well.

But one day he told me to follow him to the fields that belonged to his mother. Two other people came with us.

While hiking to the field, the dry leeches again fell from the trees and jumped onto my skin, biting me on the neck. I shook all over, tearing them away and waving my arms as though I was caught in a spiderweb.

Tang Ang just laughed at me. "The leeches are so small. Why are you scared of them?"

"I hate leeches. They are slimy and bite and crawl in every part of your body. They are my enemy." I quickly looked around for fruits to make a soap that would protect me from the worms, but Tang Ang directed me and the two soldiers with us to go into the fields where his mother was already working.

For the entire day we pulled weeds and stalks and planted new seeds and picked squash, peppers, and cucumbers; and on other days, Tang Ang told us to go up to the rice paddies and do the same. His mother fed us from her gardens, and we always returned to camp as the daylight colors faded into gray.

H'Bo often left with her group to help others, and our similar routines were repeated frequently so that the six months we were there seemed much too short to me. Members of the tribe treated me with respect, and I learned a lot about respect from the seven older people who lived at the camp.

I sometimes made mistakes and hurt myself using a knife, a rope, a sickle, or bamboo strips to make baskets, but I kept trying and benefited from the care and love that my friends showed to me.

## *Faith at Dong Knoh*

Numerous Montagnards were of the Catholic faith; however, Dong Knoh was the first camp where I had been that had set aside a place for worship. Half of the camp was Catholic, and on the site they built a wooden bench for sitting, a table to hold a crucifix, and a bowl for the Communion Host (blessed wafer representing the body of Christ). The other half of Dong Knoh was Baptist. They also built a bench of wood with a wooden cross set in the ground in front of their area. Every Sunday there were services where each religion practiced its faith.

The Baptists sang more hymns and had longer talks from their leader, and I enjoyed their singing, and their songs had comforting words that I could keep with me during the weeks. I felt sure that there would be only love and support between us when difficult times came.

The Catholic service was conducted in the Kaho dialect (which I learned to speak), but the Latin prayers were more familiar to me. These Catholic members formed a line to be served with small preblessed wafers by a caring man from the camp during their communion, but he was not a priest. I had not seen that before, so I watched. I do not know where they got the wafers, but messengers in the jungle often seemed to deliver the unusual.

Even though Communion became an important Sunday ritual for me, it was not correct for me to take part, as I had never been baptized. Even in a Catholic school, one needed a parents' consent, and not all were allowed to be a full participant in the services.

I sometimes stood at the edge of the "church" and watched my friends eat a part of the bread of life and thought of Sister Helen, my priest teachers who cared most about me, my friends in the dorms of the schools I attended, and my family.

I remembered that Sister Helen had taught me how to make the Host and the wafers for the church services when I was in the third grade at Thanh Gia. We filled a small machine, shaped like a pencil sharpener, with a white bread mixture and turned the handle on the side to press out thin square wafers. Sister Helen and Sister Benjamin told me that I could taste the crumbs, but there was no taste, and the tiny bits just melted in my mouth. I was to be extra careful with the round three-inch wafer, the one with the symbol of Jesus on top. That was used by the priests and was broken during the Communion service as a symbol of Christ.

As I struggled to embrace my relationship to Jesus to my memories and to my surroundings, I thought of our lives, strong but fragile, demanding but often broken, and sometimes my heart would cry out to this Christ.

*Where are you? What am I doing here? What are all of us doing here—hiding, running, hiding, always scared, trying to hang onto hope? What hope? Danger, dreadful killings, hunger. Peace, safety... safety...peace! God, we pray that we can stay whole. Please share your strength with us and help us find that peace!*

## *H'Bo Left Me*

Colonel Paul Yuh sent a note to Tang Ang saying that H'Bo Eban was to come to Da R'ngit camp as soon as possible.

I was so happy for her. "You have a lot of good luck to be with him and his group. He is a good man."

"I have heard that, but I will miss you. I wish that he had asked for both of us."

"Maybe one day soon!" I hugged her before she and five soldiers disappeared down a path. I had managed to say a weak good-bye. She controlled her tears with a smile.


I moved into the tight little house with H'Nhien and Jeremy and was able to help H'Nhien more when I tied Jeremy in a sling to my back while I did chores. It freed her to have some rest away from the stresses of being a mother and allowed her to do more of her own work.

# CHRISTMAS HORROR

## *Flight into the Night*

B ut that was only for a short time. Two weeks later, a soldier who had been denied a higher rank of captain (which he had wanted for a long time) took his anger out on our camp leaders and betrayed all of us at Dong Knoh.

The man Ama En had been missing. Soldiers and camp members had looked for him everywhere they could imagine and prayed for his safety. I missed him as he had helped me and H'Nhien with food and rice. A quiet man, he was shorter than most of the soldiers, and others thought that he surely must be dead. But later we learned that he had taken his revenge to the enemy.

For a week we had learned and practiced carols to sing with other villages for the Christmas celebration. The last night of preparation seemed unusually dark, but I made my way back to our little house by midnight, falling asleep almost immediately.

About two hours later, I awoke suddenly to what must have been a gunshot. The sound came from the area where H'Bo and I had had our hut built. I did not imagine any danger. Life had been stable in our camp—and it was almost Christmas. I lay back down to sleep. Surely I had been dreaming.

Another gunshot noise roared in my ears, and I sat up quickly, feeling around the floor for H'Nhien and Jeremy. They were gone.

Outside there was a rushing of shadows, but I did not recognize any of them. Then as my eyes adjusted to the night, a glimmer of light seeped through the blackness. I could see H'Nhien, her skirt lifted over her knee, and I wondered why she needed to relieve herself at that time. Then she ran off with Jeremy, not saying a word. All I could hear were night insects, almost in loud warning sounds, keeping time to my racing heart. I went back inside and grabbed my backpack and lifted it to my shoulders to be prepared if someone gave directions.

As I made several steps from our hut, I could hear things dropping behind me one by one. I stopped and realized that I had put my open pack on upside down. In frightened confusion, I bent down to the ground and crawled back toward the house, collecting my belongings and zipping my pack. Suddenly, I glanced toward the glow that allowed me to see; I paused long enough to watch three houses burning in the distance. Thoughts flickered through my mind like the quickness of the flames. *What caused the fires? Why are people running and disappearing so fast? Were those really gunshots that I heard? Where do I go? What if I get shot? No one will know or look for me. I'm so stupid. I don't know where to go. Someone could be watching me. I cannot stay here.*

There was no time to wait for instructions. I had to move on my own—but where? Bullets flew over my head, and I started to shake and walk at the same time. I could barely feel my legs that seemed locked into a nightmare of slow motion. I knew where the stream was, and my mind took me in that direction, away from the guns. When I reached the sound of water, I saw people low to the ground.

"Who are you?" I asked.

Someone jerked me down low next to him and said, "Don't talk so loud!"

I was relieved to hear a friendly voice, even though it contained anger at me.

Gunshots rang again, piercing the black all around us, and explosions set huts on fire. The flames caused more shadows to run and branches to reach out with long arms in a race to catch them. Above us, the sound was like rocks attacking the thick growth of trees. A voice whispered, "They have M79 rifles with grenade launchers."

People scattered in all directions. Some went downstream, some went up, some went across, and others just disappeared.

No one said, "Come with me!"

There was a hillside that I could barely see, near the stream. I went there and started to climb. The first branches and roots that I grabbed broke under my weight, and I slid in the mud to the bottom. I reached again, clawing in the dirt to find other branches and soon learned that two in each hand would hold me until I could grip the next group of roots. My feet clung to the dirt and pushed me upward, while my pack pulled me backward. But as each branch and root held, I found my arms and legs working together. I slipped again, only halfway down, but regained my foothold and again groped for the roots. I called in a low voice, "Help me! Can someone help me?" Only silence.

When I got to the top, I could still hear the steps of people in the stream below, but another flowing water in the distance caught in my ears, and I went toward the sound.

As I walked, the sound of my own footsteps gave me a chill. *Where am I going? Where does this stream lead? Should I stop and wait? Should I keep walking? This stream could go back to the camp. I must try to find my footprints again.*

I turned around and began to walk in the direction that I thought was the hillside. I had not gone far when I heard leaves and snapping twigs crackling in a rhythm of footsteps. I froze; I prayed to God and then crept silently toward the soft steps on my left. I crouched down and waited. The six ghostly figures moved rapidly through the forest, away from the camp, so I took a chance that they were fleeing villagers and followed behind, keeping my distance until I recognized one of the men and was sure that it was safe to join them, no matter where they were going. They accepted me with few whispered words.

No more shots cut through the darkness, and all of us seemed to ease to the ground at one time, collapsing in heaps where we dropped our backpacks. I sat quietly for a few minutes, and after hearing the sounds of sleep, I moved to a quieter place and wrapped myself in some thin clothes that I found in the top of my pack. It was not enough to stop the shivering. I imagined that somewhere back in our hut, the blanket that Dam Per Quay had given to me was burning up into smoke.

I could feel moisture around my wrists, and when I touched them, they stung. I touched my tongue to one and tasted blood. I wound my clothes around them, curled up next to my pack, closed my eyes, and drifted in thought. I took a deep breath, pleased that I had made it this far, not understanding all that had happened and realizing that somewhere, somehow, I was not alone. There were angels giving me strength, protecting me, and wrapping their spirits around me. I briefly thought of the name that the nuns had given to me: H'Tien (holy one or spirit). And with that assurance, my aching body warmed into rest.


My body shook, but not from the cold. The leader of the group, Bhir R'ong, was moving my shoulder back and forth to wake me. "Get up now. We must be going."

My covering fell off as I stretched, and I saw that blood was on my clothes, but it had dried, so I folded the cloths, pulled a pair of pants from my pack, and found a place to change from the skirt I had been wearing.

When I looked over and down the earth bank that I had climbed the night before, I could not believe how high and steep it was, or how I managed to get to the top. The memory of my escape was as blurry as the fog that covered the top of the mountain where we had slept and continued to embrace most of the surrounding areas.

At the site, I was grateful to recognize more friends: Krieng, K'ang, Bong, and Sao. They were just as glad to see me. I had the only backpack. There was rice but no pot, so we began our journey keeping an eye out for anything that we could gather along the way. By evening, we left the mountain and went down to some farm fields, but most of the crops had been picked, and the cold had shriveled up the rest. We found a discarded pot, but building a fire was too dangerous. We ate the few vegetables and corn that we had raw.

For a week, we had only bits of food. At first we looked for berries or leaves that we could eat that would not make us sick, or grub worms or yellow ants, but the land was barren, and a fire was still out of the question.

A stream provided us with water, but we became weaker and thinner, and my jaw slowly became rigid. I slept under bushes most of the time, not caring if I died. Hearing my heartbeat was the only thing that assured me that I was alive.

At the end of the week, Bhir R'ong and two men decided to take a chance and hiked several miles to a village where they thought they had relatives, but after they found a familiar house, the door was not opened to them. The villagers were too scared and whispered to Bhir R'ong that they had been threatened by the VC and told that they must stay close to their houses and not speak to anyone, or they would be killed. The confinement was for a month. The men struggled back to us with nothing, finding only two dried cucumbers in a nearby field, but by then, our stomachs would never receive raw, dried food.

Since they were not followed, the men suspected that the Viet Cong were still not around to punish the villagers. So near the end of the second week, Bhir R'ong decided that he must try again. We were starving to death. The air around me became blurred, while strange figures flew through my mind or went from tiny spots to blotches that covered my sight. Some of the others brought me water and let droplets find their way between my lips into my mouth.

This time, Bhir R'ong was by himself and walking slowly, and when he reached the village, his relatives let him in. They fed him small bits of food and asked him to stay; they told him that the VC seemed to have gone, but he knew that it was only a matter of days or hours until some of his friends would never leave the jungle.

He returned to us with two relatives and a gourd bottle filled with nourishing soup. They were very glad to see us and were shocked at our condition. There was enough porridge for all of us to have a tiny bit and other small amounts of food mashed into a paste. They helped me with a few drops of soup mixture in the side of my mouth and repeated this every hour.

The next day other members of the village found our hideaway and brought blankets and more food. With what little strength I had, I massaged my jaw for hours each day, a kind woman helping me whenever I stopped. After a couple of days, I could open it wide enough to put in some soft fruit. I made myself bite down, and gradually my jaw returned to its normal function, allowing me to regain enough energy within a week to talk about finding our other friends.

The villagers were so kind to us. They hesitated at first to tell us any news, but finally revealed that six of our leaders had been stabbed to death, and one was missing. They knew where the largest part of our group had settled and that several smaller groups, like ours, were joining them. That information made me so happy that my body almost felt fully recovered. I knew that Jeremy had to be with them. He would be six months older.

## *Reunited*

A few of the men stayed in the village, and a couple who knew the way hiked with us through the forest at our slow pace. The first day we stopped often. The second day was easier. Suddenly, in a clearing, I saw a small pond. It didn't have much water and looked a bit muddy; however, I stopped everyone and went to the edge, bending over and moving some leaves where water had accumulated. Underneath the leaves wiggled four-inch-long, dark-colored tadpoles, lots of them, with only an occasional foot beginning to grow our of their sides.

We were like children, running from side to side to catch their squirming bodies and sliding them into a cloth bag so that we could have meat to eat. We threw caution away and lit a fire, while we rubbed each tadpole between our hands until we had squeezed all of the waste from their bodies. After they were cleaned, we boiled them in a pan that I had in my pack. I had never tasted tadpole meat. It smelled a little fishy, but I decided that tadpoles were much better than grub worms or even monkey brains, and they were a lot softer to eat than frogs.

The larger group had already heard that we were coming, and some rushed out to meet us. My eyes searched the crowd, but there was no H'Nhien and no Jeremy. We kept walking until we came to the center of shelters and laundry and women preparing food. And a few yards away, I saw Jeremy holding on to someone's leg and looking scared.

I walked quickly with my arms reaching out to him and then realized that he might not recognize me. But when our eyes met, he started crawling toward me as I swooped him up and smothered him with hugs and kisses. It was one of those happy memories that I cherish.

By the time we arrived at the new group camp, we felt stronger, but I prayed that there would not be any sudden moves for a while. The physical strain had pushed my body to a limit. My exhaustion was deep. I slept a lot, but the closeness of my little Jeremy put energy back into my life. I made clothes for his naked body from what I had left in my pack (which someone had carried for me). When he was not wrapped in a blanket and tied to H'Nhien's back, he was left to make his own way. She was still depressed and glad to have me in Jeremy's life again to take care of his needs. He seemed to smile all the time when I was holding him. It felt as though I had given birth to him myself.

# IMMEASURABLE LOVE— VIGILANT CARE

## *Buon Ja Dih*

(Tribal Village like Buon Ja Dih - Courtesy of Bill Thaxton)

Relatives and friends from other nearby groups came to share what they had with us. An older couple, Par Ksa and his wife K'Srang Konso, from Buon Ja Dih had heard that H'Nhien and I had the last name of Ksor. Her mother had our name, and they gathered us into their family as their daughters. We called them Ama and Ami—our dad and mom. They walked the miles several times from Buon Ja Dih to visit us.

After I grew a little stronger, our leader came to me and to H'Nhien and said that there were new rules in the jungle. "There will be no babies—no exceptions."

I stared at him and pulled Jeremy closer to me. He turned his head from side to side and looked off into the trees. Finally I got the words out, "What do you mean?"

"Seven of our leaders have been killed recently. Babies make noise. The whole camp can be killed if there is one mistake. Babies are a mistake. You must make arrangements now."

I could feel the moisture coming up from the inside and moving from my eyes down my flushed face as I rocked back and forth holding Jeremy closer to me with each motion. I glanced at H'Nhien—her eyes blank and her body rigid. Thoughts raced through my mind, and the one that burned in my heart was that someone would take him away. "No, no, you cannot do that to him. We will think of something. No, don't do that. Let us think! Give us some time!"

"H'Tien, you don't have much time. It is a new rule of the jungle. There will be no babies." And he walked away.

I don't know how long I sat there. H'Nhien took Jeremy, nursed him, and gave him back to me. She took her knife and went out to cut wood. I wrapped myself in the blanket with Jeremy and prayed. *What are we going to do? They throw babies in the river when they make noises. Jeremy does cry, but we try to keep him quiet. But if the enemy hears, we all will be killed. Oh God, help us!*

Two days later, Ama and Ami returned from Buon Ja Dih. They found us immediately. Someone had already spoken to them about Jeremy, and they were there to take him.

He and I had become one. H'Nhien had fed him, but I had lived with him outside my womb for those precious days.

K'Srang Konso began first, "H'Tien, the new rule about babies has been explained to us, and we want to give Jeremy a home where he is loved. We will take good care of him."

"He will be treated like one of our children and grandchildren," Par Ksa said to H'Nhien. "And he will be safe—and so will all of you in the jungle."

Jeremy could feel the tension and began to cry, but H'Nhien fed him, and I put him on my back in a blanket, where he snuggled down while I walked. There was little conversation. I felt like a caged animal that paced with its young until the keeper grabbed the little one away. After he fell asleep, H'Nhien took him, kissed him, and helped K'Srang put him on her back. He woke up briefly and reached out, but he was a blur through my eyes. I stood silent as I watched the three of them disappear into the darkness of the tall trees and tangled vines.

My feet would not move; my heart ached as my grief pulled me to the ground. H'Nhien's tears were quiet. She went to our shelter and knelt by the hot coals in our cooking pit where a pot of water was heating for our next meal.


There were no longer any unexpected sounds in our camp or anxiousness over food for the baby. But H'Nhien was often in great pain. Her breasts began to throb and to swell with too much milk. I soaked cloths in warm and then cool water to help reduce her discomfort. I even tried to suck some of the milk out myself, but that was a total failure that at least made us laugh. I thought of Jeremy, hungry with no milk and H'Nhien with too much and no baby and wondered what God would have us do now.

I did keep praying every day and knew that there was an angel, maybe more than one, who continued to watch over me, but sometimes I just wanted God to hold me in his arms and to rock me back and forth and tell me that we would all live through those unthinkable times.


I also prayed for H'Nhien. She had had too much happening to her in one year—her extralong pregnancy, escaping from bullets as she swam the river with her baby, losing her husband, and then Jeremy.

It took a month for H'Nhien to feel better. Her milk dried up, and we moved often with our group. It was difficult to hide that many people, but those numbers helped to keep us strong. H'Nhien and I were never in one place long enough to build a hut, but we did have a shelter cloth to keep off the rain and sun.

Communication in the jungle was usually very quick, with messengers and scouts slipping through the forests like big cats stalking their prey. Soldiers sent requests for food to their relatives in cities and camps, and friends sent supplies and food back to the camps. H'Nhien and I had no connections, so we were scavengers in any fields that we passed and hunters for fruits and leaves that we could eat. No visitors came to see us, and our days became routine, still as a pond early in the morning—cook, eat, sleep, cook, eat, sleep. We missed the joy that Jeremy brought, but, yes, we were safer.

## *Bhir R'ong Lost*

Our scouts found a large old camp that was abandoned and would make a nice stopping place for all of us. There were even a few huts still standing. Beside the camp ran a deep trench that sometimes filled with rainwater and made a place for us to enjoy bathing and playing to help relieve the heat.

One day, H'Nhien and I followed our brother, Bhir R'ong, through the trench and into a nice area to gather some fruit. When the fronts of our shirts could hold no more, we got ready to return but did not see him, so we thought that he had gone ahead of us. We arrived at the camp, but he was not there. A few men went to look for him before it became dark but came back alone. We knew that he had a gun, a knife, and a few bullets, but we did not know if our enemy was closer than we thought—or if maybe he had had an accident. Extra guards sat up that night, but there was no sign of him the next day or for the next five days. Scouts went out when it was light, but we lost him. It made me very sad and ashamed that we did not wait for him.

Early in the morning of the sixth day, we heard a gunshot. All of us ran for our packs, but there was only one shot, and we froze where we were. No other sound came, so two of our soldiers crept low in the direction of the shot, while we lay flat on the ground. Silence. And then, a cheer from the soldiers' direction and three bodies broke though the forest wall—two soldiers carrying Bhir R'ong, wearing only his underpants. We were too stunned to look away at first, but a soldier found a blanket close by and wrapped it around his mostly naked body.

In a weak voice, Bhir R'ong told us that he got lost, must have gone completely in the opposite direction from us, and kept walking for miles, thinking that our camp was just ahead. The animals that he saw in the forest were new to him, but he wanted to save his bullets to signal to us his location. He wandered and slept and walked and slept and hesitated firing his gun often because it could alert the enemy. The shot that we heard came from his last bullet.

He collapsed in complete exhaustion and dehydration. H'Nhien and I boiled water and washed his thin, bleeding body and spent hours and days feeding him soups and small bits of food until he recovered his strength. I was so grateful that the soldiers brought him to us. We could nurse him into good health as he had done for me.

# CHOOSING UNCERTAIN INDEPENDENCE

## *Last Days at Dong Knoh Region*

Our group (maybe close to a hundred) had become too large to move through the jungle safely. Tang Ang called a meeting to discuss our options. We did need to split into at least two units. One group could keep moving through the jungle toward Cambodia, where it would be safer from the Viet Cong, but food would be a greater challenge. Another group could take an easier way and stay in the Dong Knoh area, near families and farms and villagers who could give us news, but it would not be as safe.

"If we find a place close by Buon Dong Knoh, we will have to have more security and all be trained to be scouts and guards." Tang Ang looked around at the anxious faces—friends who had run together and fought together. There was an urgency to make choices.

My mind was jumping from danger to threats, from terror in the night to beautiful high mountains and green and yellow fields, from protection for close friends to companions in distant places to sadness of being away from family. Jungle life was a challenge, and the thought of going to a different country was a tempting adventure, but was it really any safer, or were they the same?

Tang Ang turned his eyes to me and H'Nhien. "What do you want to do?"

I looked at the ground and shook my head. H'Nhien said, "I don't know."

Then my heart spoke, and I lifted my eyes to his and said, "I want to go to Ja Dih and be with Jeremy if they will give me permission and someone can take me there." I sat very still, waiting for an answer.

"Do you mean that you do not want to stay with all of us?" Bhir R'ong looked shocked.

I found his face among the group standing near Tang Ang. "Bhir, I do not want to leave you, any of you. You are my good friends—always sharing and helping, caring about one another." I could feel my eyes filling with tears. "Jeremy's voice calls to me every day. We are all trying to make life-and-death decisions, planning to live, not knowing if we will die. I want to spend that time with him if they will have me. I can't speak for H'Nhien."

There was silence, then low murmuring, and then sadness. Tang Ang called to a scout who was ready to take messages wherever needed.

"H'Nhien?" Tang Ang looked at her bowed head.

H'Nhien hesitated, and then she said, "I want to go with H'Tien—to be near Jeremy."

Tang Ang sent the request (and other communications) with two different carriers. It would take a few days to receive a reply.

## *Joy and Sorrow*

It was only two days later when a message was received from Buon Ja Dih: "We will have them come."

Tang Ang came to our hut in the late evening and told us the news. I jumped up, smiling, when he spoke, and then my body stood, not moving, letting the weight of my decision fall around me. "When are we to go?" I almost whispered.

"I think in two days. We have so many others who will also be leaving soon."

"Thank you! Thank you for allowing me, for allowing us, to go!" I looked directly at him and held out my hand.

"You have decided what is best for you."

The next day, H'Nhien and I repacked our backpacks and prepared rice and dried food that we might need. In the evening the entire group met together to speak of our concerns for each other and for ourselves.

I tried to have a steady voice and not to look directly at anyone to disguise my tears with encouraging words. "We all hope that we are leaving one another for a short time and that we will meet again in a safer place. I will remember each of you and how kind and helpful you have been to me. My prayer every day will be for your health and your safety. I will keep your friendship close to my heart."

I slipped back into the darkness, sat by our shelter, my head bowed and aching. *How can joy have so much sorrow?*


Tang Ang advised us to leave early in the morning. I was ready before dawn. H'Nhien was awake and gathering a few more things in her pack. Tang Ang said that he would carry mine, and we walked toward the edge of the still-sleeping group. There, waiting like shadow statues, as the forest creatures began their morning chorus, were Krieng, Bong, and Bhir R'ong. Krieng took my pack from Dang Ang, and Bong took H'Nhien's. It was a touching moment—another cherished memory. They would see us to the Buon Ja Dih farm fields at the end of the day.

It was February 1979. The cold went through my old school uniform and to my thin-sandaled feet as well. But there was no time and no desire to complain. I just kept walking, thinking of Ama and Ami K'Srang Konso and little Jeremy and of the privilege of having these men escort us to our new home.


At the Ja Dih farm fields, there were people waiting for us. After being introduced to Ha Tong, K'Srang Konso's son-in-law (where I would stay) to Rita, his wife, and to her two brothers (where H'Nhien would stay), we realized that we must say good-bye as well as hello.

There were long handshakes and eyes that spoke in silence. Words were few: "Take care of yourself!" "God bless you!" "I'll miss you." And the men turned and walked back into the jungle, stopping only at the edge for one last wave.

# LIFE REPLENISHED

## *Buon Ja Dih*

We walked along the side of the farm acres and spoke in short sentences. There was not much sign of life—no camp, no Dong Knoh campers, only cold wind blowing across the barren fields. I asked about Jeremy, but Ha Tong said that we would see him in a day or two. H'Nhien looked as surprised as I was.

We met two of Ha Tong's friends, Ha Krong and Ha Krang, who smiled and asked a lot of questions about the jungle. Ha Tong said, "I will call you my sister, like my wife's K'Jong Konso's sister. We will try to see both of you happy here."

Rita was a nurse, and she kept walking with H'Nhien to her new living space, while we went up the side of a small mountain to a cave. I had been in a cave before but did not understand when Ha Tong said, "Here we are. This is where we live. Go in!"

As I stepped into the opening, warm air welcomed me as well as K'Jong. Hot coals from the fire kept a pot of porridge steaming, and dried meat hung from the roof. There was a stack of wood and a place to put our backpacks and enough room for five or six people to sleep. I could not imagine anyone being unhappy here. I thought of my friends back in Dong Knoh region and hoped that they would find a place as nice.

"Thank you for letting me share your home with you. How long have you been here?"

"Two months," answered Ha Tong. "We have a lot of protection."

"I can cook and wash and sew and can help whenever you need me," I offered.

K'Jong smiled. "We will talk about that tomorrow. Tell us about the jungle."

"First, tell me about your food. You have so much."

"Ha Krang and Ha Krong are very good with a slingshot, and we have lots of birds here. I make traps for small animals. We have enough to take to others in the area and to sell in the village."

"But where are the people? I don't see a camp or huts or any people."

"Since the big fight at Dong Knoch camp, all camps and groups have split into small families so as not to draw attention to the area—and we can survive." Ha Tong's face was a mixture of hope and sadness.

"Where is baby Jeremy? Will we see him tomorrow?"

"You will see him when Ama and Ami bring him to the field. That will be your only chance for now. I must go to our hut in the field before it gets dark. I sleep there with our two sons so that we can work in the field very early. You will stay here with Ha Tong and our two friends for now."

I had thought that I would see Jeremy immediately and was confused, but the day had been long, and I would soon sleep through all of the questions until tomorrow.

It was the right decision. The people were as warm as the cave, which was a dry, protected home that I did not have in the jungle. My head was the only thing that had lessons to learn—don't stand up too quickly and too tall. It only took a few good knocks to teach me the "cave walk."

On the first night when I went out to relieve myself, I realized not only how low the ceiling was but also of the cold, chilling nights in the jungle. I stood for a moment taking in the brightness of the stars and of hidden memories I had brought this far—of months with the protection of Dam Per Quay; the beautiful, peaceful Yang Reh Mountain; running, guns, fire, starvation; Dong Knoh destroyed; friends dying; terror. *Blessed Virgin Mary, pray for me! I have warm and good, new friends and Jeremy, and I need rest. I need you. Pray for me, Holy Mother!*

When I fell asleep, it was long and deep and was late morning when Ha Tong woke me. I heard him calling, "H'Tien, wake up! Jeremy is here."

The word *Jeremy* kept repeating itself in my head as my eyes slowly opened, closed, and then came opened wide. I stood up quickly, remembering the ceiling, and went to the door of the cave, blinking my eyes to adjust to the sun. Dogs were barking, a sound that I had not heard in a long time. People were talking, and I could hear wood being cut for fires.

"Where is he?" I asked Ha Tong. I was hesitant to step out.

"Come with me. They are waiting down by the field."

From a distance, I saw K'Srang Konso with a baby wrapped in a blanket and tied to her back. On my bare feet, I ran straight to them at the edge of the field. We hugged for a long time and hugged again. It had been many months since I had seen so many smiles and felt such a celebration. The bundle on K'Srang's back looked heavy for her sixty years. Jeremy was asleep, and I asked if I could hold him. She said, "Of course," and we moved the baby from her shoulders to mine. He woke up briefly, but I walked him around until he closed his eyes again.

I was stunned to see that Jeremy wore no clothes, and his legs were very thin, his belly quite large. *What is wrong with him poor baby? Is he sick? I must make clothes and help him get strong. Sleep now, Jeremy. I'll take care of you.*

Ami called us for a meal, and I unwrapped Jeremy and washed his face and body. I spoke quietly to him, "Jeremy, do you remember me?" He smiled and hid his face but did not say anything. I realized that I must learn more of the Koho language spoken here so that he could better understand me.

Jeremy could feed himself with a bamboo stick and cup and ate the chicken that K'Srang had pounded into tiny pieces. He liked it and ate a lot for his size, but I worried that, at almost one year old, he should have been more lively. We would go to see H'Nhien soon.

## Mother K'Srang's Worthy Necklace

In a month's time, the weather warmed, the fields begged to be tended, and flowers and green leaves began to bloom and grow. Spring was a happy time of the year. I missed the bamboo shoots and mushrooms from the jungle, but we had lots of fresh vegetables and meat here, and I became stronger and healthier.

Ami K'Srang stayed in the village of Ja Dih while looking after Jeremy. She came to her old rice fields about every two weeks and would bring him with her. Ha Tong and his family enjoyed hunting together, and I helped pick the wild vegetables. His wife, K'Jong, now my sweet sister, went to the village to sell the vegetables and dried meat and always cooked food for her husband before she left. I had not experienced such a happy family before.

On one visit to the fields, Ami said, "H'Tien, I want you to come to the village and live with me and not go back to the jungle. I love you and worried so much when I heard about the shooting at Dong Knoh. We are all in danger, but we could be together."

I went to her and hugged her and thanked her for her love and her kindness and said that I hoped to take Jeremy back one day with me when he was older.

She looked sad and opened her mouth to speak but turned away. Before lunch, she came to me and said, "I have something of mine that I want you to have." She took out a necklace of beads from a skirt pocket and tied it around my neck. The shade of brownish red shone in the sunlight, and the heaviest beads were carved with different symbols.

My first words were, "Oh no, I couldn't take anything so beautiful from you. I have nothing to give in return."

She put her finger to my mouth and said, "I will be happy to have you love this and think of me when you wear it. I hope that it will always keep you safe."

I never took it off and kept my fingers on it each night and morning to be sure that it was still there.

Later in the month, a friend inspected the necklace. "Where did you get that?" he asked, leaning over to get a closer look.

"Mother K'Srang gave it to me. It is a forever gift that will remind me of her."

"Do you know anything about it—how much it is worth?"

"No, I didn't ask. It was a love gift."

He continued to stare at the fifteen beads. "Each of those beads has been bought for a large price. One bead is worth one buffalo, five beads are the price of a husband.

That made me laugh. I could not tell whether or not he was truthful, but he encouraged me to ask K'Srang more about the symbols on the beads. I said that I would, but I was unsure about wanting to know its value in money. I loved it because she gave it to me with love. When he said that the price of five beads would buy a husband, I think he was wondering how much teasing I would believe.

## *Ja Dih Camp*

Ja Dih camp was smaller than Dong Knoh and most other camps, only about seven houses. I watched Ha Tong grow stronger with his friends. I wondered if it were not only his physical hunting skills but also his prayers to God before he did anything, eyes closed and mouth moving, that made him always seem to succeed in his tasks.

Families made their own living areas wherever they felt safe and went to the main camp only to trade for food or necessary

items. It reminded me of Buon Ra Tieu with Y-Wer and Y-Wo—
kind of like an island.

Ha Tong and his two friends, Ha Krong and Ha Kiang, supported
themselves and their families by hunting. They loved the sport
and often went back and forth to Ja Dih camp with their meat
and skins. Trading meant survival in the Highlands—a lifeline
throughout the jungle.

There also was a larger Ja Dih village that was more permanent
than the camp but farther away. They usually had a wide variety of
things to trade, and K'Jong made the long hike there often to trade
fish and rice for soap, clothes, pots, shoes, and items for the family.

One day I asked if I could go with her to see Jeremy and Ami
K'Srang. My heart danced in circles when she said, "Yes." It would
be a different experience for me, since I had seldom been in a
village. I helped K'Jong with the sewing and hoped that she would
let me trade for some material to make Jeremy clothes for his
naked body. He was growing older and would soon be walking.

We began in the early afternoon with her two sons. To hide my
identity, I filled a basket with dry wood, carried vegetables in a
sling, and walked behind her, as though I was a village girl. We
followed a trail that led to the Krong River. K'Jong saw me stop
and hesitate at the edge of the cold water.

"How deep is it here?" I asked, my eyes widening to take in
the possible danger.

"It is shallow—only to your knees." She smiled but looked
puzzled.

"I never learned to swim."

One of her sons walked beside me as we crossed to a sandy
shore, and again, I was so happy to be with this family.

Even though a footwalk was made at the side of the steep
hill that separated us from the village, I had to stop several times

going up to catch my breath. It brought back memories of Yang Reh, but the air seemed thinner in these mountains.

At the top, the village looked rectangular, lined with small houses and small trees—a dusty road in the middle throwing circles of fine dirt in our faces as the breeze blew. It hugged the side of the mountain, safe from most floods and shielded from the strong windstorms of the Highlands.

It was late evening when we arrived. Unlike our house in Cheo Reo, K'Srang and Par Ksa's house was built close to the ground. It was much smaller and very dark inside but had a comfortable feeling. People sat in one of their three rooms, but I only knew Ama and Ami and, of course, Jeremy, who slept next to her.

Even though coals burned in each of the three fire pits, it took my eyes a bit to adjust. I went to Ami and kissed her, then sat down beside her, and ran my hand gently across Jeremy's face. Ami offered each of us a small bowl of rice, and our conversations about the day were short. Soon their friends went to the back of the house to sleep, and our bodies rested on bamboo mats offered to us around the fire.

Morning was a good trading time. K'Jong spread out a blanket in the center of the village where other marketers had set out their wares. People knew K'Jong and the freshness of the food that she brought. In less than two hours, she had traded for material for clothes, thread, and new needles; one pair of shoes for a son; one toothbrush; a tube of toothpaste; and some medicine for Jeremy. It was the first time in months that there had been any to make his stomach feel better. K'Srang told me that something inside seemed to be taking away the food he was eating.

As soon as we had repacked our baskets, K'Jong, her two sons, K'Srang, Par Ksa, Jeremy, and I returned to the fields, down the hillside, and across the river. We stopped in the Ja Dih camp so that Jeremy could visit his mother, H'Nhien, but he did not know her and was afraid to let her hold him. They had never bonded from the jungle, and his life and hers had dramatically changed in the following year. K'Srang was the mother he knew best, and I had to respect that relationship.

Par Ksa and K'Srang insisted on taking turns carrying Jeremy on their backs to the fields and to our cave home. I could play with him, but Ami acted as a shield and seemed to sense something that I could not understand. She knew the size of the cave and decided to sleep in the field hut with Jeremy and let K'Jong and her sons sleep in the cave. I joined K'Srang.

Loyalty, friendship, and love bound us together and surrounded me in sleepless hours.

My mind, during some nights when I awoke, listened for the enemy outside or heard gunshots in the distance or imagined water covering me in a river. Other nights my two lives—safety to terror, escape to starvation—raced through the darkness until morning.

But on that night, Jeremy went to sleep quickly. The stars that I had not often seen warmed the cover of darkness as Ami helped me roll into my own blanket of protection against the coolness of the evening. Two lights flew across the sky, and I imagined them to be angels, dancing in a garden of happiness.

Ami and I talked. I told her what my life had been like, and she gave me a few thoughts to ponder on what she learned from her own life, but she mostly tried to persuade me to move to the village and live with them. Her tone became one long line, and my eyes stammered more than my voice. The sounds blended into a hum, and there was no more talk about my leaving the jungle...permanently.

Each time I saw Jeremy, I noticed that nothing had changed—same skinny arms and legs and large stomach. It did no good to keep mentioning it. There was no doctor and no money to pay one if there were. I prayed that he would keep growing and would someday return to the jungle with us. He did wear the clothes I made for him and had a pair of sneakers like mine that Ami had acquired by trading her handmade baskets.

## *Clearing Spring Fields*

By early March, the air grew warmer, and the farmers and villagers began to walk off the area to prepare a new rice field and to sharpen their tools—saws, knives, axes, and even two chain saws. About three weeks later, the fields were being cleared. Those were long hours with exhausting work, as tall trees fell and smaller bushes were thrown into piles to burn. Sometimes the sound of saws from the side of the mountain echoed like a giant storm or a convoy of large vehicles. It made me think of the noise in Pleiku when the VC army trucks passed by our school for days.

I asked Ha Tong during a lunch break, "Aren't you afraid that the smoke will attract the Viet Cong?"

"No, they already know that we are here. In fact, they have camps not far away and sometimes come and look to see what we are doing, and then we hear a gong ring, and they go back to their camp. The VC know that we have no soldiers in our village and that we are just farmers and hunters, so they leave us alone."

It was difficult for me to believe. I still watched and lived on the edge as more burning occurred. The years of hiding our small fires when we needed to cook were not forgotten.


I assisted with the ground cleaning by taking down trees and bushes that only reached about four times my height. I could cut with my long-handled, five-inch knife, which I sharpened every day, but my arms often ached until I thought that they would fall off. Then I would find Jeremy and sit with him for a while, trying to teach him new words and to build stick houses in the dirt. But everyone worked hard, and rest periods were short.

Then, into my second week, I decided to take down a bamboo tree. I knew that it was tough, and I didn't have gloves, and although I was careful, my caution did not produce the best results. I moved too fast, and my hand slipped down to the blade that left a slice between my thumb and first finger, where blood quickly spurted out and down my arm. I put pressure on top of the wound, then sucked on it, spitting out the blood, trying to stop the flow. I tore a piece of cloth from my skirt and wrapped my hand tightly to close the cut. Blood seeped through, but this time it was much slower than after the first slice. By then, I was under the shade of a tree near my pack and realized that if I did not sit down, I would faint. No one seemed to notice, which made me feel less embarrassed, but at the same time, I wanted someone to care. I drank water from my bamboo bottle and fell asleep.

Most of the blood had dried when I awoke, so I knew that I would not die. I tore a fresh piece of cloth from my skirt and rewrapped my hand. Even though the sun was going to bed, I still had chores to do. Having a wounded hand was no excuse. I would wash it out and rewrap it when I could get to the stream.

That spring, smoke also came from other cleared fields on the mountains, which were shaped like triangles or rectangles. Deep wrinkles of furrowed earth marked their faces as they waited for corn, rice, and vegetable seeds to smooth over their creases. Ha Tong's family prepared those for planting, hopefully right before the seasonal rains arrived. We watched, worked, and prayed.

Some days, Jeremy rested on my back as I walked along the rows, dropping in seeds, covering them with my foot. With no more trees to cut, my hand survived without an infection, and my knife stayed in my backpack by the field hut.

As in most of the Highlands, the dry rice fields were especially difficult on the sides of the mountains. Balancing Jeremy, leaning over to set seeds, and swinging my foot over the planted holes was like, I remembered, first riding a wobbling bicycle to school with my backpack full of books. One time I slipped and clutched at a log that tumbled down with us through the dust and dirt, but I grabbed a second fallen tree that held us in place until I could adjust Jeremy, stop his crying, and climb back to the rows I had left. No one complained about the work. It was what we did. It was our life.

## Discovering Cave Water

Once the fields were planted, most of the families stayed near their homes to do other chores—sewing, cutting piles of wood for their fires, drying meat, and cleaning around their camps from the winter winds.

As we waited for the rains, Ha Tong, his two friends and I went back to the fields to finish cleaning the dead bushes and wood. The nights were cool, but the days were sunny, and our bodies warmed quickly. Most of the field tools and pans for cooking had been taken back by the villagers, and we had come unprepared for the sun. On a particularly hot day, we noticed that our bamboo water bottles were empty. The more we worked and talked about having no water, the more our mouths became parched like the dry earth.

During the preparation of Ha Tong's rice field, I had noticed a series of large rocks that were shaded by the remaining forest. I called over to Ha Krong, "I'm going up the hill to look for water." He laughed, and the other two joined in the fun. I went anyway.

It was beautiful from that high distance, looking over the tiny green shoots of rice that had come up after the first rain and hearing the birds' songs that sounded grateful that no more of their homes would be destroyed. I climbed around the rocks, sat very still, glanced out at the view, and listened. I moved to another place—and listened. All was quiet. I lay across the rocks and studied their curves. Most were large boulders, shaped like our hut, but there were also medium and small ones as though they were generations of one family.

I first saw it and then heard it—hidden near the bottom of the huge pile of stones—*drip, drip drop, drip* trickling from a small cave. I held my breath, slid to the ground, and stuck my head into the opening for certainty—*drop, drop drip.*

The short run to the edge of the field was more like flying. I called, "Ha Tong, Ha Krong, come quick—I found it!" Silence. *What is wrong with those boys? Did they leave me out here by myself?*

I half-ran, half-slipped down the mountain to the field hut. As I came closer, I heard another familiar noise—snoring. I shook them and brought them to their feet like rockets, but instead of exploding, they stood straight like waiting launchers.

"If you are interested, I found the water. How could you go to sleep?" I turned and started back across the field and up toward the rocks with their footsteps dragging along behind me.

"How could you find water up there? Are you sure?" Ha Krang was breathing hard from his walking speed.

"You'll see! But I'll need your help to get it."

"I knew that there would be some work to it." Ha Tong smiled as he caught up to me.

We reached the cave, and all three had our eyes and ears opened. The boys immediately went to the edge of the woods and cut dry bamboo stalks to make torches. I didn't leave them much time to think about who would go first. I said, "Don't worry, I'll go down and get the water. You light the bamboo and keep the torches burning."

I crawled through the hole, and Ha Tong handed me a torch that he lit with a butane lighter. I carefully brought it through the cave opening and could see the water right below me and his head looking down from above. My feet soon touched the wet rocks, and I slid down into the pool, picking up a pebble to test for clean water. It was clear. I drank and filled up the bamboo bottle that Ha Krong had brought, then lowered myself into the cool freshness, and bathed, using the light from another torch that Ha Tong had moved into the cave.

I could feel the cave shrimp crawling on the bottom and picked one up, snapped its head off, and ate it raw. Then I asked Ha Tong to throw down the pan that Ha Krang had grabbed from the hut as we began our adventure. I filled the pan with shrimp and reached my arm up for Ha Tong to pull me through the passage. There was plenty of height, about eight feet, but little room for more than one to sit at the opening.

Before the evening became too gray, the pan over our fire cooked the shrimp, enough to satisfy all of us, while we had time to enjoy a rest, drink fresh water, and be happy for my good fortune.

# PAUL YUH SUMMONS—
# PROFOUND LOSS

## *The Passing of Seasons*

The people in the Ja Dih area were very poor, and there was little formal education, but they wore their hearts like Ami's worthy necklace—simple, generous in spirit, sweet, and good. I loved working and living with them and was grateful for their friendship. But I knew that I would not stay forever. I was still loyal to my friends in the jungle and missed H'Bloanh, H'Bo, Bhir R'ong, Tang Ang, and all of the freedom fighters who were on my same journey.

As the fields blossomed with new growth, and summer months spread their heat, a letter arrived to the leader of Ja Dih from Colonel Paul Yuh. I was pleased to hear that he wrote but surprised at his message. It said that the fields were not safe and were too difficult for good communication back and forth and that if anything happened to me, he would hold the leader personally responsible.

Ha Tong did not understand what it was like being a part of the forces in the jungle, running from the VC, protecting and bonding with one another, but he immediately took me, Ha Krong, and Ha Krang from the fields and settled us in Ja Dih camp, along with H'Nhien. He considered us part of his family and came often to share the meat that he slaughtered, while K'Jong brought vegetables to us on her way to the market in Ja Dih Village.

I felt caged. H'Nhien and I were not close, but we lived in the same hut. I missed the beautiful fields, the family, and even the hard work, and I thought a lot about Jeremy. I had stayed away from him so as not to confuse him as he grew up as Ami K'Srang's son. He turned two, and my arms ached for that little body. As H'Nhien had struggled with her difficulties, I loved him as my firstborn, giving birth to him in my heart. I had heard that he was walking and saying words in Kaho, pointing to lots of things and smiling—when he was not crying.

By late August, restless thoughts of Jeremy controlled my mind. And then a message came to Ha Tong—one that he could deliver only through the camp leader: "Jeremy has gone to live with God."

Jeremy had become sick—and then very sick. His little body gave in, and that sweet, beautiful child found peace and rest from the parasites that infested his stomach.

It was a time of great loss and grief. H'Nhien could not speak. Her eyes were clouded with sadness that tears from both of us could not wash away. I was grateful that the baby no longer suffered, but for a while, I was hurting and prayed that one day my heart would heal. I also prayed that his father, Y-Dhun Nie Buondap, would recognize his son and welcome him with loving arms.

## *Mother K'Srang Konso*

A month later, I heard that Ami K'Srang Konso was not feeling well. I told H'Nhien that I must go to the village to see her.

"Ask permission first!" she advised.

"H'Nhien, I have lived in the jungle with no food, with scorpions with pythons, bullets, fires, killings. I do not care anymore. I am going to Ja Dih Village."

Ha Tong was at our hut that evening, and I told him my plan. "I see you are determined to go, but do you remember the way ? You must disguise yourself a bit and be careful near the soldiers."

The next day, I took a rag from a scarecrow in the garden and wrapped my head like a woman in the camp. I rubbed dirt on my face and carried what I would need in a basket with vegetables and wood on top. I spoke to no one. The Krong River was the only place that I feared. Even so, I had crossed it twice, and that day there were many people going the same way—up the same steep steps. I rested twice before I reached the top and walked straight into the village.

I was not sure of Ami's house, but I remembered a tree out in front. There were several houses with trees, and I chose the wrong one the first time, but the woman who greeted me kindly took me to K'Srang.

Her rooms were dark except for the fire. I called her name and spoke softly. She lay on her bed with her hand reaching toward the fire for warmth.

"Who are you?" she said in a weak voice.

"It's H'Tien, Ami. I've come to help you." I sat down beside her and unwrapped the rag from my head.

"Oh, I can't believe it. Who told you that I am not feeling well?"

I put my fingers to her mouth. "Have you eaten today?"

"No!" She hesitated, and I squeezed her hand as I got up, removed the fresh vegetables from my basket, and looked around to see what there was to cook.

Soup did not take long to fix, and I gave her an Advil that I had been saving for a long time. I only had three, but they would make her feel better for a few days.

As I took care of her, I met a number of youth in the village who liked to hear the way I talked and invited me to join in their music and games. Their acceptance made me feel younger than my twenty-one years and allowed me to think of songs from my school days and from the music of the jungle. By sharing tribal cultures, we could better appreciate our similarities and differences. Since there was little formal education in the Ja Dih region, they needed a teacher. I considered that possibility, but my mission was far away.

Every day at noon, I could hear the gong from the VC camp calling to its soldiers to come back, and after they were gone, I would go out to fill the water containers and to wash my hair in the stream. I cooked and washed clothes for K'Srang and talked about Jeremy and about my need to keep searching for freedom, even if it meant leaving Vietnam. She thought that I was brave. Her words of love were comforting, but I do not think that she really understood my deep desire.

And every day I would pound rice, as Ami told me, so that I could fill a large bag and buy my way to Da Lat to see the city. She knew that I dreamed of that since the previous year. The thought of the adventure made the pounding an easier job.

The bag of rice was full, and a few of the youth were going to Da Lat in two days. Before I could leave, another letter arrived to the leader of Ja Dih Village from Col. Paul Yuh. It stated that he heard I was in the village and should return to Ja Dih camp immediately.

I felt like running away. I was tired of being told what to do and very angry about missing my dream trip to Da Lat.

K'Srang spoke softly to calm me, "H'Tien, you could be in great danger. I will walk with you back to the camp."

The next day, the young people came to say good-bye and to ask me to come back to the village, and they would come to the Ja Dih camp to visit me.

I disguised myself again, and we started our walk by midmorning. Mother K'Srang felt stronger, but I carried the bag of rice and gave rice to the people in huts and shelters along the way. There was so much need. The offering of food took away some of the sting from my disappointment, and Ami was happy to be returning to the fields.

## Last Days at Ja Dih Camp

A short time later, a messenger came to the Ja Dih camp with a long list of those who were to go to Dak Nong from the Da Lat and Ban Me Thuot areas. My name and H'Nhien's were there. Ha Tong was happy to stay with his family and hunt and farm.

"H'Tien, I saw your name on the list. You must go. I want you to go, but we all feel very sad and will miss you in our hearts."

Ami talked to me the most. "H'Tien, please stay here with me. You will be safe. The government where they want to take you is not stable. Some of the sons from our village have gone. A few have returned, and others have never been heard from. Their parents are still waiting and waiting. There is little food and no supplies and is very dangerous."

My heart seemed to tear in two pieces. Our group would leave in a week. I trusted that God was watching me and would help me to be strong and make the right decision.

I knew that I could stay at the camp and teach. I loved K'Srang Konso, and I could help her. I loved my friends from the jungle; I could not abandon H'Bloanh and H'Bo and felt that freedom was still our goal. I could stay in Ja Dih and live peacefully there as long as the Viet Cong would leave us alone. I could go with the fear of death following me or search for freedom that was just out of my reach. The thought bothered me in those six days.


The night before a group from Da Lat was to come through Ja Dih camp, I went to the field hut to be with Mother K'Srang. She heard my voice calling to her and came out to wait for me beside a small fire.

We just stared at each other, and I finally said, "Ami, I will be all right. I will not be alone."

She started to cry, and I hugged her, my tears adding moisture to her face. "I love you." I had never used those words before with her, but they helped warm the cold aching inside me.

We sat down near the fire. I took the "worthy necklace" from my neck and gave it to her. She closed her hands. "No, I don't want it. It is yours to keep."

I wrapped my fingers over hers and slowly said, "Please keep this and remember me—and pray for me."

She paused, went into the hut, and brought out a package. "H'Tien, my daughter, you have worked very hard in the fields and have looked after me well. After watching you this week, I thought that you might go. Take this with you! It will help for a while. Inside the wrapping is some of Ha Tong's meat, dry fish, salt, and rice."

We sat mostly in silence, staying up only as long as the last flame flickered, and then we slept close through the night.

In the middle of the morning, we heard voices across the field and saw Ha Tong leading a group of men and women toward the hut.

"Who is there? H'Tien, is that you?" a voice called.

The faces were unfamiliar, but the group's mission was evident in the way that they walked. "Yes, I am ready, but I have been expecting H'Nhien." I looked at the leader, and he shrugged his shoulders and glanced around.

"We cannot wait," he said. "There are groups connecting with us from lots of areas—some from the north, some behind us, from many camps; some are already at our destination. We must go."

I turned to Ha Tong. "If H'Nhien comes in time for the next group, they can bring her." I hugged him quickly, thanked him for his kindness, and looked at the ground, my emotions heavy. Then as the twenty gathered people began to move, I put the familiar backpack over my shoulders, hugged Ami K'Srang Konso, and whispered, "I love you."

"I love you," she softly breathed in my ear.

She stood in the field until we were out of sight. I turned for a last look, and the jungle foliage covered our tracks.

# Journey Toward the Border

## *Following Orders through a Deadly Region*

Scouts who were familiar with the area and Y-Soan Eban led us through forests and across shallow rivers. We walked all day toward Dang Jri camp. My steps felt lighter, and there was cautious excitement hovering in our trail. We had little hesitation in following the directions of Paul Yuh. He had proved himself on many occasions to be strong and trustworthy. The news was that he left Da Lat after he sent the letter and list of people from Buon Me Thuot and Da Lat to come together in an attempt to escape, and we would follow his appointed leader.

His orders were to stop and camp at Dang Jri and to wait for others to join us. I kept my eyes opened for people I knew but only recognized a few faces, until I saw H'Bo enter the campsite. I ran. I ran through groups sitting by fires and others trying to find places to settle. We hugged and laughed and hugged again—happy that we were both safe and could touch each other. Two nights later, H'Nhien arrived with the second group that came through Ja Dih. Her group was the last and had little time to rest as we moved out the next morning. But the three of us were together again.

Day walked into night, into day, into night, and our enthusiasm drifted away, our bodies ached with fatigue, and our stomachs were almost empty because we found little food along the march. Each step seemed a repetition of previous years—four, five, six? I allowed my mind to retrace that eagerness, the optimism of a young teenage girl, dreaming of adventure, rushing toward freedom, accepting the unimagined, questioning her own judgment.

We hiked for two weeks. All sixty of us crossed the Krong River (the same one I had waded across near the Ja Dih camp), but this part of the river was waist deep and swift. Some went across first to mark a trail, especially for those of us who could not swim. We were weak and exhausted and allowed to stay a full night on the other side.

The next day, as we entered the forests around the river, the ground was damp, and the thought of leeches returned. My energy level increased, and I walked fast in front of the line— my prayers answered when we did not have to spend another night in the area.

The forests became thicker, and hills that rolled into one another gave an appearance of protection. There was a signal for a sudden stop, and four men, armed with AK-47 rifles, greeted us. Identification was swift. They had been on alert for our group and guided us quickly to the base camp, which was hidden well next to the foot of the tallest hill in view.

The men directed us to join another group that had numerous women. Our leader, Y-Soan Eban, soon became responsible for both groups. He called H'Bo and me to meet with him. "We are in an area where there is no rice, no potatoes, only *kloi*, a very poisonous root that must be prepared in a certain way, or it can kill you if you eat it. That will be our main food, probably our only food, and I want you to learn the methods of cooking from these women here."

## *Kloi—Poison Root—Preparation*

Someone had told us about *kloi*, but we had no experience cooking it. The next morning H'Bo and I began our "poison root" training classes.

An older woman took us to a field covered in vines and showed us how to dig down under the vines to find the roots. I still had my long-handled knife with the five-inch blade, so I began the search as soon as I watched her for a few minutes. No roots were the same size—brown on the outside, like sweet potatoes, or big and round like small pumpkins, all yellow on the inside. She filled a basket, and we filled two that she had given us. "Take those to the camp and come back with your empty baskets. We have more people here now, and it takes a long time to gather and to prepare these for safe eating."

Our stomachs were as empty as the baskets, but we returned to the camp with our second load of roots. Three other girls joined us and our lessons began. "Listen carefully," the woman warned. "People who do not listen die."

I had heard about the danger, but it was hard to believe that some could still poison themselves after learning how to treat the roots. How difficult could that be? But hunger can cloud one's judgment—as I later found out in a personal way. The five of us sat in front of the woman who was surrounded by piles of roots as she lit the wood in her fire pit. She put several roots beside each of us and made sure that we had knives.

"There are three ways to make these safe," she said. "Boil, sun-dry, and pickle. We begin by peeling the root. I'll put a pot of water on the fire so that it will be ready."

The skin was stronger than most fruit but not as thick as a potato's. We emptied two of our baskets, finishing as the water boiled.

"We put the *kloi* in here and boil for several hours until they are a bright yellow and soft—but not too soft to slice. While boiling the roots, the poison will begin to rise to the top as a slippery film, and the smell will be like decaying garbage. After the roots are tested for tenderness and have cooled, we slice them into baskets and set the baskets in the pond that is a short distance walk from here. We must rinse the root-filled baskets in the water often during the day and at least three times during the night. The poison will continue to come to the top of the water giving off a foul odor. When the water is clear, and the roots are no longer slippery, the roots may be taken out and boiled again into a mush that we can eat, mixing it with whatever you have— salt, fresh ferns, or vegetables.

"It will take this *kloi* awhile to cook, so you may go and rest, and I'll come for you when they are ready to be sliced. Then I'll show you the second way."

In the middle of the afternoon, H'Bo and I found her and the three other girls sitting in the sun with even more roots. "I was just coming for you. Take this stick and poke the roots in the pot so that you can tell how tender they are. They should still be firm enough to slice. Here is a slicer to use. I have three for you to share. We pour this water off, remove the roots to cool, and put fresh water in the pot along with the slices. Remember, tonight and for the next two nights, the water must be rinsed three times. When you finish the slicing, we will begin learning about the second way to make the roots safe."

I looked at H'Bo, and there was nothing to say. We both knew that this would be one of the most difficult times that we would face in our years in the jungle. The slicer was not new to me, but I had not sliced cooked vegetables on one before. It took both of us a little practice to stroke the root across the surface of the flat metal so that the slices were the same size—about a quarter inch thick.

"Is this really all that we will have to eat while we are here? Are there not any fruit trees or tender ferns?" I asked the woman.

Her mouth was straight; her eyes had little life. "No! No fruit, nothing else. That is why you must be very careful. You will be feeding others as well as yourselves. Learn well."

After all of us had peeled another pile of roots, our teacher instructed us to slice them and to lay them out on the ground in the sun. There, she explained, they would stay for three days until they turned white, and the three-day soaking process would begin. Afterward, the slices would dry and harden and could be crushed into a powder (easily carried in backpacks) or could be mixed with water to make a pancake-type patty, cooked over a fire.

Later in the afternoon, our teacher returned to the fields with us to collect more roots and to show us where to find sour leaves for use in pickling our next collection of *kloi*. The leaves were also vines, but they crawled in and out of bushes and up the sides of trees, or wherever they could attach themselves. The scent from the finger-sized growth was easy to recognize—much better than the putrid odor of the soaking roots.

Later, we placed our full baskets of sour leaves beside the soaking and drying slices that had taken most of the day to prepare. We sat on the ground with our heads touching our bent knees and with little energy to speak. We could hardly think of eating anything ourselves, but our teacher gave us slices of *kloi* that had been prepared several days before. It was difficult to keep my face from looking ugly as I tasted the strong, bitter root, but we both thanked her and took the slices back to our area to eat our "poison" slowly.

"We will need to work hard to accept our new life-threatening diet," said H'Bo.

"Yes, but we don't have a choice. It seems that there is only one way to survive, and if we are the cooks, we are responsible for life and death," I answered as I searched through my pack for anything I might find to eat. My disappointment was emphasized by a long sigh.

We nibbled the roots we had been given, wrapped ourselves in our blankets, and fell into a deep sleep, both of us waking in the morning with roots still clutched in our hands.

Our main job the next day was to learn the third method for extracting poison. "Surely it cannot be any more difficult," I said to H'Bo as we walked over to our "cooking school." Our teacher already had peeled a number of roots. "Maybe we can be that fast with practice." I smiled.

"Is today like yesterday?" H'Bo asked.

"Yes, but not exactly the same. Sit down and start taking the skin off! Then we must go to the fields to dig up more and to gather more sour leaves for the pickling. I changed the water last night. Tonight and tomorrow you will change it all three times. You must see the bubbles come to the top and feel the slippery liquid to understand about the poison and when it is no longer in the root."

There was already a batch of slices in a hole behind where our leader sat, but she directed us to dig another one, about three feet in diameter and a foot deep. Again, we had to use our knives, which, by now, were not very sharp. She explained that we would line the hole with the sour leaves and spread a layer of roots on top, then repeat the leaf-root layers, ending with a layer of leaves. This looked like it would be the easiest preparation, but we would have to learn more about finding the correct leaves for this procedure.

"It takes about three days for the poison to begin to come out and turn the leaves a dark brown. The roots soften and the layers shrink and sink down into the hole. They will still be slippery and will need to be soaked for three days as more poison is eliminated.

"These lessons are very serious for you. Many people who try to be too quick die." The woman frowned. "Take your time, watch carefully, and you can survive."


We trained for two weeks while waiting for orders from Paul Yuh. It was comforting to have a teacher who constantly reminded us to watch every detail. She never hesitated to correct the slightest error. And our bodies began to accept what we could not change.

The message came: we were to move out and follow Y-Soan Eban, but this time forty people from Dak Nong had been added. Now the preparation of the roots was even more important; we numbered a hundred, and most did not understand the process for survival.

## *Knuk Division*

These marches were different from others. There were so many of us, and more seemed to join each week. Our directions were specific; the low tones of conversation mentioned the Cambodian border. Our steps seemed to have purpose; Paul Yuh was going in that direction.

Hunger and thirst accompanied us into the third week away from the hills and into flat, dry land, with smaller trees and bamboo bushes. A distinct strong odor greeted us in a thin forest where trees were twisted and broken, and vegetation was scattered. I had never smelled or seen elephants, but others knew immediately where we were. The ground was covered with dark green elephant dung. A gunshot made all of us freeze and get close to the smelly ground, but word came that our men were hunting for food and had taken down an elephant. I saw a mother and baby run off into the woods and watched our group push toward the noise.

When I arrived, the scene was gruesome. The elephant was on its side, dead, and knives had cut him in half. Blood was everywhere, running across the ground and pouring from every part of the huge animal. Men and women ripped into the flesh with their knives, cutting out pieces to take with them, never seeming to mind the red dripping down their arms. Our leaders yelled, "Take what you can carry and move. We cannot stop. We must hurry."

My stomach was both sickened and rumbling, so I stepped through the bloodied earth and with my dull knife cut a small piece of flesh, but it was mostly fat, then I cut another piece. My knife was not in condition to slice much of the tough meat. At least I could char the skin and have something to chew, cook what meat I had, and keep it in my thermos bottle to eat later.

## *Knuk*

Across the Dak Dam River, we stayed the night to prepare our elephant meat, and after crossing the shallow Plai River late the next morning, we were told that the Knuk area was only a two-day march.

The Knuk soldiers, not rude but firm, made sure that all one hundred plus of us formed a straight line into the campsite. We were obeying their orders when I heard a man call my name. "H'Tien, H'Tien!" I saw him but at first did not answer. He kept calling, "H'Tien!" He got close enough that I waved my hand in his direction. He came quickly toward me. "I am Philip Ksor. You are my niece. Give me your pack! I will give it back later." I did, and he walked away, leaving me with lots of questions.

When I got close to the front of the line, I saw that the soldiers took packs and searched each person, asking them many questions. The commander, Y-Dreri Eban, looked hard at me. "Do you have a letter from Da Lat?"

"No."

"Are you sure that you are not carrying a letter from Da Lat?" He glanced at the soldier beside him.

"I am sure." I stared at him. *They must be looking for a secret message, but why would I have something like that?*

He reached out to search my body, and I pushed his hands away. "Don't you touch me! I won't let you treat me like that." And I turned and walked rapidly toward our group waiting in a large pavilion.

No one came after me, but soon six soldiers came to the pavilion and divided us into two groups. H'Bo and I were not to be together. They divided us into even smaller groups—ten in mine. Our leader, Y-Kro Nie, was a good person from the way that he treated us. It was late, and he found an area where all of us could sleep. With no pack, I had to wrap my clothes around me and lie down on a few fallen leaves, but as cold as I was, sleep was my immediate warm friend.


A silhouette in the dim morning light shook me awake. It was the man, Philip Ksor, from the day before. He placed my backpack on the ground beside me and whispered, "If I had not taken this from you, the soldiers would have seized it, and you would not see it again."

"Thank you! Thank you for caring about me, Uncle." He disappeared back into the forest.

I could see that the other girl in our group, H'Kroai, was waking, and we slipped out to the woods together before the men raised their heads. She and I would have to look after the preparation of the poison roots, but we would have to find them first. She said that she had been sick for a month, with a black rash and redness all over her body, but she had no medicine, and she could only pray that she would get better.

I told her that I would go look for the roots and sour leaves if she could start digging a pit and explained the size to her. A man in our group knew where to begin, so he and I took two baskets in search of *kloi*. He dug, and I began to peel until our containers were full.

He had seen the sour leaves when we marched into the camp, and we gathered enough for a large pit. When we returned, H'Kroai had finished a hole, almost as good as my teacher's, and we sat down to slice what we brought. Soon we would also have a pot of boiling water for some additional roots that she had peeled. She already knew a little about survival, but I wondered if her rash was the result of eating some bad *kloi*.

In the evening, I went to the nearby Rovai River to bathe, but when I came to the bank, I saw baskets and pots along the edge, filled with the roots. The smell was overpowering. I could barely make it to the edge to test the water, and my hand came back with a slimy film dripping from my fingers. This was not the place to fill up my water bottle or to rinse the layers of dirt from my own body. I studied the river stream and hiked up to an area where the water was clear and moving fast. It was not deep, so I slipped in cautiously from the bank and steadied my balance in the flowing stream. Several times I dipped my pan in the current and poured the refreshing water over my head and through my hair, turning my braid loose and rubbing my head to release the field dust and hiking sweat. H'Kroai would be waiting, so I stood up and wrung out my hair and the clothes hanging from my shoulders. All would dry by evening.

## *A Poison Root Drunk*

Early morning arrived along with a request from Y-Kro Nie for H'Kroai to go to the fields and for me to stay at the camp. Her eyes looked down as she asked to stay. Her pain showed in the way she moved her body, and I quickly said that I didn't mind going. Her gaze still did not meet mine, but her mouth moved slightly upward as she whispered, "Thank you!"

Y-Kro sent Y-Dhut with me again. As we picked up our baskets, we ate a few of the prepared roots and took a couple with us for a snack. The river felt cool as we crossed. Our decision to separate, each taking a basket, seemed reasonable at the time, so he went upstream, and I walked toward the forest. As I reached the edge, I blinked my eyelids to clear the view; my head seemed to sway back and forth on my shoulders. My stomach churned until it stopped as though someone had grabbed it and squeezed. And then anything that was on the inside quickly rushed to the outside. I fell to my knees in pain and crawled to a nearby tree in the shade, gagging and gasping for air. I heard voices, some passed by, but none were Y-Dhut's, and no one wanted to help—at least I didn't remember. I slept; then I woke to voices. I tried to answer; I slept again. I heard *drunk.* I slept again. Something pounded my head.

The dark shadows of evening came, and images began to come—wild animals, black widows, leeches. I tried to get up; I fell back down. *I am going to die here. I* have *to get up. Where is Y-Dhut? Where is the river? I have to cross the river. Get up! Get up! The river, I hear the river. Is anyone there? Scream! I am screaming. No, it's the river. Go, crawl, go!*

The cold water shocked me, but I could not stand up. I don't remember reaching the other side of the river, but I did know the voice of Y-Kro Nie when he got me to my feet. Other soldiers were there, and next I was sitting by a fire wrapped in a blanket, my eyes opening and shutting, but my grateful heart steadily letting me know that I was alive.

I was teased about being "that drunk in the woods," but I knew if that was what it was like, I would never, never drink *nam pai* or any other drink that I am not familiar with.

A lot in our group got sick, including Y-Kro. The roots that were given to us were still full of poison and had not been rinsed long enough. The water could not have been clear, but hunger made people hurry through the process, and often they paid with their lives.

I was hit the hardest and was weak for several days, but H'Kroai and I struggled to get up during the night to ensure clear water and no odor in our pots. Our group only ate what we prepared, and no one else got sick during that month.

No longer did we question our teacher's strict rules as to why we *must* prepare the *kloi* like our experienced countrymen before us. It was a deadly plant, and I learned in the months ahead just how fierce it could be. A great many friends and travelers were not careful, and when we had to rush along the trail, we had to leave them where they fell.

# FEAR, SURVIVAL, AND Y-KING NIE

## *Inexperience Claims the Young*

Y-Soan Eban received orders from Paul Yuh that it was time to move in his direction. Two large groups, like platoons, including ours, began another march toward Cambodia, with Y-Tlung Ayun as our leader.

From Dha Prong Village and other camps, numerous young people joined us as we moved through the forests. They did not have backpacks, did not know about preparing *kloi*, and knew little about surviving in the jungle. They became numb and hungry and discouraged.

After a week of marching, we stopped to provide ourselves with a new supply of food and to allow a time to rest.

Our leaders seemed to disappear, nothing was organized, and no one directed us to fields where roots grew. Young and old came to our site and left again, slept and visited whenever they wanted, wandered in the jungle, but returned with few new supplies, became hungry, and then complained. We had no commanders to keep order.

I had little experience with the purple potato-like *nagaimo* and with the sweeter taro roots, but if we could find them, it would help all of us. We could at least make soup without being poisoned. Something had to be done—or all of us would die.

I explained to our small group of ten that we would be the leaders and teachers. Their eyes seemed to focus on every word, and their bodies showed a willingness to begin immediately.

Two of the men left to find bamboo strips to make baskets. H'Bui, a girl from our last place, knew how to prepare the *kloi*, and several knew what *kloi*, *nagaimo*, and taro roots looked like.

"Take the baskets that we have and some of the new people and spread out to find these plants and any vegetables or leaves that we might cook," I instructed. "Bring some of the girls to me and H'Bui, and we will train them how to take the poison from the root. And do not be too long. I see sickness and starvation all around us."

Searching the forests, fields, and streams took most of the first week. By the second week, we had everyone involved—peeling, slicing, boiling, roasting in hot coals, and emphasizing the importance of complete preparation. Not only were we gaining food, but the group found a purpose. Many friendships came together, and everyone learned the poison root process. On the third week, I crushed dried *kloi*, shared it, and instructed them to *keep it* for as long as they could in their packs or pockets so that it would be there in case of an emergency like we had just experienced.

For us, no longer was the Knuk area called the Place of the Dead. We were survivors, and soon after we became a stable community, a soldier arrived with instructions to take me to meet another leader, Y-King Nie. I would miss all of my new friends, but it was a relief to move away from that desperate place.

## Y-King Nie's Battalion

I sometimes wondered what all of our marching and hiking and changing directions and numbers weaving in and out of the jungle would look like from up above. Oftentimes I felt as though we were scattered ants, scurrying from nest to nest, frantically trying to find the one that would swallow us up into a safe home where our lives would be surrounded by kindness and honey and restful days.

The small group that I met was mostly from Dark Nong, and it was comforting to know that at least they knew their way around the jungle. Together we crossed the O-Chi-Bad River and then the Krieng River and settled along its very dry riverbed. Rain was needed, and many groups used what little water ran through its bottom, but used wisely, it was enough.

Y-King Nie, who led this modest battalion, had heard that I could cook the roots, wash, sew, and take care of his needs. I made quick work of my chores for him, but he refused to let me go with my friends when they left the camp, looking for enjoyment. I was bored; I stayed alone much of the time, and my mind became depressed from inactivity. I would fix a dinner for several men in our unit, but they would eat some other place before they came back for the night. Then they would be hungry before they went to sleep and want fresh-cooked food.

In the jungle, one learned to be obedient. Refusing the leadership could destroy you. I ate little, slept a lot, and wondered if God cared for caged animals.

One afternoon, a friend, Y-Bunh Mdrang, found me asleep under a tree. "H'Tien, wake up! Come with me and walk along the riverside. You will see lots of new things, and you won't be alone. Y-King has gone."

My eyelids were slow to open, and his words sounded unclear, but he took my hand, pulled me up, told me to get a few belongings, and led me away from the hut.

"I waited until Y-King Nie went to another camp and said that he would be there for some time," was Y-Bunh's answer to my questioning eyes. "You don't have to think, just come with me!"

We found *nagaimo* and taro roots and looked for insects to eat. He killed a large snake, bit its head off, and charred it over a fire that he built. The taste was not as important as the small bites of meat that warmed my body as I swallowed. I knew that all was not well inside me because of the black waste that often came from my painful stomach.

"Thank you, friend! You have made my day much better."

I ate a little more, and he finished eating the snake on our four-hour walk to the *kloi* fields to gather roots with other friends. We rested often, and just being away from Y-King Nie gave me strength to smile.

Where they were camping, the Krieng River was full and deep, and I could lie down in the shallow edge of the water to soak away the boredom. But in the river, I ran my hands over my body and felt bones where flesh once was. My friends were astonished to see the walking skeleton.

"You cannot live much longer, H'Tien. Surely you will die soon, maybe in a few days."

I could tell that it was true, but I wanted to live. *I want to make it out of the jungle. I have to survive. I am too young to die. We have come so far. No, I will not die. I will not.* And I prayed to God for life. I drank from the taro root, soaked the poison roots from the field, cooked, and laughed with my six friends. I would not die.

The two weeks with Y-Bunh and those faithful companions seemed like two days. My emotions spilled over as we all hiked back toward Y-King Nie's camp. We met him on the way, as he had returned and heard from others where we were. I could not tell his mood as we approached. He just stared at me and said, "I have a message for you from Y-Kler Eban, Y-Nguan, and Y-Siu Hlong.

Those were familiar names to me, and I was curious that Y-King mentioned meeting with them. We hiked back to his hut in silence. I cooked his meal and prepared for bed.

Y-King spoke out to me. "H'Tien, Y-Kler is looking for the girl who sings and can read. They want you, but you do not have to go. You can just say no."

I could not show my surprise and happiness. *Has my prayer already been answered?* I said that I would give him my answer in the morning, but I already knew what that would be.

While eating his morning meal, he added, "Y-Nguan did say that they chose you and that you would have to come."

I breathed in the putrid air from the soaking pots by the river, almost choking on the odor, and tried not to pack my things too fast.

Y-King sat by the fire as I spoke. "I thank you for your protection here, but I will be happy to honor their wishes. I will be ready when the soldiers begin their return to Y-Kler."

His look of surprise became sad and then distant.

Three soldiers came for me by late morning. I had time to see my friends, especially Y-Bunh, and to give each my thanks for saving my life. "I pray that I will see you again—maybe soon— and that we all will be safe."

The two months that felt like two years of weariness from serving Y-King Nie eased off my shoulders with each step I made toward my new camp and my old friends.

# A Special Place—an Abandoned Wood Mill

I had only heard of Y-Kler before. He was a good leader and kind to our group but mean to his soldiers. I had noticed that characteristic with other leaders and thought that fear must be a way of controlling obedience.

He told me that he had known my name at Da Lat and at Dang Jri. And I finally had the opportunity to thank him for a skirt that I had received from him during those years. He seemed glad that I remembered and gestured with his hand that it had been Y-Nguan, Y-Siu Hlong, and his idea to rescue me from "the old man." I expressed that I was grateful.

Two other girls, H'Dam Arul and H'Tot Eban, in our group of twenty, managed to rise at 3:00 a.m. most mornings and get to the fields before anyone else. They returned to camp with baskets of *kloi* and occasional mangoes and *nagaimo*. By going out to the jungle fields early, they selected food supplies first. Other divisions around us would have to search farther away to satisfy their needs. It took me a month to build up enough strength to join them in that early hour, but it was my joy to be active with chores, preparing *kloi* and gathering pure honey from trees in the forest with H'Dam. The bees rarely stung me. Even the yellow ants' colonies were close enough to the ground to gather, and we could use them to give a spicy flavor to our food.

Two men hunted the forests for meat—birds, monkeys, snakes; three provided wood while others built huts. Two men supplied fish from a nearby river; another sharpened blades and straightened knives.

It was a time of pleasure. All of our members were active and supported one another. Our Saturdays were free, and Sundays were blessed with prayers and thanksgiving and with tears for those we left behind. Respect and friendship bound us together while we waited orders from Paul Yuh.

Late one evening, word came to our camp that another group from Pleiku had arrived about a half-mile away. I thought that my heart had stopped beating when I first heard the news, and my arm froze in the middle of stirring a pot of soup. *Was it really from Pleiku? Could she be with them? I must go now. No, I'll wait until morning, but how will I sleep? Could God be answering another prayer so soon? Don't be too hopeful! She may not be there.*

But she was. A soldier led me to the new arrivals, and I saw H'Bloanh immediately, walking from her temporary shelter. Everything seemed to be in slow motion as our arms reached out toward each other and bodies met in a long, unbelieving embrace. Tears, laughter, and caresses blended into joyful delight, only interrupted by moments of prayerful silence.

The years that had separated us since Dam Per Quay sent her to Pleiku melted away. Sadly she had no news of my family and had been unable to communicate to them that I was alive. Now, although she was to stay with her group, she was in our battalion, and we could see each other every afternoon, sometimes meeting by the fresh waterfall in a bamboo forest. We ran back and forth in the cold water, sunned on the stones along the bank, and often returned with cinnamon ferns that we picked by the stream. She shared the salt she had brought, and I lavished her with pure, sweet honey.

A month later, Y-Kler spoke with me seriously about going forward to Thailand. "Don't go, H'Tien! Stay in your own country! Everything is so uncertain there. How will you get across the Mekong River?"

"I don't know the answer to all of that, but I cannot stay here and never have freedom again."

His eyes focused on the ground. "I have an opportunity to go back—go back to my family. I really miss them. I do not see how I can live the rest of my life without them. Come with me!"

"You are a good friend, Y-Kler, and I pray that God will look after you." There was little else to talk about. I had come too far to retrace a single step. I would not reconsider.

Several months later, the jungle messengers brought news that Y-Kler's safety depended on the Viet Cong government. I never saw him again.

# ANXIOUS COMMANDERS—
# DIRECTIONS FROM THE TOP

## *Y-Tlung Ayun's Command*

Y-Tlung Ayun took the leadership after Y-Kler left. With regret, we moved to his area. His camp was more like an army company of over seventy people, and H'Bloanh was then about one and a half hours away. He rearranged our division again and put twelve girls together into one unit, between Y-Daler Nie's battalion and his own. We were happy with that plan, especially when we found our accomplishments to be more than we expected.

We were strong, seasoned jungle women and could depend on ourselves to take care of our own needs as well as those near our camp. Our bamboo baskets for our leader Y-Tlung's company were strong and woven well. The huts that we built were sturdy; the food we gathered was sufficient. Y-Tlung's soldiers came often to collect their share to supply his men. We gave willingly, but often discussed the need for his people to act responsibly for themselves.

We accepted the sick men, the ones with diarrhea or malaria, stomach disorders or simple starvation. We nursed them with what we had—cool cloths, hot broth, bits of food, exercise to help them regain their strength. And after they healed, they stayed close by to guard our unit. But every few days, other soldiers borrowed our shovel to bury their dead.

Paul Yuh's messengers, bringing salt and dried meat, came straight to our women's unit before communicating with our leaders. We sent them back with properly prepared *kloi* and fruit from the forests. Friends visited, and in the evenings, our voices echoed through the camp, inspiring others with our favorite songs and hymns.

Additional groups located near our batallion and the number in our company increased every few days. H'Nhien finally arrived under another commander and settled only a half-day away. Although I had known from couriers' mouths that she was okay, having her and H'Bloanh close by gave the three of us comfort that we had not shared in several years. That lasted barely a month.

However, after several weeks, our girls drifted away one by one to be with different families, until there were only four of us left.

## *Communications Stir Expectations*

Something was happening in the jungle. Messengers from Paul Yuh came more often, but Y-Tlung spoke little about the details he received. He was tense and repeated harsh words to those around him. Even though the messengers stopped by our hut for a meal, they hid their secrets well in their conversations.

When Y-Tlung heard that our unit now only numbered four girls, he tried to send H'Dam and me to some very distant rice fields, but I looked him in the eye and said, "I won't go that far away. We can look after ourselves. H'Dam needs to stay here."

He said, "There is not a place for you here. You must go. We need your huts." His eyes seemed not to focus on me as though his mind was far away.

"Why are you angry with me and H'Dam? What have we done, and why can't you talk to me about it?"

"I cannot talk to anyone." He jerked his head around and looked at me. "You see all of these people? And more are coming. We must have food and shelter, and...I don't know for how long." His mouth became very thin and tight.

I struggled to find some way to keep the conversation going, but I did not ask questions. "It feels as though all of us will be moving soon."

"Go back to your hut with H'Dam! We'll talk later."

And we did talk on occasion for the next week, the kind of talk that had manners. Before I left with the next group, I gave him the shirt that Y-Kler had given me but kept the army pants that saved my legs from thorns and bamboo when we marched. Also, I gave him a pen and thanked him for becoming a friend and for changing his hard actions.

## *Directions from Paul Yuh*

Finally, H'Bloanh and I received a message that Paul Yuh wanted us to join him at his division headquarters. Messages and rumors circulated through all of the platoons, which increased in number every week. Food was our main concern, and H'Bloanh and I knew to make the most use of our backpacks for storing crushed *kloi*, dried meat, taro roots—anything that would not spoil and could keep us alive for the move to Cambodia.

If we were to be in Paul Yuh's division, we must be close to the border. Everywhere friends talked in low voices: "When do you think it will be?" "Have you heard anything?" "Have any of the camps moved?" "How will we know when we are in Cambodia?"

"Our destination is Thailand," read our communication.

My eyes read it again. "H'Bloanh, are we really going to Thailand? How will we get across the Mekong River? It is so wide, and I...I cannot...and there are so many of us."

My strong and loyal friend frowned and then lightly smiled. "You can do it. We will do it together, and we'll make it across."

I slept comfortably next to her through the nights that followed. Our hike to Paul Yuh's company village only took half a day, and the other surprise was the house that he provided for us with seven other young women. The roof, bamboo walls, and floor were luxuries that we had forgotten for years.

"This looks permanent," I whispered to H'Bloanh. "Do you think that our lives will end here? There are so many more people."

"No, but there is not the rush that we thought. This will give us time to prepare more food."

And over the next two months, we again cooked and washed and made preparations and tried to keep ourselves cheerful and enthusiastic.

From somewhere came a supply of rubber inner tubes (from old tires) that we learned to cut into flat sandals held on by rubber straps around the heel and up from the sole through our first two toes. We had a pattern to follow, but not all feet were the same size. Soldiers told us that the march ahead would be through tall grasses and prickly paths, not like the floors of the jungle. We were pleased to have foot protection, but the straps made blisters, and getting used to with our floppy footwear did not come easily.

## *A Flag for Food*

- Blue

- Red

- Green

FULRO Flag for Paul Yuh

Paul Yuh asked me to make a small FULRO flag of three colors (dark blue, red and dark green with three white stars on the middle red stripe) and sew it to his green beret.

"I know it will take a long time, and I must gather food every day so that all of us can eat," I answered him.

"Then I will pay you with food to make it," he offered.

I stared at him and at the huts and the people—busy with surviving. Paul Yuh had been good and fair to me, so I finally said, "Okay, I'll make one."

He had scraps from a very worn flag that he had carried in his pack, so I had the colors and found a needle and thread in a metal bottle that I used to carry small items. The left-hand rectangle was a royal blue, and the three rectangular stripes attached to it on the right were red, yellow, and green. They were not as difficult as the white crescent moon and star sewn on the blue background, but with no pattern, they were as even as I could make them. It took me a week to finish his request, working between chores around my camp. Attaching the flag to his hat had to be done at night so that he would not be without his green beret during the day, but his smile of approval and gratitude when I returned it to him made me happy.

Paul Yuh's brother-in-law, Y-Blol, gave me a bag of poison root powder in payment. It did not look like much, but it was generous as I did know how long it took to prepare it. I thanked him and was pleased the next morning when I saw our commander proudly going through his battalion—his back straighter, his stride confident.


Occasionally I visited my uncle Klut Siu and his son Kan Nay in their camp. They were like close family from our earliest days in the jungle after my mentor H'Tlon Nie left us and was soon killed. We spoke long about where we almost lost our lives and how our survivals might be an act of God. I had little to take to him, but if they had fish, they shared enough for me to take back to H'Bloanh.

# Radio Message from Cambodia

Rumors, messages, whispered talk went quickly through the battalion. A radio communication had been made between the Cambodian leader and our division leaders—Y-Khot Nie Krieng and my uncle, Nay Rong. Our group was given permission to join Cambodians in a massive march toward the Mekong River and on to Dangrek, but only seventy of our people were allowed at that time; those chosen names were on a list. That list was sent throughout the area, and all seventy were instructed to assemble in two weeks at the edge of our division with Y-Khot, Nie Krieng, and Nay Rong.

I was stunned to hear my name called and H'Bloanh's omitted. I could not accept that, so I disappeared. Almost a week later, Paul Yuh's soldiers found me hiding, with H'Nap, at a *kloi* field and took me back to him, where I found a very angry man threatening to send me back to Pleiku.

"H'Tien, I didn't choose you. This list came from Thailand. Their directions were that we would include four BJRK girls: from Bahnar, Jarai, Rhade, and Koho tribes. The four names are H'Ngam, H'Tien, H'Wat, and Bron. There are 66 men on the list, all joining the first wave of 1,500 to cross into Cambodia and to the Dangrek resistance camp on the border of Thailand. There are many who beg to go, but I have orders to send you. Why are you acting like this?" His face was red, and his fist was closed.

"But I can't leave H'Bloanh."

H'Bloanh had come with me to see Paul Yuh. "You will go first, and I will come later."

"But I…"

H'Bloanh turned to Paul Yuh. "When does the first group leave?' She held my hand.

"In a week." He turned sharply and walked away.

# Frightening Endurance

## First Two Weeks—Tropical Savanna

Montagnards on the move - (Courtesy of Ed Sprague)

Y-Djot Mlo was our commander (in charge of the soldiers and of safety), and Y-Panh Ayun was the leader of our group. They moved us in the direction of the Mekong River, but first we would have to cross the Ho Chi Minh trail—with 1,500 people.

I soon was to find out what 1,500 people looked like. I knew that my village near Cheo Reo did not come close to that number. What little information I had about our march came from Uncle Nay Rong. There always seemed to be a kind of uncertain certainty in the eyes of our leaders and our soldiers.

H'Ngam, H'Wat, Bron, and I stayed close together, and after two days of marching, we were ordered to set camp—each of us assigned to different units. Our leaders selected a savanna with tall green grasses, small trees, ponds, and a creek that supplied us with enough clear, flowing water—enough for occasional bathing and for soaking poison roots from the surrounding fields. We were tired and needed a few days to adjust. We had had visions of going straight to the trail, but our days there turned into weeks.

I cooked for seven soldiers, three leaders, and myself. Numerous people around us complained about not having enough to eat, but our group was good at searching for food, and I knew how to process the *kloi*. Even though we could now find some *nagaimo* and occasional fruit and palms, we understood that the poison roots would be our main diet for a long time. Even so, I always saved some of the powdered root that I pounded and stored it in my pack for the long journey in front of us.

At first in my unit, our leaders wanted meals served from their own pot, but several days later, I declared that I did not need to build two fires or to wash and cook in two pots—that we would all eat our meals from one pot. One leader opened his mouth to say something, but my eyes widened, and not moving, I stared straight at him. Mouths closed, eyes closed, subject closed.


Rejoicing came one day when Dri Y-Siu returned to camp with four monkeys. We shared our bounty with the six other groups and ended the evening with songs of thanksgiving.

The next day, Nie Kpa Wick, one of our leaders, said, "H'Tien, last night you should never have shared with the soldiers the salt that you were given. That is for the leaders."

"The soldiers work very hard to hunt and to protect us. It is not fair to keep it from them. They are like brothers to me." It made me so angry that I left the group the next day. They could fix their own food. I found Bron and joined her group.

All of us were getting tense. The strain of the previous months of adjusting to new places, different units, lack of water and food, sickness, and death were adding to our uneasiness and desire to push forward to the Mekong River and on to Thailand.

# The March to Ho Chi Minh Trail

Every day, near our camp, we noticed companies of Cambodian soldiers and villagers swelling the numbers already gathered nearby, until the area looked like a woven rug of muted colors.

Anticipation built as we continued to collect and prepare food and to stare in the direction of the unusual mixture of people. We spoke in low tones, listened to the sounds of children, watched soldiers hurry around the camp, and questioned the appearance of men and women who could barely walk.

Soon, early on a warm, dry afternoon, all rumors stopped; all uncertainty stopped. Y-Panh Ayun and Y-Djot Mlo went around our sites and recounted our seventy members. "We leave tomorrow morning. Set the camp in order. There is no more time to cure poison roots or to look for food."

Even though my bag had remained packed, especially with enough food (so I thought), my mind only calmed for short periods during the night.

In the morning, there was no cooking, all fire pits were covered, and the campsite looked abandoned except for the 68 people gathered to hear instructions from our two leaders.

"Listen carefully! We are marching with 1,430 Cambodians— our allies, our friends. Our group will stay together. I want you to follow one another closely, the four girls in the middle, one behind the other; do not stop, but if you have an emergency, notify us immediately! While marching, we will be in a line of one hundred—twenty Cambodian soldiers in front of us and ten behind. I will walk in front of our division, and Y-Djot Mlo will follow the last one. The other Cambodians will be in fourteen rows of 100 each and will be responsible for themselves. I hope that this is clear." And Y-Panh Ayun began to organize us into a straight line.

I looked across the savanna and watched our new allies arrange a variety of generations and abilities into orderly, marching companies.

"How is this going to work?" I spoke to Bron next to me. "It seems impossible for all of us to go at once."

"We have been moving this way for many months. I guess that the Cambodians have too." Bron paused. "I pray that the commanders are prepared. To turn back now is to die."

I knew that she was right, but before I could add my thoughts, a signal came for us to move out.

*God, I am a little scared, but I know that you are with us. I am also excited about finally seeing the Ho Chi Minh trail. It has been a dream in my heart for so long—for so many years. The Mekong River is my greatest worry, but today, please be with us in crossing the trail.*

"Today" went into night, went into another day and night, and I was hungry and thirsty but took only tiny sips of my water. Our pace slowed with exhaustion, and our short rest periods were more in number. I began to question whether there was even a trail, or maybe we were just lost.

Finally, the command came that we would camp for a night and that it was safe to cook over small fires. I was able to mix some of my white-powdered *kloi* with mud and cook it in my pot. It was not meant to give taste but to make my stomach feel full.

Deep, quiet sleep came throughout the camp. Any sound from the Cambodian children was swallowed up in the night air. I remembered what happened to babies in the jungle. They were unwanted, dangerous liabilities.

Our guards listened and watched and protected us through the dark hours. We heard that they took one-hour shifts so that each could have a small amount of rest.

Morning came with only a short time to have a snack of dried fish, a small piece of taro root, and a sip of water. But after a few hours of marching, we came upon a river—narrow and green and moving slowly. My thrill at having something to drink was soon cut short after I stepped into the water to cool my aching feet. A terrible smell came up from the bottom, along with chunks of green floating objects. The odor was immediately recognizable as elephant dung, and I thanked God that I had not swallowed the water that I heaved out of my mouth. I spit and spit and spit until I could spit no more. I found a taro root in my pack, cut a small piece, and sucked on the stem to rid my mouth of the taste.

We marched again before I had a chance to even consider that I might still be thirsty. In front of us was a dry field, a small forest that had been cleared, burned and left to decay, but the sharp, prickly stubs did not bend with our steps. They seemed to attack my feet like needles and stick through my rubber sandals. Even though my friend Y-Suiah HLong tried to fix the broken straps between my toes, my flip-flops gave me more trouble than going without. I put the left-foot broken one in my pack and wore the right one for as much protection as I could get. I didn't know that the barbed stubs were not as harsh as the trail ahead.

On the other side of the field, we entered an area of tall elephant grass, so tall that the only way you might know that there were people in it was by the swaying motion. The clumps were thick, and the stems were razor sharp. When we came out on the other side, our arms and faces, especially, were ripped, sliced, and bleeding.

My friend Y-Suiah tried to comfort my tears of pain by telling me that the trail was not far. "We cannot stop, and there is no stream or anything to ease the hurt."

Before I had time to study my complaints, we were through the next softer field. I was barefooted and more comfortable. My one pair of shoes had worn out years before, and in places, my feet were like leather.

As I adjusted to a new pace, there was a signal from the front that had all of us stop. Y-Djot Mlo came up from behind with the last of our line. His instructions had been planned weeks or months before.

"The trail is up ahead. We are going across it, but you must listen to every word that I say. All 1,500 of us are lining up into our fifteen rows of one hundred each. There will be a signal from the front when it is time to go, and we all will run together. Each one of you has come this far to save your own life. We are used to helping one another, but *your* survival depends on what *you* do. If you fall, no one is going to pick you up. If you stop, no one will wait for you. We will run until the front of the line signals that we are safe. You will run for a long time. When you are out of breath, keep going; when you cannot keep going, keep running. Remember that there is an end, and you want to be there.

"The Ho Chi Minh is a supply trail for the North Vietnamese. We will have guards on the road watching for trucks and other vehicles. Should one come while we are trying to cross, our men will signal for everyone to stop and to lie flat in the tall grasses until they pass.

"After all of us are across the trail, some of our soldiers in the rear will set mines near the road to keep the VC, or anyone else, from following us. There is to be no talking. Just focus on the person in front of you. I hope to see all of you on the other side."

I looked ahead, saw our line move, and soon the man in front of me was running, and I was right behind him, followed by Y-Suiah, Dri, and Y-Siu. I didn't look left or right. I just ran. My feet felt soft dirt for two or three seconds as I briefly closed my eyes to the dust, and I knew that I had just crossed the trail. Not far on the other side, I stepped on a woman's leg. It threw me off balance, with my backpack shifting to the right. In another second I had run past her without stopping. My heart sank, but I heard Y-Suiah say, "Keep going!"

I tripped twice, and my friend encouraged me, "Don't fall; be careful. Take it easy!" But I couldn't slow down. I began to fly, to race with the wind, to narrow my eyes in the dust-filled air. Branches of trees and small bushes brushed over my wounds. As I felt my legs trying to give up, I imagined myself to be a buffalo in a herd escaping from a lion. My backpack dug into my back, and sweat washed over the blood on my arms and face.

As my lungs began to burn, I sensed that the line in front of me was slowing. I looked up to see a hill rising in the distance—a welcomed sight. People were lying on the ground or sitting down with chests moving in and out so rapidly that it looked as though they were rocking.

My pace slowed to a walk and then to a stop, where I stood for a moment, released my pack to the ground, and joined it on my knees.

After my breath came back to normal, I asked Y-Suiah how far he thought that we ran. He said, "Several miles, maybe three or four." He looked at his watch. "Almost an hour."

It did not seem possible. I laughed out loud, and the man next to me said that I must be crazy. Maybe I was, but I could see that all four girls and most of the men were across. We rested for a while and then our leaders said that if we left then, we could get to the Mekong River by night. The bodies, scattered on the ground, slowly stretched and unfolded as new energy lifted exhausted spirits.

# *The Mekong River*

(Large Dugout Canoe Used on River - Courtesy of Bill Thaxton)

I reached into my pack and found some small bits of cooked elephant skin in my thermos. I put a piece in my mouth and took a sip of water. The skin puffed up and became soft enough to chew. I cut a piece of taro root, took another small sip of water, and was ready to start the march again.

Aching bodies groaned under the weight of the backpacks as we adjusted them on our shoulders, but there was little complaining. Our lives depended on our packs, which mostly contained survival food. "They say it isn't far," was the word passed around by soldiers. Smiles helped to bring us to our feet, as the sun began to ease down behind the hill that we would climb one step and then another, and the pace quickened.

By the time daylight faded, we had walked to the top of a ridge above the Mekong. The ground, the sky, and the river were the same—black. But I could smell the river and hear the water lapping over itself. I saw the outline of trees and bushes beside me and wondered if they ran along the river enough to hide 1,500 people.

No one cheered, as sound travels across water, but anxious relief was in the whispering voices along the banks. Word came back to us that we would begin the crossing soon. Y-Siu had more information. "We will go in small numbers to an island in the middle of the river and wait for the last in line to follow. We can build small fires during the night once we arrive, but there is little food on the island for all of us. We are encouraged to rest before going on the river." *Rest.* I wondered when our scouts, guards, and leaders rested. Their responsibility was enormous.

Y-Siuah heard that the Cambodians had provided boats for us (two for our group). One could take twelve people (including the ones who paddled), the other could hold six (two with paddles). I leaned against my pack and tried to count the number of trips, my lids drooped over my burning eyes, and sleep crept in without warning.

Y-Siu woke me. In a low voice, he said, "I think it's time for us soon. We need to go to the shore to be ready."

"What do you mean? Where are we going?"

"H'Tien, we're crossing the Mekong. It is time. Some of us have already gone."

I sat up and rubbed my head and shoulders. Y-Siu held out his hand, pulled me up, and helped me with my pack. A chill ran through me, and my stomach was churning, but I followed Y-Siu Dri and Y-Suiah to the edge of the river. I heard paddles cutting through the water and could see the outline of two men and a small boat, a man at each end.

"Are we going on the little boat?" I could hardly speak.

"Yes, we'll be okay. I know that you can't swim, H'Tien. A lot of us cannot swim." Y-Suiah's voice was only slightly reassuring. Suddenly H'Bloanh's words spoke through my memory: *You can do it. I will come in the next group. We will make it.*

A soldier on shore reached out for a paddle and pulled the boat closer. The two men with paddles got out, and two more got in. My heart seemed not in my body. "Okay, let's go," a soldier onshore said to me. I handed someone my pack and stepped into the middle of a boat that was hardly wide enough for me and swayed from side to side so low in the water that I thought we would all immediately sink. I began to shake as I sat down in the bottom and hugged my bag to steady myself. Between lots of rocking as we tried to settle, the others sat in front and behind me, and one of the paddles pushed us from the bank.

I think that I held my breath for the first ten minutes, and then my rigid body began to ease, but my mouth was as dry as field dirt. As the boat slid quietly through the river, the water lapped against the sides, sometimes with a slap but often with a soft splash. The smell was different, heavier, older than the fresh small rivers we had crossed in the jungle, but I reached one hand over the side to feel the water and then the other. When I brought my hands to my mouth, I licked the moisture from my fingers and did it several more times. The drops rolled down my tongue and calmed my fear.

My prayer to God came from me in a Vietnamese song— almost a hum with whispered words, *"Lay Me la Ngoi Sao Sang"* ("Star of the Sea").

> Dear Mother, who is the bright star, please shine on me as I cross the ocean of my world.
>
> Dear Mother, who is the bright star, guide me straight to the place of blessings.
>
> Alive or dead, I rely on your countless, supportive strength—on you, Mother, ever ready to look after me, taking me safely home, taking me to heaven.
>
> Dear Mother Queen, please understand my plight, as I am in this fragile hour about to be capsized by high waves.

Dear Mother Queen, please understand my plight, please help me always to be safe at your side, surrounded by your love for me.

According to Y-Suiah's watch, it took us fifty minutes. Soldiers who had been first to come to the grassy island helped us from the boat. I was so grateful and said, "Thank you! Thank you!" to the two soldiers as I stood on solid ground and relief moistened my eyes. Y'Suiah said that it was already 1:00 a.m., and they could make only two more trips that night. All crossings would stop at 4:00 a.m. and continue the next night at 9:00 p.m.

We walked toward the center of the island and put our things down near others who had crossed first. I took my blanket out, wrapped it around me, and slept into the rising sun.

During the next two nights, our fires lasted long enough to cook small pancakes of our white-powdered *kloi*, mixed again with a little dirt to make our stomachs satisfied. We boiled and drank the river water and ate small amounts from our packs.

The second night, all made it across, including our soldiers who had set the mines, rowed the boats, and guarded us throughout our march. They pulled our boats ashore and hid them in the grass for our escape across the second half of the river. In the daytime, we listened for planes and watched for boats on the river, always alert and hiding flat down in the tall grasses or under nearby bushes. The island was long and narrow, and there was no food or privacy.

Early on the third morning, Y-Djot Mlo gathered our group. "All of us made it across the trail and across this much of the river. We must wait here for further instructions, probably tonight. Whenever we begin to cross the other part of the river, we will probably have an hour's notice."

I lay back in the new green grass, stared at the clouds, and breathed in the cool, fresh air. A mountain range was in the distance, across the Mekong. *I wonder if we have to climb that first. We could be in a worse place to wait. But I do pray that it is not much farther and that we will be safe. Thank you for all of the brave soldiers!*

The orders came before 9:00 p.m., and we began to cross the other half of the Mekong. Once on land, we kept marching in small groups, led by a few soldiers and unpredictable moonlight that moved in and out of the clouds. We hid in the forests when a hint of daylight allowed us to find a resting place. Again, it took two nights for everyone to arrive at the site.

Y-Djot Mlo spoke to us the next day. "We will wait here as long as we are not spotted by low flying planes or VC scouts. Our group is like a large company and needs direction from the Cambodians to map a safe march to Dangrek mountains. It could take several weeks, so be careful with your food. There will be those who have not prepared well for this trip. If you have food, guard it. In small numbers, you may go back a mile or two and fish in the Mekong, but stay alert and hidden. You might find *nagaimo* roots, berries, and a few animals, but you must not use your rifles. The sound will carry to far places."

## *Mountains as Shields*

Days dragged on into a month, and even though we had been prepared and had rationed our supplies, our food was dangerously low.

Orders came that we were to continue to travel alongside the mountains that were giving us protection. I was amazed that there had been no planes or enemy rockets so far.

While we made our camp look as natural as possible, Y-Suiah spoke to me in a very serious voice, "H'Tien, you have always tried to help people around you and share what you have. I must warn you that I have seen many in the other groups begging for food and water. You have spent all these years in the jungles to save your life so that you can live in freedom. We still may not make it because of our numbers and little food in sight. Be strong and walk past the empty hands held out to you. As difficult as it is, you must save the bits you have for yourself."

I understood, but when I marched straight ahead, not looking left or right, brushing by the weak, starving bodies, my heart was heavy, and I prayed to God for forgiveness.

Into the first week, we were allowed to rest for a day. Our bodies were bent, and our pace was slow. There was little strength left in any of us. Y-Suiah and Dri followed a unit of Cambodian soldiers to look for food. While they were gone, they met with gunfire, which we could hear. We immediately buried our fires and struggled up into the mountains, dragging Y-Suiah's and Dri's packs with us.

I felt that the sides of my stomach had met. Y-Siu and I began to wonder if our friends had any food in their backpacks that we could share until they came back with more supplies. But soon they returned with no food and news that Cambodian Communist scouts and Khmer soldiers had engaged them in a shooting. The scouts and Khmer soldiers had been killed.

The routine in our camp had been disrupted, so we reorganized and hiked on for four more hours before we set up another hiding place. Hunger was briefly forgotten but returned again along the trail, as we kept on the watch for *nagaimo* or any greens or berries that we could quickly gather.

During the second week of marching, we were suddenly stopped. A creek in front of us had been planted below the water's surface with sharp bamboo stakes (points up) so that anyone who blindly entered the water would be seriously wounded or killed. The Cambodian soldiers were wise and sent messages throughout our company, directing us to form a single line before we waded in, carefully following the person in front of us. They went ahead, pulled up the stakes to make a path, and warned us again at the creek to stay one behind the other.

The Khmer soldiers were helpful, and we were slow and deliberate. Our numbers were no longer 1,500. People, mostly Cambodians, had already died along the trail from exhaustion and hunger, and it still took three hours to get all of us to the other side.

The rainforests in the mountains offered plenty of space to cover our mass of people; however, we camped not far from the edge where the land was rich with good soil, and streams and ponds were only thirty minutes away. There were animals up in the jungle areas, but shooting rifles was not allowed, and elephants were too big to take down without a gun. Small lakes an hour or two away provided fish for roasting and drying.

Y-Djot Mlo's words encouraged us during our month-long stay: "The Dangrek mountains and the camp are only a fifteen-day march." With the use of walkie-talkie radio contacts among the Cambodians and Montagnards, communication was as accurate as our travels would permit. Guidance was necessary. Our number could not be absorbed easily—as we would be needing food, water, and shelter. Dangrek soldiers would come when the camp could safely accommodate us.

While we hid half-starved, Y-Panh Ayun hiked out into a Cambodian village to look for food. In Vietnam, he had acquired ivory (maybe from the elephant that was killed) and had traded that for gold. As we grew weaker, he used that gold to purchase rice that he brought back to our unit. I cannot forget how generous he was to share it with us or how warm and healing it to our bodies.

# Unimagined Liberation

## Long Wait Over

Y-Djot Mlo gathered us one evening and said, "Soldiers are on their way to lead us to Dangrek. We should provide for our march." It was unbelievable news.

Twenty-seven men came—with smiles, handshakes, dried meat, fruit, and reassurance. They led us from our hidden camp and turned north toward the Dangrek range. Our scouts still watched for the enemy, as they were not convinced of our security until we were over the Thai border. There was time to sleep and to cook on our march, but all of us were anxious to push ahead, and our pace quickened.

I had only imagined what it would be like to count down fifteen days to safety. But there, in April 1982, I was counting each step at the beginning of what I thought would be our last journey from the Viet Cong, from the Cambodian Communists, from land mines, from severe hunger, and from poison roots.

The sun was still asleep when our anxious group gathered to begin our last hike to Dangrek. I awoke with expectation in my heart and doubts in my thoughts. *Is this real? Are those years of nightmares behind me? Will this really mean freedom? What will we do here— and for how long? Are the Thai people good people?* And with each step up the sloping mountainside, my mind raced in and out of my body, focusing on the ground, lifting my eyes to the beautiful view back into Cambodia and ahead to the land where God had brought us. When I realized that I was near the top, I thought of Ami and Ama when I left them eight years ago with my last words: "I love you, I will miss you. I am not coming back. I am going to Thailand."

Abruptly, I fell to the ground when gunshots rang through the air. Y-Siu bent over me and said in a voice that spoke over more gunfire and cheers, "Get up, H'Tien! It is a celebration. They are welcoming us to the camp. We're here."

I stood with my hands over my ears and looked down a wide dirt road that led into a community that looked like more than a village. Bamboo houses lined the way under tall trees that reminded me of the Da Lat forests and of Dong Knoh camp. A mixture of tents and small houses spread out as far as I could see, and people—men, women, and children dressed in similar clothing—ran to meet us or stood in front of their houses, clapping their hands and laughing in happiness, as our worn and exhausted battalion of almost 1,500 walked down the road into our new home. The men who greeted us wore red striped scarves, and the children and women looked bright in colorful skirts and blouses.

"Is this really Dangrek? It is like a city," I raised my voice to Y-Suiah over the noise.

"Yes, H'Tien, we have made it." His moist eyes met mine. It would take time for me to believe all that I saw.

The Montagnards had their own area, the Montagnard Dega Camp. We four girls had a small house with two beds for two people each. As we lowered our packs to the floor, my body said, "At last we can sleep." But we were kept awake by people bringing food and handshakes and joyful welcoming words that we often could not understand. We smiled as they rejoiced and thanked each of them.

Soon the sun cast shadows through the camp as it set behind the mountains to the west, and our generous new friends brought new blankets to H'Ngam, H'Wat, Bron, and me—fresh, warm, and not filled with damp earth and jungle odors. We hardly spoke, as our good-night words hung in the air over deep breathing and grateful spirits.

## *Adjusting to Change*

Daylight had been in the sky for a long time when my eyes opened, and I saw Bron next to me. I sat up, confused, not knowing where we were. She woke, and we whispered as though our voices would suddenly make our surroundings disappear. H'Wat and H'Ngam joined us, while we looked out trying to decide what we were supposed to do.

Someone must have been watching for us. For as soon as we stepped down out of our house, three women came to us with clothes, colorful uniforms, rubber sandals, food, salt, sugar, water, soap, and personal items.

We spent the day cleaning ourselves, trying on our new clothes and collecting thread and needles to alter the material to fit our thin bodies, and walking around the city-sized camp to look at our surroundings. At first it was a bit frightening. We stayed close to one another; there were so many Cambodians. Voices spilled from stores and gardens, and children ran and played near their houses and tents. Our eyes did most of our speaking as we stared in all directions. When I stopped someone and asked how many people lived in Dangrek, the answer made the four of us gasp at one time: "About 140,000."

It seemed that only a few steps later we decided to turn around and find our house again. It was already evening, and we were overwhelmed. Far down the road, I could see some of our countrymen talking. I relaxed and smiled, but I talked fast.

"Bron, can this really be true? I wonder how long they will let us stay. Maybe we can plant a garden. Can you believe the supplies they brought to us? There are no more poison roots or grub worms or ants or monkeys—or leeches."

"Maybe, I don't know, maybe yes, no, yes! H'Tien, slow down. The answers will come." We reached our house, and the girls laughed at me, and I at them, and at the air where there were no gunshots.

We went again behind our secure house to use the toilet facility, a four-sided little bamboo shed with a door. It did have a wooden seat with a hole cut in it and reminded me of the toilets at Thanh Gia at the orphanage school. Like the school, there was no paper, but everyone brought their own stick. Even though it was a relief from our past years in the jungles, the odor often overpowered the air, and in a few days, friends and I frequently went to the woods after dark.

Every day small bamboo bathhouses, with wooden floors, were built for our growing population. A well in the center of each allowed two or three of us to dip containers and to pour fresh water over our dusty bodies at one time. It was not as much fun as the streams, but not as cold either.

In the beginning, each day at Dangrek was unexpected. My body was overwhelmed by the food—new food of Thailand (Ramen and Mama Noodles, bean sprouts, *onchoy*, *montry*, taro root, and banana blossoms).

At night, I mixed a little sugar with water and let it sit until morning. The cool, sweet liquid became my favorite treat. We had been without for so long that we had to restrict our meals to small portions several times a day, although a week later I heard that some people used too much salt too quickly, and their feet and legs swelled so large that they could not walk. Our adjustment would take some time.

My feet relaxed, and anxiety left my mind. I thought again about school, about learning languages, math, reading, a way to teach in the camp, but there was little interest, and there were no books. My heart said that we were wasting the time that God had given us. I longed to read and to have a paper and pen again. Part of that came true later when I moved into Uncle Rong's unit that had arrived two years earlier.

In the Montagnard Dega Camp, there were a number of houses along the wide pathways that branched out from the main road, and more around a generous garden where vegetables grew. The soil was rich, and water from mountain streams was easy to find—useful for irrigation, wells, and even for house use. The garden had been planted by the first Montagnard refugees in 1980, when Uncle Rong had come with a small group of fifty, which multiplied into five families.

All of us immediately began to take turns doing chores. The men even helped with the cooking as there were too many chores for such a handful of women. In an extended garden, with seeds provided by the camp, we planted corn, eggplant, cucumbers, hot peppers, baby shanghai, watermelons, and banana trees. From eggs, we raised chickens and ducks, and our bodies became healthy and strong.

In a few weeks, we four girls were moved into a new longhouse that had a kitchen where we cooked for our unit. Everyone ate together in another building that later added a kitchen. Uncle Rong had his own house near the center of all activities, with a well and fire pit inside. All around us were houses, including the ones that housed the five families who had come two years before. I helped in all areas and especially looked after Uncle Rong. He was good to me, and I respected him as well as my new friends and family.

# LIFE AT DANGREK CAMP

Type of Long House at Dangrek - (Courtesy of Surry Roberts)

## *Sixth-Month Surprise*

Because Uncle Rong was a general in the FULRO army, he had a big role at the camp and was consulted often. But he accepted more responsibility than his body could handle. I often found him bent over his desk in pain or barely able to rise from his bed. Terrible headaches accompanied him for days. He frequently struggled to finish his meal and became very weak. I prayed every day that God would not let him die and cried with him through his agony.

Although he did not discuss any significant information with me, we had been at Dangrek for six months when he spoke to me late one evening. His eyes seemed brighter, and his mouth curved upward into a kind smile.

"H'Tien, I have news for you that I could not tell until now."

We sat near the fire, and my heart beat fast. *Is it sad, or is it bad?*

"A group of twenty-three men has gone down the mountains to welcome sixty more of our countrymen—and women. H'Bloanh is among them."

I remained still, looking at him and wanting him to repeat what I knew I had not heard.

"They will probably arrive in the early afternoon tomorrow. I know that you will want to be there when they enter Dangrek."

I covered the smile on my face with my hands and caught the tears that rolled down to meet my fingers.

"There are forty-seven men and thirteen women, more than any other group. All seventeen of you will stay in your house. I'm sure that you can make room."

I cleared my throat. "Thank you, Uncle Rong! Thank you, God, for her safe journey! I have prayed long for her these many months. I can hardly believe this. I'll go tomorrow morning and prepare things for their welcome if you'll permit." He was pleased with my response. And I ran back to my house, shared the good news with the other girls, and fell asleep while planning our reunion.


The next morning, I fixed Uncle Rong's porridge early and prepared his lunch. I went to the Thai officials who gave out the clothes and supplies in order to find the smallest skirts and blouses to be sure that the girls would have all that they needed. Bron, H'Wat, H'Ngam, and I moved our things to make room for the girls, made everything fresh, and arranged the provisions brought to our house. My cleaning and cooking tasks were suddenly interrupted by the gunshots of welcome at the entrance to the camp.

I raced toward the celebration and shifted from foot to foot until they came over the top of the mountain, soldiers leading. I searched the faces and lean bodies of the young women, and a rush of memories covered me. H'Bloanh saw me first and waved.

As I rushed toward her, the crowd disappeared; we wrapped our arms around each other and stood for a long time, holding on to the past and the future.

A week after the third unit arrived, all seventeen women were called to the Montagnard Dega camp meeting house. Uncle Rong and several of the leaders were present. I looked at the faces around me and thought how sad that so many women had been left in the Highlands.

One of the leaders began, "We are very thankful that all of us have made it to Dangrek. You are aware that among over two hundred in our camp, you are the only women. Many of the men have left families behind and have been in the jungles for a long time. Often they can desire someone other than their wives, and you are in their sights. We have set up strict rules of behavior to keep you safe. I will ask each of you if you have a boyfriend in this camp."

The answer from each of us was, "No!" I did remember in the Da Lat area that I had liked someone. It was the first time that I had had an interest in a man, but he was there, and this sounded much more serious.

"There will be no steady association between men and women, and I hope that that is very clear. The men are aware of the rules also."

*What if someone sees love in another person? How will they be able to speak of it?* But that was the end of the conversation.

## *Activities in the Camp*

The leaders had their own office spaces in the center dining house where they worked most mornings, directing soldiers, scouts, and battalions through messages and two-way radios. I could read and write and was chosen to be the secretary for Y-Bhi Kbuor. H'Bloanh and her friend H'Oanh helped Y-Djot Mlo and Y-Pat Buonya. It was work that I enjoyed, and I was able to see H'Bloanh more.

When there was extra time, I joined H'We Nie, H'Juaih Buonya, and others to learn about nursing. Bandaging, dressing wounds, and wrapping ankles were the easy parts. Putting needles in arms and hips gave me a chill, but I learned to do it without closing my eyes. There were pills and instruments that we never had in the jungle, and it was comforting to know that they were there for us now.

I was happy for this freedom and good friends, food, and medicine. Dangrek was a fine place to live—until the men broke the rules.

I talked to my friends about the men's needs and desires and did not want to blame them, but I had myself to protect. Several men secretly asked me to be their girlfriend, and I always replied, "No, I cannot be promised to you." I prayed that at the right time God would choose the right person for me.

One evening after dinner, a soldier came to H'Bloanh and me and said, "H'Tien, Y-Ngong Knul wants to talk to you."

I looked at H'Bloanh, and without speaking, we both got up and went together. We reached the house with the soldier, and I asked, "Where is Uncle Ngong who lives here?" He pointed to the house of H'Wil and Y-Bhuat (a husband and wife). "He is visiting."

I knew that she was at the hospital looking after Y-Bhuat and that they were not at home. "But where is Y-Mao Eban, the keeper of the house?"

He gave me a short answer, "He has gone and will return later. H'Bloanh, you can go."

I had an uneasy feeling, but I knew this man and trusted too much. H'Bloanh slowly left, and I went into the house, lit only by a candle in the dining area. I sat down quietly to listen to Y-Ngong's words when suddenly someone grabbed me from behind around the neck. I drew in my breath, frightened by the action, and bit down on the hand at my neck as hard as I could. The hand released me, and the man yelled, but I jumped up and hurried across the room, pushed open the door, and ran all the way to our house, holding my neck and sobbing through my panic.

"What has happened to you? Are you all right?" H'Bloanh put an arm around my shoulder, and we went outside.

"Yes, but you must not tell anyone!" I cried and talked at the same time. "Someone tried to choke me, maybe kill me, maybe do something terrible to me. I was so scared, but don't tell anyone. I don't know who it was, but you know that I'll get the blame. Promise me you won't say anything."

I had been with men in the jungle for years. I had been protected first by Y-Nguan, then Y-Klut Siu, H'Tlon, Dam Per Quay, Y-Kler, by Paul Yuh, but here I had no one. Uncle Rong was as close to my protector as was possible. He was kind and generous, and I looked after him, but Dangrek was different. It was a large city, with the Montagnards there taking care of themselves, abiding by their own rules. The women were victims of slander. There was no one to speak up for them, and the men took advantage by saying things that were not always true.

I learned from the years before to listen, not talk, to know people well before I gave them my trust, to look after myself, to keep running—over the mountains, across the Ho Chi Minh trail, the Mekong River—to safety. *Is this a safe place? I have no one to trust in my heart except H'Bloanh and H'Luok Mdrang. I am scared. I just want to live in peace, to be able to trust, to have caring love in our Montagnard family. But I must act as though I have not been betrayed.*

## Uncle Rong

Uncle Rong Nay was like a second father to me. He worried about me. He worried about the way others teased me or ignored me or said things to me that he did not like. Sometimes I was a problem for him. But I never told him what happened in the dark house or who I thought might have hurt me. One time, though, he hit me on the back with a stick because he was bothered by the attention to me and didn't know what to do. The women, no matter what, were to blame for all conduct.

I felt sorry for Uncle Rong. He was a sick man at the time; the stress preyed on him like a vulture. Sometimes his headaches blinded him; his stomach pain became intense, and all I could do was accompany him in his house to be near him as he became weaker. All in one day, I watched him as his voice became a whisper, and his eyes looked blank. I continued to pray to God, and Uncle Rong held on to life with a powerful determination.

He was one of the heroes of our journey. There were so many, especially soldiers, who set their lives out front to protect all of us. They guarded us at the expense of their own safety. They were young, courageous through frightening engagements, determined not to complain (where anyone could hear), deprived of sleep, and brave beyond their years. We owed them our lives; we prayed for the souls who left their bodies in the jungles.

## *Appendicitis*

In the fall of 1982, our first year at Dangrek, I felt something wrong in my belly—the right side was painful, and I was cramping on and off there. A friend brought me medicine that made me feel better, so I tried to forget it, but my discomfort must have shown on my face. Uncle Rong was growing stronger, and he and others began to worry. Finally, he took me to the Dangrek hospital that served numerous camps in the area. After a week there, with medicine every morning, I was better, and they dismissed me. My friend H'Luok Mdrang walked the thirty minutes back to camp with me.

Two weeks later, Uncle Rong spoke with his trusted Thai advisors about my condition, and soon I was in Kampa's car, with Ta R'ya (a Laotian), for the five-hour drive to the district hospital at Nam Yun. After the first hour and a half, we stopped in a small village where a kind woman cooked a delicious meal of frog legs for us. They were bigger than the ones that we caught in Vietnam and much tastier.

But then, there was a much longer ride over rutted, dusty roads at thirty to thirty-five miles per hour. The swaying and jarring bounce of the car did not help my pain. It was as though the frogs had decided to leap up and out.

Finally, we approached a gate where four young men directed us in to a small house that was raised on tree posts. I felt better after we left the car, and Ta R'ya showed me where I could wash and the porch where I would sleep, while the men strung hammocks under the house. At least one man was on guard at the gate at all times, and two prepared our meal while all of us laughed at our attempts of communication. They warned me not to leave the house, as I might get lost, and danger was close by. I did not know exactly where we were, but I thought that it was a military place where officers stayed. I did understand that I was to wait for my turn to see a doctor.

I slept very little that night with all of the bright security lights shining but was happy to have guards and new friends. The next day, I saw a lady, not far from the house, motion for me to come across the garden to see her. Kampa and Samphon went with me and said that she had a school dormitory and that I was welcome to stay there while I waited. Since I did not understand the language, Samphon translated and asked Kampa for permission. I didn't know how she knew anything about me, but it was a blessing, as I spent the next two weeks in less pain and enjoyed the company of the high school girls there.

The girls and I exchanged exercises in languages, songs, and laughter and enjoyed a trip to their market. When I left, they gave me some of their stylish clothes, toothbrushes, toothpaste, and powder for after a bath. I could only say thank you over and over and give them a lot of hugs and gratitude for their generosity.

The day of the appointment finally arrived, and Kampa, Ta R'ya, and I went to the doctor's clinic. The doctor pressed on my right side, gave me some medicine, walked out of the room, and that was the end of the visit—no x-ray taken, no blood pressure data, no diagnosis. I was so surprised by the nonexamination that my old stuttering returned when I went to Kampa to explain.

We returned to the officers' house where a wonderful meal was prepared and had a pleasant evening before the rough road back to Dangrek the next morning. During the long, bouncy trip, I had happy thoughts about not having some kind of surgery in Nam Yun. I did not know anyone at the hospital, and my friends couldn't be there to look after me. But the pain came back and then stopped.

The girls, H'Bloanh, Bron, H'Di, H'Oanh, and Phi greeted me with worried faces that turned into smiles and giggles when I showed them the more stylish clothes from the high school students. We all took turns trying them on and deciding who would wear what the next day.

Uncle Rong was still unhappy. He saw me when I doubled over and moaned during my chores, and he was puzzled when I seemed okay. A week went by, and he took me back to the Dangrek hospital.

A new doctor saw me and said that the cause of the pain was my appendix. He did not say to me, "You must have surgery very soon." He just assigned me to a ward and said that he would check on me later.

The hospital was not very clean, but the nurses were beautiful and offered me help every day. They brought me soup and taro root with syrup—and my medicine.

The facility covered several acres, with different sections for men, women, children, and old people. The floors were dirt; a straw roof hung over the bamboo walls. Wooden beds, about a foot and a half high (covered by bamboo mats), lined both sides of the rooms in each dormitory. I had a blanket and a shelf where I kept my few belongings.

There was much sickness there, so many injuries, and few doctors and nurses. Fierce storms often rained over the camp, and very large trees fell on houses and crushed people. Some never recovered. When I went outside at night for my personal relief, I walked past small graves marked for babies or children. Once I passed a pit containing partially covered body parts. I not only felt sick from the putrid odor in the air, but I also cried for the loss that was ours to share and to overcome, in that sad and struggling place of devoted compassion.

When the patients needed a shot, the nurses went down the rows with one needle and gave each person their dose. Friends came every day and night.

During the morning of the fourth day, after I finished my soup, a nurse came by with a syringe and gave me a shot, which she did not explain.

"What is this?" I asked, looking down at my arm.

"You need vitamins," she told me without expression.

It only took a few minutes for me to realize that the "vitamins" were more active than I could imagine. I became light-headed, and my eyes began to blur. "Just go to sleep now, and you will be fine." My nurse smiled.

*I don't want to go to sleep. Is this for an operation? No one mentioned an operation. I need to get out of here. They might cut me—or kill me.* I got away from my bed and walked like someone with too much *nam pai* to find the doctor or someone to talk to me. I went into a room beside a door marked Surgery Only, walked through some white curtains, and saw H'Bloanh, Mik, Y-Siu Vien, and Uncle Rong. A Chinese doctor and a nurse with a needle appeared from behind another curtain.

I stumbled up to the doctor and said, "I have had two bowls of soup today. If I die, you will be responsible. If I live, it is okay.

You look good. I want you to surgerize me." And that's the last I remember until I awoke, looked up, saw the IV in my arm, and felt the bandage on my belly. It was done.

That night, Dr. Lhon (we called him Pet Llon) said to me, "You are the only person I have 'surgerized' who had two bowls of soup before. But I am now safe because you will live." He smiled and put his hand on my shoulder.

"Thank you!" I mumbled. "I'm sorry that I was trouble."

"I am glad that your appendix did not burst. There was a lot of infection. You will be here for a while."


Dr. Llon was right. A month later, in late November, I returned to my house with my faithful friends who, one by one, had slept with me at the hospital every night on my wooden bed made for one person. They had not told me about the operation because they thought that I would run away, and I might have.

I went on working as the secretary of Y-Bhi Kbuor and caretaker of Uncle Rong—but between hours of rest. I thanked him many times for not giving up on my pain. The doctors and nurses at the Dangrek hospital did their best with what they had, and angels were at my side.


A new girl, H'Nglat, about seventeen years old, moved into the longhouse with me, where there were kitchen and dining facilities. She had been requested by two of our Thai advisors and translators, Kam Run and Kam Pa, to be their cook. Ta Roya and another man, Y-Lanh (whom I did not know), were assigned to help also. H'Nglat was a beautiful, smart young girl and was soon a part of our family. She called Uncle Rong "Grandpa," and me "Aunt."

As I healed, my prayers gave thanks for Uncle Rong's strength and for H'Nglat.

# UNPROTECTED RELATIONSHIPS

## *Cautious Friendship*

N ear the end of the year, it seemed that a friend of mine, Y-Plier Enual, and I had more conversations together than usual. I had known Y-Plier since the "deadly place," the fields where I taught others how to cook the poison roots. His dad, Philip, was the one who snatched my backpack from me when I was in line to be checked in at Camp Knuk and saved all of my belongings. At Dangrek, I called Y-Plier my young brother.

One day he began our conversation, "H'Tien, I want you to know my 'brother' Y-Ji B. He is a good man, and I think that you will like each other."

I stared at him a few seconds and looked away. I had noticed Y-Ji, and I even had saved him a meal when he was late for dinner one night. He ate in the kitchen where I worked.

"Y-Plier, I cannot think of being close friends with a man now."

I would not even trust my good friend Y-Plier as I did not want to take blame for something that I had not done. I remembered how it was in the camp, and only H'Bloanh knew about the man who tried to choke me. We wanted the rules to change, but it was harmful to the girls to break those rules. No one spoke of love.

In the following weeks, Y-Plier teased me, "Take Y-Ji to be your husband!"

I always turned away and said, "No!"

Y-Plier and Y-Ji were like brothers and were from the same village. They spent a lot of time together and often were not far away from the places where I did my secretarial chores. Y-Ji was close to the leaders at Dangrek and had been a translator in

Bangkok for many months. I listened when I heard his voice, but I did not dare speak to him. When he looked my way, I tried to hide my eyes from his so that no one in the camp would suspect any attraction between us and might talk about us. It could mean very big trouble for me.

Finally, I told H'Nglat about my feelings and asked her opinion but made her promise not to say anything to anyone. She had also noticed him—his quiet ways and strong-looking face—and was excited that we could possibly marry.

Y-Plier surprised me one day in the kitchen where I was cooking. "H'Tien, I have something for you from Y-Ji." His eyes were laughing, and he handed me a beautiful scarf to wear around my neck. I looked at him and down at the gift in my hands and had a difficult time controlling a smile.

"Are you sure that this is for me? It is very pretty."

"Yes, Y-Ji wants you to have it. I told you that you two belong together."

I could not speak to him of my own feelings. I trusted Y-Plier, but I could not fully trust him. I was confused but said, "Please tell Y-Ji thank you for considering me with such a nice gift!" And I carefully folded the scarf and put it in my pocket. *Does this mean that he really likes me? How will I know if we cannot talk? What should I do now?* I remember trying not to smile when I saw him at the evening meal, but he could see that my face was happy.

A week went by, and I did not hear any talk about me and Y-Ji, so I began to trust Y-Plier more. But I was particular about what I said and how I looked.

I prayed, "If I am to marry someone, please let it be with a man I love."

## Altered Rules—Disturbed Marriage

In 1983, the rules on dating and marriage changed, and a few of us were allowed to get married to each other, one couple at a time. Y-Ji and I were the fifth ones to have that permission from

Uncle Rong. He signed a paper with our names on it, stating that we belonged to each other, and I stayed at Y-Ji's house. But there was trouble coming from a man who seemed to be unhappy about our union.

The strong still ruled the weak; men still dominated women. And this man had decided to break our marriage by spreading rumors that I had promised myself to him, even though I was married. I told Y-Ji that it was not true, but I could see the doubt on his face. Being together was quite an adjustment for both of us, but frustration and mistrust were working their way into our relationship.

Having more freedom between men and women was good and bad, and H'Nglat also was not having a good time. She had been slapped and shaken when she denied marriage to one of the men and was totally humiliated. She didn't know what she did wrong when people talked about her and blamed her for what happened to her.

H'Nglat and I shared our feelings with each other but did not know what to do. We decided that the best thing for everyone involved would be for us to disappear and take our unjustified shame with us.

Our plan began to unfold one morning at eight thirty when, with backpacks full, we walked out of our camp. We had already finished our cooking chores, and Y-Ji was out in his garden and would not miss me for a while. We were not sure where we were going, but we thought that a rough path through the woods would lead us toward Nam Yun. We passed close by the hospital dispensary, and H'Nglat remembered my appendix operation, but I assured her that I was okay, even though I was often tired and weak.

A few miles and hours later, we saw the Cambodian camp and some of my former nurses washing clothes. Our legs ached, and we sat down to rest.

"Where are you two going?" my friends asked.

"Oh please, can you help us? We want to stay here," I begged one of the nurses.

She smiled. "Stay here, and I will find someone and ask for permission."

Soon she returned with a man who had a serious face and who asked us many questions. "We would be pleased to have you both stay with us, but the politics of our groups in the jungle will not allow it. I am sorry that you will soon have to leave."

Our frustration and reaction welled up in our eyes; our disappointment was great, but there was nothing to say. We accepted their offer of food and a place to rest for a short while, but my mind raced toward the night and the thought of two young women sleeping in the forest—alone. *We can do it. No one will care, and what if something happens to us? Y-Ji will find someone else, and H'Nglat will no longer have such pain in her sadness.*

But there was little time to think about our future as about twenty minutes later, a jeep arrived from our camp, with Kam Run and two men who had come to take us back to Dangrek. I could only assume that someone had radioed Uncle Rong that we were there.

There was no arguing, no attempt to run away, just two young women silently escorted into the car to return to their unknown fate.

## A Jail for Two

We were charged with betrayal. The camp's security soldiers directed us to a small hut that was called a jail and told us that we would stay there three days without talking to anyone. People from our group did bring food but did not speak to us. We ate and slept and sang songs to reassure ourselves.

After the three days, H'Nglat was taken back to her Thai kitchen to cook, and I went to the longhouse to cook and do my chores. I worried more about H'Nglat than about myself. We both felt abandoned. We did not trust the people around us, and they were having few conversations with us. Y-Ji and I did little to communicate. Uncle Rong had difficulty facing others in the camp because of my actions. I had shamed him. It was a painful time for everyone.

Finally, two weeks later, I went to Uncle Rong. "I have a favor to ask from you." My eyes tried to meet his straight away. "I request that you call a meeting that includes the man who accused me of something that I did not do. Let him stand before you and me and repeat his charges, and we will find out the truth."

Uncle Rong stared at me a few moments, his eyes sad, but then he nodded his head.

"I want H'Nglat to come. She has been wronged also and has a right to be heard."

He agreed, and the meeting was set for two days later.


Twenty men (including Y-Ji), H'Nglat, and I assembled in a room that was called the courthouse. At first I held H'Nglat's hand as we both were shaking, but after the first question, I had to calm myself from anger and stood straight and tall.

A man raised his voice. "Why do you promise yourself to another man when you already have a husband?"

"I never did, and I need to see proof."

There was a lot of mumbling, and my accuser said, "I have proof. I have proof that you wrote me a letter, promising to be mine."

I said, "Show me that proof! I did write you a letter, after you wrote to me, asking me to be with you. My reply letter asked you why you were writing to me when you yourself already have a wife and children, and I am promised to someone else."

"I have the proof right here." He held out a tiny torn piece of paper with the word *promise* written on it and showed everyone.

"You are a liar," I said, glaring straight at him. "Produce the whole letter, and we will see who is right."

My words seemed to knock him backward, while the rest in the room stared in his direction, and the air grew still. I did not move.

Only the man's eyes shifted from side to side, and Uncle Rong's low voice spoke through the silence. "Show us the rest of the proof!"

As if a road abruptly ended, the man said, "I do not have any other proof. H'Tien did not promise herself to me. Someone used me to make up the story. I am sorry for this misunderstanding."

The tension left the room as the men stood up one by one and slowly left the building. Y-Ji was first.

"But what about H'Nglat? She needs to be heard."

They only commented to the man, "Get out of here! You have wasted our time and caused a lot of trouble." And the three of us, H'Nglat, Uncle Rong, and I, stood alone in the empty stillness, while my accuser walked out with the others—a free man.

## The Dark Side of Lies

I was relieved but still worried about H'Nglat. She was more depressed than I was, even though we thought that our days in the jail hut were over.

I stayed with Y-Ji, but we talked very little. We were not happy together. Within a week, a letter was delivered to me that said that H'Nglat and I were to return to the jail. Surely it was a mistake, but Uncle Rong said that he was powerless to stop the further investigation of our actions.

H'Nglat met me in the evening and handed me a small bag containing a handful of white pills. "These are for when you cannot take it any longer."

"But what are they?" I glanced at her, knowing what I did not want to know.

"I have given you half of what I took from the medicine box. I only know that they have power. I have mine down in my underpants. It is safe to keep them there."

I put my tongue to one of the pills to see what it might be. The pill was extremely bitter, and the tiny taste took awhile to leave my mouth.

Two days later, before our lunch time, a man escorted H'Nglat back to the jail, and a man took me from my chores to a courtlike place for additional accusations. I was there more than an hour. Something inside me became very uneasy, not just from the questions about my personal life. I told the men that I needed to cook the evening meal and to finish my chores, and they released me—"for now."

H'Nglat was alone. I asked someone from our group to go to the jail to check on her.

"She has something on her body that is harmful. She needs to be searched, even inside her underpants." I felt like a traitor, but I was caught in a helpless net.

They sent a man to investigate, and she said, "Don't touch me—I am having my period." Another in our group took water and food to her and told me that H'Nglat was sad but seemed not to be sick.

When I arrived at the hut in the late evening, the hut was as dark as the sky. The guard lit a lantern for me and said that he had not heard from H'Nglat in several hours. My stomach tightened as I walked in, but she was alive and lying on her bamboo mat, with a little food and water by her side.

"I have been waiting so that you can write a letter for me."

After looking through my pack, I said, "There is no pen."

She sat up. "Then use a piece of charcoal," she said, her voice sounding urgent.

H'Nglat had watched me search for the pen and paper while she ate some of her food and water. I sat beside her with the charcoal and began to write on a paper the best that I could in the dim light, using three different dry coals.

She began hesitantly, "A man slapped me for"—she coughed and continued—"for refusing him but told others that I was his." She paused. "I did nothing wro…"

She stopped, and I turned to see her twisted face and wide eyes. She lay down and pointed to her mouth.

"H'Nglat, what is wrong?" I then saw a few of the white pills beside the food that she had eaten and immediately thought of the handful that she had saved for herself but were nowhere in sight. "You took the pills. How many? My God, are you dying?" And I screamed for the guard outside. He came in and saw and ran for help as I held her and rocked back and forth. "I'm so sorry. Don't die, don't die!" But I could see that her stomach was swollen, and her breathing was very slow.

As H'Nglat's life left her, I wanted to warm her body, but mine felt cold and lifeless; my prayers to God were in mumbled whispers. I wept and prayed and rocked until someone untangled my arms and said that she was gone. It was H'Bloanh.

We walked out into the darkness together, her arms trying to comfort my pain, but there was only deep, intense grief.

"H'Tien, I know about the pills, and I think that you have some too. I want you to give them to me."

"No, I don't know what you mean," I objected.

She turned me around, reached into my underpants, and took the bag of pills that I was hiding. I was too weak to struggle.

H'Nglat had no relatives in the camp, and the custom was to bury her with her belongings. We had exchanged numerous pieces of clothing, and her backpack contained some of my things, but I did not mention that when they took her pack, along with her body, to her last resting place. One of her blouses that I had worn the day before would be my everyday companion.

*May God forgive her sweet soul and keep her in everlasting peace!*

# SILENCE—FORGIVENESS

## *Hearts Heal*

New beginnings took place in our Montagnard area of Dengrek over the next several months. H'Nglat's suicide had shocked the men into silence, and a few seemed more respectful.

The longhouse required a new kitchen and foundation, and I needed to restore my relationship with my husband. Numerous men came together to take down the longhouse and to build another house next to it, reusing the materials that were still solid. It would have a larger meeting area next to a comfortable kitchen and an extra room where I would stay when it was finished. For a temporary time, I moved into my friend Uncle Rmah Dock's house.

Y-Ji came to visit me, and we had long talks about our relationship. He apologized for doubting me and for causing pain to my heart. He said that he had learned from the hurtful experience, that he did love me, and that he wanted to be a real husband to me.

The stress of the previous weeks slowly eased, and as I forgave Y-Ji, my heart softened and healed, our friendship grew closer, and our union became stronger. After the new longhouse was finished, he moved into the extra room with me. The space looked very nice, but the dirt floor of the house was cold, and in a month's time, we began to talk about a house of our own. The idea made both of us so happy that Y-Ji and some friends built a new place in three weeks. They added a kitchen separate from our small house so that the smoke from cooking would not always be inside with us

The builders went out into the jungle areas to cut bamboo for the structure, and I was grateful each time they returned and had avoided the dangers from poisonous snakes, falling trees, saws, and old landmines. Some men from the camp already had died. The construction of our new house was so successful that others built nearby, and H'Luok and Y-Duen Mdrang built beside us a month later.

Uncle Rong blessed my marriage to Y-Ji and gifted us two chicks (male and female), and we added ducks, planted a garden, and had enough to share. I still cooked in the longhouse and helped Uncle Rong in his garden—all of us exchanging hot peppers, squash, pumpkins, lettuce, green beans, and other vegetables. Our happiness grew. I felt secure with my husband.

Often, whenever I worked in the dirt and saw new seeds spring to life, I thought of Ami and Ama and their gardens and fields in our village. I remembered the generous neighbors who paid me to work that summer so that I could go to school, and the many friends who cared about me during my long journey. Ami and Ama did not know that I was still alive nor anything of my escape through those years in the jungle. I had been bold to tell them that I would not come back. They did not know that I was married—without a ceremony, without a ring, without parents or promises of faithfulness, but only with Uncle Rong's approval and witnessing and signing of a marriage paper. But I knew that they would be pleased with Y-Ji, with his quiet, assuring smile that said, "I will always be with you and support you and love you."

*I pray that God will forever guide us in our love and that angels will be at our side.*

# UNEXPECTED ASSAULT

## *Broken Peace*

Our Montagnard group was small in comparison to the thousands of others at Dangrek, and we knew that a lot of those in the resistance camp were the Khmer Rouge (a militant group of Cambodians), but we had lived in peace with them for several years. Even so, our good friends and interpreters Kam Run and Kam Pa had gone to Bangkok and never returned. Rumors circulated. Something was not right. Y-Ji became concerned when a FULRO soldier arrived carrying a communication from Paul Yuh in Vietnam. All tracks and trails to Dangrek were being watched. and radio signals had been blocked by the Viet Cong or Communist Khmer. Paul Yuh could no longer send anyone out of the jungle safely or check on our security, and we were very concerned about him and all of those left behind.

Our leaders in Dangrek immediately had a meeting and organized a group of around forty men to scout out new passages for Paul Yuh, possibly through Laos. Y-Ji's name was included. My whole body seemed to shrink with disbelief when I heard that he had been chosen, but I knew that he had years of experience and could be an interpreter. Y-Ji said that they would leave in two weeks. I began to pray every moment that he would not have to go, and every night and day I heard gunfire echo through the jungle below Dangrek.

And then, Dangrek was attacked.

Rocket fire exploded in and around the whole area. There was much noise and confusion, running back and forth, fires to be put out, and loud voices from every direction. I ran toward a crowd and fell into a zigzag trench that led to a camouflaged shelter, built with four sides of wood and a flat wooden roof covered with mud and trees. Y-Ji found me there and squeezed into the ten-feet-square structure with others in our community. Every day, when the shells began to explode, those who could, raced for the shelter. Dangrek was so big that there was no way for us to tell how many people were hurt or killed, but our hiding place remained untouched.

After the first day, the shells did not land in the early mornings, so Y-Ji went out and eased his stress by tending our garden. But I knew that the assault could start again any moment, and I often sat holding my knees close to my body, with my head bowed in conversation with all that was holy. Fortunately, not one bomb fell on the Montagnard camp.

Then it stopped. It stopped after the third day, and our commander, Y-Djot Mlo, called a meeting of the Montagnards. "Go to your houses, cook as much food as you can carry, and pack what you really need. We must leave Dangrek as quickly as possible."

There was a moment of stunned silence, and another moment in slow motion, and then a rush began back to our homes.

I first cooked the rice that we might need, trying to keep focused on food, but my mind flashed back to previous years—to leaving Yang Reh Mountain when under fire, to not having enough rice or food, to all of the uncertainties of running through jungles and rivers. Now we were so many—215 they said. Mines had been set all around Dangrek. How would that many people get through those fields? And now there were children.

This was so different. I packed my husband's clothes and mine. He packed pots, pans, sugar, salt, water bottles, and things that had been accumulated in our first year of marriage. What would we choose to leave behind with our warm and beautiful first home? The packs filled too easily, and we repacked, making difficult decisions.

Outside, the ducks quacked through the rushing motion, and the chickens ran back and forth—a mirror of my mind and heart. Something white caught my eye—a memory of the curtains at the dispensary, my appendix out, the high school girls in the dormitory at Nam Yun, friends who might already have left, and sweet H'Yoy who shortened her life at the end of a rope and who would stay behind beside H'Nglat.

I folded the scarf that Y-Ji had sent to me by Y-Plier and slid it down to the bottom of the pack so as not to leave it. And the eyes of twenty accusing men pierced my memory. *I forgive you for the wrong that you caused. I ask Uncle Rong to forgive me for the days of trouble that I brought to him. I am thankful for all those who loved and protected me through the bad times.*

I finished cooking and packed the last pan. Y-Ji closed the backpack, and we both stood in our house, silent, avoiding each other's eyes and struggling against the fear of uncertainty. He put on his pack and helped with mine. Then I smiled at him. We had each other, and I put my hand on my belly as we walked out with our first child, cradled two months inside.

## *The Final Escape*

Not all could fit into the shelter, so some slept outside, but most of the night was peaceful. Then the earth shook as a slight hint of dawn uncovered the dark sky. Y-Djot Mlo alerted the group immediately, "Tanks are coming up the mountain. Don't ask questions, just follow me."

I heard him say to Y-Mong B., "Release the mines!"

Y-Mong was an expert with landmines. Y-Ji had told me that we would need to cross the planted fields to get away, and even though I had confidence in Y-Mong and his men, my heart raced as if to escape my body. Our cover of darkness lifted enough for me to see the quiet, empty streets and abandoned houses of the place I had called home for over three years. For as far as I could see, we were the last to leave. Behind us, the drone of tanks vibrated against the silence, and Dangrek trembled in anticipation of its new visitors.

My pack was heavy, but I followed the crowd toward our escape route, and pushed my tangled thoughts back into the dark shadows of a deserted city. As I watched my feet step by step, I focused on a prayer that God would grant us all safe directions. The packs became heavier. Y-Ji stopped to take some things out to lighten his load. I wanted others to wait for him, but there was no pause, and he had to hurry to catch up.

## *Fear and Horror*

We met up with a group of one thousand at the minefields. A lot of those did not know or take caution, and we heard mines go off in different areas. Y-Mong B. knew how to find, to avoid, and to deactivate the ones that were set. When he signaled, the first person in our group followed his exact step, and the next person followed the first person's footprint—and the next, and the next—over the dry fields, through bamboo forests, into the woods, sleeping one night, cooking when permitted, back into the fields—step by step by step. It took four days to pass through the mines.

We reached Pet Um, now almost a ghost village. Some of the group of a thousand had already passed by, leaving crying children abandoned in the jungle—children who would not survive. Parents knew that the cries from their babies were forbidden and could endanger the lives of all on the march, and they could not bear to watch their leaders take the life from their babies. Three young ones cuddled close to their mother, tears pouring from their eyes. Their mother was dead. It was useless to stop. It was heartbreaking to watch.

No one knew what to expect where we were going or even knew for sure if any of us would survive. I marched and cried and covered my belly with my hands, mourning those poor little souls and thanking God that our baby had not been born yet into this cruel world. Eyes focused on the ground—step by step by step.

From a group behind us, we heard occasional gunshots. Three Montagnards were lost to the mines, one going back to look for his hat. There was a sea of people, too many to be managed, and no one was in charge.

Our commander, Y-Djot Mlo, had a compass that gave him an indication of our position and a pencil-drawn map of where we might find a village that would help us. He divided us into four groups of about fifty, each with a leader, and instructed us to take different paths to reach the top of a mountain not far away. If we had stayed with the remaining mass of people, we would have had no direction and no commander, and our group could easily have gotten separated and lost. Also, the Khmer Rouge who blended with the crowds might not be as friendly toward us as they were at Dangrek. We followed Y-Djot Mlo's orders and quietly separated from the other fleeing refugees into the woods on four different trails leading to the top of the mountain that he had indicated.

Y-Djot Mlo was a wise leader. By the end of the day, we all had reassembled and camped for the night, grateful for the rest. It had been six days since we left Dangrek. The next morning two men went down the mountain to a distant village to ask for help. The police of that Khet Don Village did not at first trust the men and kept them jailed overnight. After much conversation, the men made friends with the guards and returned to us with the good news that we could cross over their roads and could camp for three days to cook and to wash in their stream.

Someone from the village must have informed the Thai Red Cross about us. They came and interviewed Y-Ji (who could translate) and two of our leaders, who told them that we were Montagnards from the Dangrek resistance camp, that our entire group numbered 212 and that we needed their help. Nam Yun was still our goal, and for the first time, we were given hope that our destination was possible.

From our location, there was a large dirt road to the Nam Yun region, far enough from the Cambodian border. After much discussion and advice, we decided to carry a white flag (of surrender) and to march out in the open. The Thai police with us could tell that villagers along the way were frightened. Our long line of bent-over, displaced persons from another country, carrying guns and bulging backpacks, was not something that they saw every day. So the authorities led us to an area off the road that had a pond, where we stayed for one week. Then they took us by bus to a site near a creek for another week. Our only choice was to follow their instructions.

A jungle area filled with large boulders was our next stop, where we waited for one of the women to deliver a tiny baby girl. It was exciting and scary at the same time. By then, others were commenting on my size, and Y-Ji and I showed that we were happy, but I prayed daily that we were far enough away from the deadly jungle of the forgotten children.

# PROTECTION FOR THE WEARY

## *Nam Yun Region*

Finally, the officials led us to a more permanent camp near Nam Yun, and we remained there for several months. The men helped one another build huts for shelter. Ours, about five feet by seven feet, was made of bamboo, with a roof and walls woven from *sambong* leaves. It had a wooden floor, with a fire pit outside for cooking and for keeping the bugs away. We had enough room for the two of us to sleep, even after the baby came, and space to keep our packs. There was an abundance of *sambong* leaves to make all the huts, and the plant's fruit, like snow peas, was good to eat.

Y-Ji found work, an hour's walk, in Nam Yun Village, where we met a couple, Pho Me (ami and ama, our parents in Thai) who loved us as their children. We helped them in their yucca root field, and they helped us with food. Y-Ji went into the surrounding jungle and cut wood logs that he sold to the village people for one thousand baht and shared the baht with his friend who helped. It was hard work and dangerous because cutting the wood was illegal in that area, but we had to eat and to make a living for our growing family.

The Red Cross came often to the nearby camp of Kmer Sre, so again, we had help with any illnesses, and of course, the nine months that my baby had grown inside me were almost over. At the camp, there was a nurse, H'We Nie, who saw that I would need help and told Y-Ji to come and get her when we thought that it was time. She was the same one at Dangrek who taught me and a few other girls some basic medical practices such as taking blood pressure, giving shots, healing wounds, and other methods of assistance. Our reunion was one of great surprise and happiness.

## *Spring Arrival*

On April 25, 1985, I told Y-Ji that my body felt unusual and that from what the other women had told me, the baby was going to come. I thought that I needed to relieve myself as water was soaking my clothes, but when I went to the hole he had fixed for me outside, nothing happened. He could see from my face that I was struggling with pain and could barely speak. Earlier he had prepared a sharpened bamboo stick to cut the umbilical cord, but it was not time for that, and he rushed through the camp to find H'We Nie.

They both arrived quickly when contractions were coming more often. H'We sat on the floor beside me and helped me breathe so that it would not hurt so much. By 2:00 a.m. on April 26, a baby girl cried her first breath, and I gave thanks that we were in a place where she was allowed to cry. Y-Ji used the bamboo "knife" to cut the cord and our little H'Thuin had a life of her own.

H'We stayed and helped clean me and the baby with cloths I had prepared, and she instructed me about nursing our hungry little one. I thought of the stories that I had heard about me and my mother in those early months of my life twenty-seven years ago. I held our baby close and promised her that I would never leave her.

After H'We left, Y-Ji asked me to stand up so he could fix the mat where I lay, but my head began to spin as soon as I stood up, and I fainted. He was very frightened, and as soon as I could speak a whisper, he went out in the dark to find coconuts for juice to make me feel better. I had been told to be careful not to eat strange leaves and to try to eat a little at a time and only the foods that I knew. I did that but kept drinking the coconut juice and bleeding from the baby's birth.

After two days, I sent Y-Ji for H'We, who came right away. "Where did you get this coconut juice? You are lucky to be alive."

We did not know that it was a juice that encouraged fluids to leave the body. She told Y-Ji to make our pit fire hot and for me to sit with my back to the fire for four days. If I followed all of her directions, I should not have any trouble having more children. She thought that we already knew enough facts about having babies, but instructions were usually passed from mother to daughter—and having babies in the jungle was kept a secret.

## The Red Cross

In the area of Kmer Sre, we received health care checkups, and when H'Thuin did not seem well, I took her there for help. I was impressed with everything that the Red Cross did and very grateful for their dedication.

The Red Cross refugee camp was not very far away. Their leaders, knowing our large numbers, encouraged and advised us.

Our commander, Y-Djot Mlo, had a heavy responsibility and had to make decisions for our whole group. The Red Cross leaders held several meetings with him and others in our camp. They emphasized that the living conditions were better in the refugee camp, and the Red Cross would help us leave Thailand and settle in a permanent place—but we would have to turn over all of our guns. Even though we were a peaceful culture, we had had weapons for many years to defend ourselves.

Y-Djot Mlo called us together and explained the option. At first, there were objections. "How can we give up our guns? How will we fight?"

"There will be no more fighting," Y-Djot Mlo said firmly. "We have already left our homes and families and cannot go back. Where else can we go? The Red Cross is trying to settle our countrymen in other more stable countries, but it will take time, and they are willing to have us wait in the Red Cross refugee camp. America is one place that has been mentioned."

Eyes became wide, and then I looked toward the ground. I stared down at our little girl and wondered what kind of life she would have here, always running. But what would it be like in another country, with a new language, new customs, unfamiliar people who also might not like us? Would there be guns there? I knew my friends had the same questions in their minds. For weeks, numerous discussions gave way to fewer objections and then to less resistance until, reluctantly, no one opposed the plan.


In September, we surrendered our weapons.


Five days before we left, we walked the hour to Nam Yun Village to say good-bye to Pho Me and to spend the night with our adopted family. They had watched H'Thuin develop and were sad to see us go. Friends gathered to say farewell with gifts of baby clothes, powder, diapers, and personal items for Y-Ji and me. They were in the band of angels who had watched over us for so many years. We could never fully express our gratitude.

# Trip to Site II South

Our week of anxious preparation came to an end when we left our camp at 6:00 a.m. and walked toward a place in the Nam Yun area, near the village, where buses waited for us.

All weapons had been given to the Thai military agency, and our backpacks were heavy with our belongings.

I heard our drivers instructing over and over, "This will be a seven-hour trip, so keep anything that you might need with you. Your packs will be tied to the top of the bus."

I had already put fresh cloths in my jacket pockets for H'Thuin, and Y-Ji put a small amount of food in his pockets for us to eat.

Four buses pulled away from the side of the road at 8:00 a.m. on a journey that was occasionally smooth, but mostly rough and slow. Before the swaying put me to sleep, I watched people walking in the dust, shopping in markets, and weeding in farm fields. It came to me that this country seemed the same as Vietnam—only the clothes were more colorful, the faces were different, the Thai food was often unfamiliar. But the good people were good, and the bad people were frightening.

H'Thuin rarely cried and appeared to know that the rocking bus cradled both of us. I went to sleep dreaming that I was on the bus to Pleiku, to a new school, toward an adventure that one day I would describe to my children.

The droning noise of the engine suddenly stopped, and my eyes opened wide to see that people were getting off the buses for a twenty-minute break, and fish sandwiches were handed to the drivers and other passengers. We were glad that we had brought a little food, as a fish sandwich was not a meal that we were used to, although we had eaten many other unfamiliar foods in our survival years in the jungles.

As I took in our surroundings, I could see that there were not as many private places for relief as in the jungle; fewer trees and sand replaced the muddy, leaf-covered ground of our previous camps. We spoke with our friends in low voices—filled with uncertainties and uncomfortable anticipation.

Only a couple of hours later, our vehicles slowed to a stop in front of the Tha Han Sua Dam (soldiers in black uniforms) at a gate marked Site II South Camp. After speaking to our drivers, the soldiers swung open the gates, and our bus wheels filled the air with sandy dust as we slowly rolled past white tents for as far as we could see. The engine stopped next to a large tent where the driver directed us to get off the bus and to collect our packs.

It was about five in the afternoon when we entered the shelter. A cool September breeze accompanied us, and the exhausting trip showed on all our faces. I did not care where they put us as long as we could only lie down and rest.

The shelter reminded me of the hospital in Dangrek where I had my appendix removed. Bamboo mats for sleeping lined each side, with enough walking space down the middle for two people to pass. As soon as we secured mats for us and lifted the packs from our backs, I put H'Thuin down and lay beside her, but she was hungry, and I pulled her close to me to nurse her. Soon the whole shelter became quiet, as we all gave in to our exhaustion from our seven-hour trip. My eyelids closed out the light, and sounds faded.

I do not know how long I slept, but H'Thuin's movements and Y-Ji's touch caused me to sit up and try to understand where I was. The sun was very low in the sky, and Y-Ji had found some sticks to make a small fire where we could cook some porridge. He asked a man who seemed to be the one in charge if we could use the water from a pond, about fifty feet by fifty feet, that we passed by after coming through the gate. The man said yes but added, "You may use it for washing, cooking, bathing, but not for swimming. Always boil the water before drinking. A truck comes once a week to refill the pond, which is only three feet deep." I had planned not to look back to our jungle life, but at that moment, I missed the flowing streams that had sustained us for those long years.

Three days later, we were instructed to gather our belongings and walk about twenty minutes into the center of Camp Site II South, where we would have stable housing. Our temporary space would now be the resting place of other refugees.

Our march into the camp was like our arrival at Dangrek. People stared at us, probably wondering about our looks and our nationality. It made me uncomfortable, and I shied away from meeting their eyes, but I did answer their welcoming faces with my happy smile.

There were many houses built of wood and covered with leaves rather than bamboo. Another man in charge directed us to twenty of these and said that we would stay there. Some houses even had two floors. He divided us so that at least two families stayed in one house, each family having two rooms. A concrete stove was inside, and behind our house, the men built a bath hut that we shared with Uncle Rong's household. H'Luok, Y-Duen, and little Y-Yotham Midrang were assigned with us. Y-Yotham was two months younger than H'Thuin, and when the babies cried at night to be fed, we all understood. It had been a long time since I had felt such peace.

# *Learning to Weave and Contribute in the Camp*

(Woman teaching weaving near Nam Yun, Thailand)

We needed to contribute something to our camp for the privilege of staying there. I thought that someday I would learn to weave and had bought new thread at Nam Yun, which was still in the bottom of my pack, along with two old sweaters that I could take apart and use while I learned the craft. Y-Ji was able to construct a loom that was wide enough to weave cloth for a large purse. A new friend in the camp knew the craft and gave me a few directions. It was like fresh air and simple joy.

I found the sweaters and began to unravel them thread by thread. I tied the ends together, boiled a pot of water, and soaked the threads. As the water cooled, and the sticky sweater wool blended, I took it out and hung it on a clothesline to dry. Afterward, I wrapped the long thread in an oval shape from my hand around my elbow and back until it became untangled. As

I wove the material on my loom, I practiced keeping the knots underneath and smoothing the threads on top.

My young "brother" Y-Suaih Hlong took care of H'Thuin for three weeks while I made my first length of fabric into a purse. It was an unusual combination of effort on my part to weave something beautiful. And it was (I thought at first), but after I spent four more weeks weaving a blanket and Rmah Dock sold it to the Red Cross for four hundred baht, I knew that my dedication to the craft made my labor valuable. I shared the money with Rmah Dock and Y-Suaih and decided to stop weaving, as it took too much time from H'Thuin and my family chores. But I kept my first attempt to always remind me of my earliest lessons.


In the dentist's clinic, Y-Ji met a Thai lady who allowed him to work there for four months. He could fix things as well as translate. We both felt pleased that we were useful and that we were trusted.

## *Help for H'Thuin's Illness*

H'Thuin was growing and needed more than breast milk. I pounded rice into powder to make baby food, but when it was outside drying, the flies and dust infected the rice. The mixture gave H'Thuin diarrhea, and Y-Ji and I had to rush her to the hospital at two in the morning where they kept her four days and gave her two bags of IV fluid. I prayed hard for our sweet baby and thought of Jeremy being eaten up with stomach parasites. The doctor assured me that H'Thuin was not in that condition, but I do not think that I was convinced until we could take her back to our house.

A week later, I received a WIC voucher that allowed mothers of children under four years old to receive some monthly supplies, including eggs, rice, baby powder, and a few clothes. Our group went early in the morning to the nutrition center so that we would not have to stand in a line all day for our share. We were very grateful for any help, especially for our babies. And we enjoyed going to the center that broadcast music in different languages over a loudspeaker. It made waiting seem to pass quickly and brought smiles to many faces.

# FAITH, HOPE, AND LOVE

For the first time, Y-Ji went with me to the Catholic Church at the camp. A French priest who spoke English as well as Cambodian welcomed us as though we were old friends. H'Bloanh, Y-Pat, and about twenty more people gathered with us each Sunday. Nuns in white habits helped with the children as well as at another church at Site II South. When I first saw them, memories of Sister Helen, Sister Amanda, Sister Goretti, and all of the priests from my school days filled me with joy and hope, as if the years of struggling to survive had never happened.

Now I had time to reflect on my faith and to wonder in amazement how I knew God from such an early age and how he walked with me every step of my life. The church had been solid under my feet, even though I had not been baptized and was not allowed the closeness of the Eucharist. But the Spirit of Christ that was born in me guided me in everything I that I did. I had become more aware of this closeness in the jungle in my "home with no future," and I had trusted God in my heart—through the hunger, the anxiety, the Mekong River crossing, the false accusations, the marriage to the man I loved, the birth of our precious daughter.

The nuns whom I knew had great courage and loved me as though I were their daughter. Their faith and their strength lived within me. I watched the nuns in the church at Site II and knew that they were volunteers there, demonstrating the same qualities and love of my friends in Cheo Reo. These were the same witnesses of the holy Catholic Church who inspired me to try to have compassion for the good and the bad people who entered my life, to try to communicate in different tribal languages, to blend in with various cultures and customs, to be aware of nature's warning signs, to be at one with God, and to let the cross lead me.

*And now, I have been blessed with a faithful husband, who supports our family, and who is learning to know the god whom I trust. I am happy in our small house of leaves; we are safe. We did not have to abandon our child at Pet Um; we have an uncertain future, but God will be with us wherever we are sent, and angels will lift our fears. I will hold H'Thuin tight and cover her with kisses and dream that one day we will all be baptized and will receive the blessed Eucharist in the Catholic Church.*

## *Interview at the Emigration Office*

After we had been settled at Section 6-E, Lot Dega, Site II South for six months, a group meeting was called one evening. "We will be leaving Site II very soon," our leaders said. It was a surprise to most of us, but there had been rumors. The appointment for our group interviews was at the office of Emigration and Naturalization Service on April 7, 1986.

The night before, I felt joy mixed with nervousness and insecurity, and I slept little, but the next morning, we were all prepared and ready to be on time for the interviews. Most of us had happy faces and spoke in low anxious voices: "What will the questions be? Will all of us stay together?"

The officials greeted us at the office with smiles and handshakes and called us for interviews by families. They had officers who spoke Thai, Cambodian, Vietnamese, and English, but Anup Siu acted as our interpreter. We did not need to worry about questions, as they were general—about our ages, our nationality, where we had been in the last few years, and if we were willing to go to a different country. They took our photographs, and after our papers were completed, they informed us that the United States of America would accept us and that we would be moving to a place called Panot Nikham where we would receive medical examinations and applications for visas. They did not know how long that would take.

I looked at Y-Ji and smiled, but I could feel apprehension between us as well as excitement. We just did not know what it all meant. We had fought so hard, waited so long, and here it was right in front of us.

A few days later, we said good-bye to our Site II South friends. Through our happiness, I could see the sadness of some who still had no place to go. I tried to be encouraging, saying that they would probably be called next for an interview. I prayed that it was the truth.

## *Panot Nikham and an Old Friend*

The bus ride to Panot Nikham was not as long as the last one, and the camp was not as large. It was a place for processing emigrants who were leaving the country. Two-story houses, made of concrete floors and tin roofs, replaced the leaf houses of Site II South. Groups were not kept together, and families were assigned to houses with others who had already been processed. The officers just pointed to a house and said, "You go there!"

We walked in to find that we shared the limited space with three other families—Chinese, Thai, and Cambodian—and were relieved to hear that everyone spoke enough Vietnamese to communicate. There was a water pump from a well near our house, but the lines were usually very long. Sometimes I compared the comfort of the leaf-covered forest floor with the ungiving concrete floor. I imagined that when we got to America, the floors would be softer.

We spent the next three months having medical examinations and completing our visa applications. At that time, we had the opportunity to decide on the names that we would use in America. Y-Ji said that an easy change for him would be to Y-Jim Buonya. In my heart, I had always kept the name that my mother had given me, so to honor her, I wrote down H'Yoanh Ksor Buonya as my official title. Although I thought that H'Thuin was a beautiful name for our daughter, I wanted to honor the man, Captain Charles Judge, who had tried to adopt me many years before, and who had called me Anna. Officially, our beautiful baby's name was changed to Anna Ksor Buonya.


Again, we were blessed with church services every Sunday. The Baptists and the Catholics had the largest attendance—two hundred could participate in our church—with a Vietnamese priest.

One Sunday, I noticed a young woman crossing the road in front of me. There was something about the way that she walked that reminded me of a classmate, Nguyen Thi Dung, from Thanh Gia Elementary School and Thang Tien Middle School. I hesitated, called softly, then louder, "Dung, Dung."

She turned around and looked straight at me, surprised that someone was repeatedly calling her name. I recognized her immediately, but she had little hair on her head now. "Dung, do you remember me from Thanh Gia? I am H'Tien."

She stared for a moment, "Oh my, yes—but you look very skinny. Is it really you? And a baby? What are you doing here?"

And we fell into each other's arms with hugs and tears and laughter that echoed from distant years. Her journey had not been as complicated as mine, but the length of separation quickly vanished, and our goals of escaping persecution remained a focus for our futures.

Dung, one of my angels, soon noticed how poor we were, and having come from a family of more opportunities, she reached out with generosity to her friends. Some days, after she went to the market, she would stop by our house and share food with us. I could not return the favor, but I thanked her many times, and we visited often.

A month into our stay, H'Thuin became infected with chicken pox. She cried and tried to scratch wherever she could, and everyone in our house became tired of listening to her. A doctor gave me some cream to rub over her body, but it took two weeks for her to get completely well. It was fortunate that no one else became infected, but it was a strain on all of the families living in such a small space. Patiently we endured a hard life.

The three months at Panot Nikham seemed longer than the six at Site II, but word finally came that our next bus ride would be to the Bangkok airport in a few days. I think that the relief I felt was more than the apprehension I had about getting on an airplane. At least we were moving toward a new home. The directors at the camp told us that our stop in the Philippine islands would be our last before America.

We waited for the buses to arrive, and I heard a voice call my name. I turned to see Dung coming toward me.

"H'Tien, I came to say good-bye and to bring you something. I do not need these clothes, and you can use them where you are going." She handed me two shirts, a pair of long pants, a sweater, and a pair of shoes. I barely had room in my pack, and she helped me fold them into the top. "I also want you to have this." She handed me fifty American dollars.

I just stared at the money then to her then to the money, and tears choked my words. Finally I said, "I can never repay you for your kindness, but I will always love you and will be your forever friend." The buses came; we hugged for a long time—H'Thuin between us—and Y-Ji said that we must get in line.

"I am so sorry to leave you here." Our gaze seemed frozen in place.

"Don't worry, H'Tien, my brother will soon sponsor me, and I will go directly to the United States and will find you there."

I waved to her until we were out of sight, and I turned my thoughts to what lay ahead.

# STRENGTH IN FAITH

## *Morong, Bataan, Philippines*

The three-hour trip to the airport was short compared to previous rides. It was twelve noon when we arrived and were given lunch while we waited for the flight. My eyes could not take in all of the new things that I saw. There was so much that was beautiful and strange and fun to watch. There were places to buy food and moving stairs and stores where we could buy books and toys and clothes and jewelry—if we had money for that. I did not mind waiting, but our leaders soon announced that our airplane was ready.

I began to shake from the inside out, but I kept talking to H'Thuin, now Anna, and telling her about what we saw as I tried to calm my nerves. We walked down many steps, our ICM card passports were checked at the door, and once at the ramp, we followed carts filled with our bags to a plane larger than I could ever have imagined. My breathing was so shallow that I thought for a moment I wasn't breathing at all. After we climbed tall stairs and stepped inside, a man in a uniform showed us where to sit. Y-Ji and I sat with Anna in a seat between us, and he said that we should put the belts in the seats around us. I listened and laughed through my nerves because we were not sure about anything, but another man in a uniform came by to help each of us. Then the first man held a microphone to his mouth and kindly instructed us again. Anna's eyes were very wide, but she did not cry or try to get down. I held her hand while I tried to keep both of us calm and sat up straight when the lights dimmed and the plane began to move backwards. I could barely breathe. I watched from the window as we moved away from other aircraft and people near the building.

The plane changed its direction, and more noise made me stare at Y-Ji. He sat strong and silent, then turned his head toward me and said, "It's the engine." Our plane moved slowly for a long while and stopped several times before the loud sound of the engines and the forward motion of the plane pushed us back into our seats so hard that I gripped the armchair, closed my eyes, and prayed to God that we would not die.

When I next looked out of the window, I saw white clouds such as I had seen only in books. The ground became patches of colors that abruptly turned to blue. "Y-Ji, look, look, can you see?"

He leaned over H'Thuin and smiled. We were on our way above the ocean in a fantasy world—shades of aqua, touches of pink, floating veils of mist.


Three hours later, one of the men in uniform announced that we would soon be over Manila and should be sure that our seat belts were around us. I had never unhooked mine. I watched the land come closer, heard a loud grinding noise, and closed my eyes when I saw the tops of buildings rush past the window. My eyes popped open when the plane roared louder and pulled us toward the seats in front of us. Suddenly we slowed and moved forward as though we were riding in a car; then came to a stop at the airport's building. When I no longer heard the engine sounds, I smiled at Y-Ji and took a deep breath. Anna had slept most of the way.

People greeted us with food and drink as we gathered our packs and made our way to the buses that would take us to Bataan in Morong area. I welcomed the bus. We were safe.


The ride to our new base was not long, allowing us to arrive about five on a cool June afternoon. Our accommodations were ready for us—rows of two-story houses for as far as we could see, another very large campsite. I sighed but remembered that this was to be our last settlement.

# TRUST IN HOPE

## *Final Months*

O nce more, the living spaces were small, but this time we were allowed to stay with our group. Some even attached their hammocks to posts outside.

Our one-room house was made of concrete, but we had wooden beds above the floor. A loft with a ladder slept four of the seven men that stayed with our family. I was the only woman, and we had the only baby, but I cooked just for Y-Ji and myself. At first I helped with gathering wood for our fire pit outside, but later there was no time, and I asked to use any fire that was already built.

In some ways, the facility was better than the last, even though it was more crowded. A stream nearby could be used for bathing, but we were told that it was not safe on the other side as people had been killed by small gangs that roamed in the area. Each house had a toilet in the floor with a pitcher of water to pour down the hole and a door for privacy. For drinking water that we needed to boil, the lines were much shorter than at Panot Nikham.

For ten days we were able to explore our surroundings, wash clothes (which were sometimes stolen if we hung them outside), and relax before our ESL and American culture classes started. I heard many languages that I did not know and saw faces from countries that were unfamiliar to me. We were given a small amount of food and some baby supplies and were told to sign up for different chores at the camp—as were the other hundreds, maybe thousands, of people who were there for the same reason.

On June 20, I took the English placement tests, and the next week I started the ESL (English as a Second Language) course.

Buses arrived near our houses to take us to the school center for morning and afternoon classes, but people struggled to get on the bus, as many pushed and fought for a seat. When I finally arrived at the center, I found a nursery near my classrooms for Anna. My teachers showed enthusiasm, and of course, I loved learning, but there was a lot of homework and studying in the evenings with light only coming from a kerosene lamp and candles.

After classes, the buses were again too crowded, so in the afternoons, I picked up Anna at the day care and walked the hour back to our house. A month later, I finished my chosen class to learn food service, managed to do my volunteer work, and still made the long walk with my baby in time to cook and clean for our family.

Y-Jim was lucky. After the placement tests, Mrs. Mark Bishop chose him as an ICEC (International Catholic Emigration Commission) assistant teacher coordinator. He did not have to take the ESL classes and was selected because of his previous experience as a translator in Thailand. His days were spent doing volunteer work.

I had been able to learn many tribal dialects in the jungle, but my ear had difficulty hearing and pronouncing English sounds, even though years before I had been required to take English in school. The most fun was learning about American geography and American customs—the size of the country; many tall mountains, lakes, and oceans; eating at a table; using knives, forks, and spoons; cooking on stoves; washing clothes in a machine; and buying food in big stores. We heard about choosing clothes from many shops, driving cars, working in factories, attending large schools and colleges, and even celebrating American holidays. How could any one place have that much?

In November, five months after we arrived, we left the life that had endured countless challenges to our minds, bodies and souls and began our final journey toward a land that a young teenage girl from a village near Cheo Reo, Vietnam, would never have imagined when she left her home and her family eleven years earlier.

(H'yoanh, Y-Jim and Anna. Last stop before America)

# EMBRACED BY LOVE

## Flight to Freedom

On the commercial airline, the time to reach Seoul, Korea, was four hours and to Los Angeles, California, USA, thirteen. I knew what to expect when taking off and landing, but the size of the cities from the plane was a sight that I could not understand.

An American official met our group after we landed in the afternoon in Los Angeles and led us through all of the processing needed to enter the country. Buses took us to a motel for the night, where my relative, Uncle Kully, met us, and through tears of joy and hugs of greetings, he invited us to join his family in their home for dinner. I could barely eat, as I was a month pregnant and had been sick on the plane, but it was the polite thing to do, and we were very grateful.

The motel bed was not like our wooden camp bed, almost too soft. Y-Jim had been in the bathrooms in Bangkok, so he knew how to operate ours. Even though we tried to work the TV, we were too tired to care and laughed at our lack of skill. The next morning, my uncle brought us coats to wear after our four-and-a-half-hour flight to a much colder climate in Greensboro, North Carolina. He also handed me $50 in folded American money. "This may help a little," he said with a worried smile. Our culture classes at Bataan could never have prepared us for what we had already experienced—or what was to come.

On November 26, 1986, the plane came in low over Greensboro, with its twinkling lights, colorful trees, and fields. The sick feeling I had experienced most of the long, long journey seemed to disappear. The airplane parked away from the building, and all 212 of us walked down the stairs to find crowds of people cheering, American flags waving, and smiling faces everywhere we looked. An American Special Forces band played enthusiastic, welcoming music as we walked between lines of saluting soldiers and officials shaking hands with each of us.

My legs almost collapsed with thankfulness for being on this soil. My heart skipped in time with the music, and I could taste the tears of joy that covered my face. Anna hid her face in my shoulder, and I held her so close we became one. I could faintly see a smile on Y-Jim's face, and the cheering continued.

Looking at the uniforms, I instantly remembered my foster dad, Captain Charles Judge, who had tried to bring me here so many years before. I said a prayer that I would find him to thank him for his loving care. And I whispered, "Thank you, God, for your many blessings!"

We went inside the building, the music drifting behind us, to find more people waving banners and signs with names on them. A Special Forces soldier stood at a microphone and said, "Welcome to the United States of America. We are so happy to see all of you."

Our friend, Y-Guk Gil, translated for us, but I did not hear much of the speech, as my headache returned, and I threw up in the paper bag I had brought from the plane. Few people saw me, but someone brought me a chair, and I felt better but very embarrassed.

No one knew exactly what was happening or where we were going and did not have time to say good-bye to many friends. We only had been told that our entire group would be settled in towns called Raleigh, Greensboro, and Charlotte and that we would be in the same state and not too far apart.

Y-Jim found our sponsors, Mrs. Pat and Mr. Boon, with our names on their banner. After collecting our belongings, we got into their car for the hour-and-a-half trip to a house in Garner, near Raleigh. H'Luok, Y-Duen, baby Y-Yotham, and their sponsor were already there.

We had learned *thank you* in English and repeated it over and over with our smiles, but as soon as we were left alone, H'Luok, Y-Duen, and Y-Yotham went to their room. I lay Anna in a crib that had been provided, and my weary body found a bed with fresh covers and the sound of Y-Jim's steady breathing.

We were in a rural area that was quiet from the city noises, but the heat machine to keep us warm went off and on all night and echoed the restless thoughts of the past and future that raced through my mind. I nibbled on crackers that our sponsors had given me and gently rubbed my belly with loving hands. We could stop running, we were free, we had new friends, we would begin a new life, and we would have a baby born in America. Thanks be to God!

# EPILOGUE

## *America—Land of the Free,*
## *Home of the Brave*

L iving in America was a shock—unimaginable. Our months in the Philippines were helpful but could not prepare us for such a different lifestyle. From the time that we stepped off the airplane in Greensboro, our encounters with American life and with the American people led us to gratefully embrace full citizenship in our new country. Yes, we miss what friends and family remain in Viet Nam, but sadly, it still could be dangerous for us to return, even for a visit. We cherish our new life. It is not always smooth, but we have opportunities here that were never available to us before. Sometimes we look back and laugh at our early, innocent years in North Carolina, and enjoy recalling the paths that we have traveled since arriving.

In the beginning, kind people brought us food, but we did not know how to cook it and could not read the cookbooks that our sponsor brought. At our first house, Y-Jim and Y-Duen made traps to capture birds for us to eat. Some got loose in the house, but they were pretty flying around, until they pooped on everything. One day we saw our neighbor in our yard setting the birds free from their traps, and that put an end to nature's food supply.

Going to the market could be called "what's this?" trips. Some of the vegetables and rice were familiar, but we questioned how the store could have packages of meat that was already cleaned and cut up. I took pleasure in remembering my rooster chase in Pleiku.

While our husbands went to their new jobs, H'Luok and I stayed at home and tried to make friends with the stove. Roasting and broiling seemed best, but when we opened the door of the oven to check on our first whole bird, the chicken burst into flames, and we were forced to call 911. While smoke floated out of the opened windows in the kitchen, the firemen knocked on the door and yelled many times before we let them in. They were big and scary to us. But after the fire was out and the men were gone, H'Luok and I laughed more than we had in a very long time. Everything we tried had a funny side—even walking to church through our first snowfall wearing flip-flops and carrying our babies.

We attended Mount Moriah Baptist Church in Garner where our sponsors went every Sunday. I loved the beautiful large church and the welcoming friends, but I did miss our more familiar services, and after Y-Jim asked if there were a Catholic Church nearby, we were taken to St. Mary's. Anna Owens, Claire, and Dan Hinspeter became close friends, took us to Sunday services, and patiently answered our endless questions.


People were generous with clothes that they no longer needed, but most Americans were larger than we were, so we donated unusable items to others. Our church friends, Lutheran Family Services, and U.S. Special Forces soldiers all contributed household items and money as we adjusted to our new culture. My wonderful ESL teacher, Kathy Miller, also taught me to tell time, an important part of my new life. Everyone tried to communicate through our limited English and their lack of our language. But English—not easily pronounced like tribal dialects—was difficult. It was a relief when we could visit with other Montagnards.

Y-Jim was able to save enough money to buy a used brown Ford station wagon and soon earned a license to drive. He also surprised me with a watch to help me understand the schedule for each day.

Lutheran Family Services provided us with classes on living in America, and although I loved learning, I often felt that my head would spin off my body, taking the facts with it. I thought of the simple life we had lived in Viet Nam—the games, the singing, the dancing, Ami, and Ama. But when it thundered, I awoke with a start, shivering from the memory of bombs and guns and tanks and racing through the jungle to safety. Then I would ease back on my pillow and listen to the silence. I was no longer a child, no longer that young girl dreaming of freedom from persecution. I was free. I was strong in my heart and in my faith. And my body was ready to bring another life into a world that I hoped would offer security and peace.

When the baby, Vivian Ksor Buonya, was born at 5:00 a.m. on July 21, 1987, there was no hard floor covered in a bamboo mat, no pit fire to warm my back, no coconut milk to give me diarrhea—only clean sheets, warm blankets, healthy liquids, and happy faces.

Two months later, Anna, Vivian, Y-Jim, and I were baptized by Father Albert Todd at St. Mary's. Y-Jim and I were confirmed and received our first Holy Sacrament of the Body of Christ through the Eucharist. I felt great joy as the blessed Virgin Mary seemed to wrap her arms around our family and friends in the quiet of that peaceful sanctuary.


Y-Jim and I did not know which way to turn our heads in one bed with two children, so we rented an affordable house by a railroad track. Only one eye on the stove worked, and the house rattled several times a day as the trains passed, but Anna was happy waving to all of them. Friends helped with furniture, and for two years, we lived in a place that was far better than the huts and hard floors of the shelters we had known only a short time earlier. We often had guests, and for our first American Thanksgiving there, we "baked" the turkey five hours in an oven that only partially heated. Later our friend Kathy finished cooking it at her house, but everyone gave thanks many times for the rest of the meal and rejoiced that we were the newest pilgrims.

## *Raleigh, Jobs, and Babies*

America was not the Thailand destination that I had dreamed about with my leader and protector H'Tlon, but it was more than I could ever reasonably imagine in my mind—the houses, the traffic, electricity, water, food, telephones, schools near every neighborhood, jobs that enabled us to buy what we needed, and the generosity of people, and helpful programs that allowed us to be independent.

In 1988 Father Todd at St. Mary's had a brief ceremony to bless and approve our marriage and dedication to each other in the jungle. I could not understand much of the English, but our translator, Ms. Quynh, interpreted enough for me to realize that my faith in God and devotion to my husband were being affirmed.


We moved to the city of Raleigh, to a smaller house but closer to work. H'Luok and Y-Duen came with us. Y-Jim changed jobs, working a shift from 4:00 p.m. to midnight, and I, pregnant with our third child, found a job where I could work from 7:30 a.m. to 3:30 p.m.

When Lutheran Family Services gave me an old Dodge, I had to learn to drive. I was determined, even after the brakes did not work, and I found out that I could not keep the car from rolling into traffic by running along beside it. A cement wall saved our lives. Later, while I drove to work—eight months pregnant—on snow and ice, the car spun around several times on the highway and caused me to give two-weeks notice to my job—and to put away the keys until a month after our son was born.

## Our Permanent Home

At the time that we moved to Raleigh, we heard that several Montagnard families had been accepted into a program called Habitat for Humanity. With the aid of Mr. Swain, my husband and I as well as H'Luok and Y-Duen applied and were approved. We did not know what that meant at first, but the possibility of living in our very own home was a miracle. Having two growing families in our tiny house, with parents sleeping in one bedroom—a curtain separating their space—was a reminder of our last refugee camps.

St. Michael's Episcopal Church in Raleigh agreed to sponsor and to build a Habitat House with us in a neighborhood of twenty-two houses (newly under construction) that included five Montagnard families. The house would have three bedrooms, one bathroom, kitchen, and living area, all in about 1,100 square feet, and a big backyard where the children could play. I did not understand everything, but I, smiling with happiness, signed the papers.

Y-Jim began the second of four jobs he would have—anything to make the monthly payments and take care of his family. He and our friends, along with a swarm of volunteers, built our beautiful dream house in six months, and we moved in during a fall weekend in September 1990. A new American flag that had flown over the United States Senate and a North Carolina flag were presented to us and were attached to our bright yellow front porch. St. Michael's priest blessed our house and offered prayers of thanksgiving, "May all who dwell herein find peace!"

## America—Unlimited Possibilities

To me, education had always been the key to success. While Y-Jim worked four jobs and learned English, he went to Wake Technical Community College and earned two associate degrees—one in mechanical engineering. I worked at temporary jobs, gave birth to Cecile in November 1991 and to Maryann in January seven years later. I have taken numerous classes, working toward my GED, and now have a full-time job. But my proudest moments have come from the accomplishments of our children.

In 2007, Anna graduated from the University of North Carolina at Greensboro and in 2010 from Elon University School of Law, while Vivian also graduated from UNC Greensboro in 2009. Jimson and Cecile are working toward college degrees, and Maryann, in middle school, has taken the SAT through the Talent Identification Program at Duke University.

My story has not ended. There are hundreds like mine. But I have told this one to encourage others and to let them know that adversity and oppression do not have to control one's heart and mind. With the help of friends, strangers (additional angels), and God, the smallest beam of hope can be the sustaining light that continuously shines on one's life.

# PRONUNCIATIONS

## Names

| First name | Middle name | Last name | Pronunciation |
|---|---|---|---|
| H'Yoanh | Ksor | Buonya | Ha Yoan Ksar Boonya |
| Buk | | | Buk |
| Dam Per Quay | | | Dam Par Quai |
| Dong | | Nay | Don Ni |
| H'Blin | | | Ha Blin |
| H'Bloanh | | | Ha Bloan |
| H'Chrem | | | Ha Chrem |
| H'Jok | | Ksor | Ha Jock Ksar |
| H'Juaih | | | Ha Joash |
| H'Kong | | | Ha Kan |
| H'Lip | | | Ha Lip |
| H'Lonh | | | Ha Lowan |
| H'Luok | | Mdrang | Ha Looak Mdran |
| H'Mio | | | Ha Mia |
| H'Ngam | | | Ha Ngam |
| H'Ngonh | | | Ha Ngowan |
| H'Nhim | | | Ha Nim |
| H'Nhien | | | Ha Nien |
| H'Nhun | | | Ha Nooan |
| H'Phian | | Nay | Ha Pian Ni |
| H'Plip | | | Ha Polip |
| H'Tien | | | Ha Tian |
| H'Tlok | | Ksor | Ha Tlock Ksar |
| H'Tlon | | | Ha Talowng |
| H'Ton | | | Ha Ton |
| H'Ty | | | Ha Tea |
| Ing | | Siu | Ing Siew |
| Klut | | Siu | Kolut Siew |

| | | |
|---|---|---|
| Mtuat | Ksor | Mtward Ksar |
| Nguyen | Cao | Nguyen | Ngwen Kow Ngwen |
| Paul Yuh | | Paul Yuh |
| Puin | | Pahuan |
| Rong | Nay | Wrong Ni |
| Vien | Hoa | Nguyen | Vien Hwa Ngwen |
| Y-Bhi | Kbuor | E-Bi Kabuor |
| Y-Dhun | Buondap | E-Thun Boondap |
| Y-Djot | Mlo | E-Judge Milo |
| Y-Ji | Buonya | E-Ji Boonya |
| Y-Khiem | Ebam | E-Khem Eban |
| Y-Niam | Buondap | E-Niam Boondap |
| Y-Nguan | | E-Ngwan |
| Y-Plier | | E-Pliar |
| Y-Siu | Hlong | E-Siew Halong |
| Y-Soan | Eban | E-Swan Eban |
| Y-Suiah | | E-Shoai |
| Y-Tlung | Ayun | E-Talung Ayun |

## Schools, Places, Villages, and Rivers

| | |
|---|---|
| Bon Ama Djong | Bon Ama Young |
| Buon Me Thuot | Ban Me Tuat |
| Cheo Reo | Cheo Reo |
| Hau Hoc Van | How Hock Van |
| Minh Duc | Men Deck |
| Pleiku | Plekoo |
| Qui Nhon | Qui Nion |
| Thanh Gia | Thank Ya |
| ThangTien | Thank Tian |
| Tien Hoc Le | Tian Hock Leh |
| Trinh Vuong | Trin Vooang |

# BIBLIOGRAPHY

B enge, Michael. D. *The History of the Involvement of the Montagnards of the Central Highlands in the Vietnam War.* in "The Fall of Saigon" SACEI Forum #8. March 2011 OutskirtsPress.com

Mr. Benge spent eleven years in Vietnam (1963–1975) serving with IVS, USAID, CORDS, five years as a POW, and subsequently as an advisor to the Minister of Ethnic Minorities. He is a student of culture and politics of Southeast Asia and has published articles extensively in this regard.

Map Not To Scale